STRUGGLING WITH THE PHILOSOPHER

The Institute of Ismaili Studies
Ismaili Texts and Translations Series, 2

Editorial Board:
Farhad Daftary (general editor), Wilferd Madelung (consulting editor), Heinz Halm, Abbas Hamdani, Hermann Landolt, Mehdi Mohaghegh, Roy Mottahedeh, Azim Nanji, Ismail K. Poonawala, Paul E. Walker

Previously published title:
Ibn al-Haytham, *The Advent of the Fatimids: A Contemporary Shiʿi Witness.* An Edition and English Translation of Ibn al-Haytham's *Kitāb al-Munāẓarāt,* by Wilferd Madelung and Paul E. Walker (2000).

Struggling
with the
Philosopher

A Refutation of Avicenna's Metaphysics

A New Arabic Edition and English Translation of
Muḥammad b. ʿAbd al-Karīm b. Aḥmad al-Shahrastānī's

Kitāb al-Muṣāraʿa

by

Wilferd Madelung and Toby Mayer

I.B.Tauris *Publishers*
LONDON • NEW YORK
in association with
The Institute of Ismaili Studies
LONDON

Published in 2001 by I.B.Tauris & Co Ltd
6 Salem Rd, London W2 4BU
175 Fifth Avenue, New York NY 10010

in association with The Institute of Ismaili Studies
42–44 Grosvenor Gardens, London SW1W OEB

In the United States of America and in Canada distributed by
St Martins Press, 175 Fifth Avenue, New York NY 10010

ISBN 1 86064 693 X

A full CIP record for this book is available from the British Library
A full CIP record for this book is available from the Library of Congress

Library of Congress catalog card: available

Typeset in ITC New Baskerville by Hepton Books, Oxford
Printed and bound in Great Britain by MPG Books Ltd, Bodmin

The Institute of Ismaili Studies

The Institute of Ismaili Studies was established in 1977 with the object of promoting scholarship and learning on Islam, in the historical as well as contemporary contexts, and a better understanding of its relationship with other societies and faiths.

The Institute's programmes encourage a perspective which is not confined to the theological and religious heritage of Islam, but seeks to explore the relationship of religious ideas to broader dimensions of society and culture. The programmes thus encourage an interdisciplinary approach to the materials of Islamic history and thought. Particular attention is also given to issues of modernity that arise as Muslims seek to relate their heritage to the contemporary situation.

Within the Islamic tradition, the Institute's programmes seek to promote research on those areas which have, to date, received relatively little attention from scholars. These include the intellectual and literary expressions of Shiʿism in general, and Ismailism in particular.

In the context of Islamic societies, the Institute's programmes are informed by the full range and diversity of cultures in which Islam is practised today, from the Middle East, South and Central Asia and Africa to the industrialised societies of the West, thus taking into consideration the variety of contexts which shape the ideals, beliefs and practices of the faith.

These objectives are realised through concrete programmes and activities organised and implemented by various departments of the Institute. The Institute also collaborates periodically, on a programme-specific basis, with other institutions of learning in the United Kingdom and abroad.

The Institute's academic publications fall into several interrelated categories:

1. Occasional papers or essays addressing broad themes of the relationship between religion and society, with special reference to Islam.
2. Monographs exploring specific aspects of Islamic faith and culture, or the contributions of individual Muslim figures or writers.
3. Editions or translations of significant primary or secondary texts.
4. Translations of poetic or literary texts which illustrate the rich heritage of spiritual, devotional and symbolic expressions in Muslim history.
5. Works on Ismaili history and thought, and the relationship of the Ismailis to other traditions, communities and schools of thought in Islam.
6. Proceedings of conferences and seminars sponsored by the Institute.
7. Bibliographical works and catalogues which document manuscripts, printed texts and other source materials.

This book falls into category three listed above.

In facilitating these and other publications, the Institute's sole aim is to encourage original research and analysis of relevant issues. While every effort is made to ensure that the publications are of a high academic standard, there is naturally bound to be a diversity of views, ideas and interpretations. As such, the opinions expressed in these publications are to be understood as belonging to their authors alone.

Contents

Introduction: Al-Shahrastānī, Ismaʿilism and Philosophy 1
Note on the Translation 16

Kitāb al-Muṣāraʿa (English Text) 17

The First Issue:	On the Enumeration of the Subdivisions of Existence	22
The Second Issue:	On the Existence of the Necessary of Existence	33
The Third Issue:	On the Unity of the Necessary of Existence	44
The Fourth Issue:	On the Knowledge of the Necessary of Existence and its Relationship with the Universal and Particular	60
The Fifth Issue:	On the Incipience of the World	74

Bibliography 99
Index to the English Text 102

Kitāb al-Muṣārʿa (Arabic Text) 107

STRUGGLING WITH THE PHILOSOPHER

Introduction: Al-Shahrastānī, Ismaʿilism and Philosophy

Tāj al-Dīn Abu'l-Fatḥ Muḥammad b. ʿAbd al-Karīm al-Shahrastānī (d. 548/1153) has long been known in modern scholarship as the author of the *Kitāb al-Milal wa'l-niḥal*, a comprehensive survey of the religions, sects and philosophical schools, first edited by W. Cureton in 1842–1846.[1] Although written from a distinctly Islamic point of view, the book has continued to attract attention and admiration for its non-polemical objectivity and the wide range of its investigation of the currents of human belief and religious thought. Its chapters on the non-Muslim faiths have been described as 'the high point of Muslim histories of religion'.[2] A modern French translation of the book with full annotation has been sponsored by UNESCO with a preface paying tribute to the author's spirit of tolerance.[3]

[1] Al-Shahrastānī, *Kitāb al-Milal wa'l-niḥal*, ed. W. Cureton (London, 1842–1846).

[2] Guy Monnot, 'al-Shahrastānī', EI2, vol. 9, p. 216.

[3] Daniel Gimaret, Guy Monnot and Jean Jolivet, *Livre des Religions et des Sectes*, vols 1–2 (Paris-Louvain, 1986–1993), Preface by M.A. Sinaceur.

Al-Shahrastānī's major work on scholastic Muslim theology, the *Kitāb Nihāyat al-iqdām fī ʿilm al-kalām,* was first published by A. Guillaume in 1934.[4] It revealed his searching interest in the basic questions of Islamic theology and reflected his expert learning in the Ashʿarī school tradition in which he had been brought up. As an outstanding Shāfiʿī Ashʿarī scholar, he had indeed taught for three years (511–514/1117–1120) at the Shāfiʿī Niẓāmiyya Madrasa in Baghdad made famous by the earlier teaching activity of al-Ghazālī there.

A different aspect of al-Shahrastānī's religious thought was first highlighted by M.R. Jalālī Nāʾīnī and M.T. Dānishpazhūh in the 1960s. Both scholars noted definite Shiʿi and, more specifically, Ismaʿili views in some of his works.[5] These confirmed charges by several Sunni contemporaries of al-Shahrastānī that he, with all his erudition in the religious sciences, adhered to 'heretical doctrine'. Abū Saʿd al-Samʿānī (d. 562/1166), who had heard him teach, reported that he was accused of inclining to the 'people of the mountain fortresses', i.e. the Nizārī Ismaʿilis in Iran, and of spreading their 'heretical' teaching.[6]

Al-Shahrastānī's Ismaʿili views have since been examined in detail by a number of scholars. They are most significant in three of his extant works. The first is a *Majlis,* a sermon in Persian on the two worlds of Creation and Order, delivered by him in Khuwārizm. It was first edited by Nāʾīnī and has been translated into French and analysed by Diane Steigerwald.[7] The second is the Qurʾan commentary *Mafātīḥ al-asrār wa-maṣābīḥ al-abrār* composed late in his life. Here he mentions

[4] Alfred Guillaume, *The Summa Philosophiae of al-Shahrastānī* (London, 1934).

[5] Muḥammad Riḍā Jalālī Nāʾīnī, *Sharḥ-i ḥāl wa-āthār-i Ḥujjatu'l-ḥaqq Abu'l-Fatḥ Muḥammad b. ʿAbd al-Karīm b. Aḥmad Shahrastānī* (Tehran, 1343/1964); Muḥammad Taqī Dānishpazhūh, 'Dāʿī al-Duʿāt Tāju'l-Dīn Shahrastāna', in *Nāma-yi Āstān-i Quds,* 7, no. 2 (1346/1968), pp. 71–80; 8 (1347/1969), pp. 61–71.

[6] Al-Subkī, *Ṭabaqāt al-Shāfiʿiyya al-kubrā,* ed. A.M. al-Ḥilw and M.M. al-Ṭanāḥī (Cairo, 1388/1969), vol. 6, p. 130.

[7] Diane Steigerwald, *Majlis: Discours sur l'ordre et la création* (Saint-Nicolas, Québec, 1998).

having met a 'pious servant of God' who taught him the true methods and principles of Qur'anic exegesis, affirms the divine authority of the *ahl al-bayt,* the Family of the Prophet, to interpret the Qur'an, and in some passages uses Isma'ili terms and concepts in his exegesis. The extant part of the commentary has been published in facsimile and has been analysed in detail in a series of articles by G. Monnot.[8] A critical edition is under preparation by M. 'Alī Ādharshab, of which the first volume has already appeared.[9] The third work is al-Shahrastānī's refutation of Ibn Sīnā's theology entitled *Kitāb al-Muṣāra'a,* first edited by Suhayr Muḥammad Mukhtār,[10] and which is here re-edited with an English translation. The key thesis espoused by al-Shahrastānī in this work is the absolute transcendence of God above all being and comprehension as taught by the Isma'ili tradition. Its formulation tallies closely with doctrines he ascribed to the older Ismā'īliyya or Bāṭiniyya in his *Kitāb al-Milal wa'l-niḥal.*[11]

None of al-Shahrastānī's contemporary Sunni critics suggested that he, while holding what they regarded as heretical views, actually joined the Isma'ili community. Born and educated as a Shāfi'ī Sunni, he continued to identify with the Sunni community and followed the Shāfi'ī ritual and legal practice to the end of his life. Yet his concept of Sunnism evidently moved far away from the contemporaneous orthodox understanding of it and expanded to allow Shi'i veneration of the Family of the Prophet and recognition of the religious authority

[8] Al-Shahrastānī, *Mafātīḥ al-asrār wa-maṣābīḥ al-abrār* (Tehran, 1409/1989), 2 vols; Guy Monnot, 'Islam: exégèse coranique', in *Annuaire de l'École des Hautes Études, Sections des sciences religieuses,* 90–9 (1981–1991).

[9] Muḥammad 'Alī Ādharshab, *Tafsīr al-Shahrastānī al-musammā Mafātīḥ al-asrār wa-maṣābīḥ al-abrār,* vol. 1 (Tehran, 1417/1997).

[10] Suhayr Muḥammad Mukhtār, ed. *Kitāb Muṣāra'at al-falāsifa* (Cairo, 1396/1976).

[11] Al-Shahrastānī, *Kitāb al-Milal wa'l-niḥal,* vol. 1, p. 147. The same doctrine is described by al-Shahrastānī as that of the Bāṭiniyya and a group of the Shi'a in his *Kitāb Nihāyat al-iqdām,* ed. Alfred Guillaume (London, 1934), pp. 128–30.

of the Shiʿi Imams. In his Qurʾan commentary the breadth of his concept expressed itself in an eclectic use of Sunni and Shiʿi sources and a range of varying avenues of exegesis. In his *Majlis* and the *Muṣāraʿa* his Ismaʿili thought prevails more consistently. Al-Shahrastānī can thus be described as Sunni socially and communally, but as Shiʿi and Ismaʿili in some of his core beliefs and religious thought.

In his *Kitāb al-Milal waʾl-niḥal* al-Shahrastānī describes the teaching of the 'old Bāṭiniyya' in some detail and an objective, detached manner. He then goes on to state that the followers of the 'new preaching' (*daʿwa jadīda*), i.e. the Nizārī Ismaʿilis in Iran, had abandoned this teaching when al-Ḥasan b. al-Ṣabbāḥ began to recruit men and fortified himself in castles. Al-Ḥasan then concentrated entirely on arguing the need of mankind for a truthful Imam at all times and on explaining the way of identifying him. Al-Shahrastānī quotes the gist of al-Ḥasan b. al-Ṣabbāḥ's argument in his programmatic *Four Chapters* (*al-Fuṣūl al-arbaʿa*) and some other treatises. He charges, however, in a distinctly critical tone, that al-Ḥasan prohibited the common people from discussing religious sciences and prevented the elite from consulting older books (of the Ismaʿili literary heritage) except for those who knew the value of each work and the rank of the author in each discipline. Al-Ḥasan's theological teaching to his followers did not go beyond the statement: 'Our God is the God of Muḥammad'. He told al-Shahrastānī: 'But you say: God is the God of the minds', implying that everyone was merely following the guidance of his own mind.

Al-Shahrastānī then complains that the followers of al-Ḥasan b. al-Ṣabbāḥ, whenever he sought to engage in theological discussion with any of them, would confine themselves to al-Ḥasan's statement 'Our God is the God of Muḥammad', and tell him that they had no need of him and could learn nothing from him. Al-Shahrastānī responded, conceding the need for an authoritative teacher and asking them where that teacher was, what he would impress on him in theology and what he would prescribe for him in rational matters. A teacher, he suggested, is to be sought not for himself, but for his teaching. In his view, they had thus closed the door of knowledge and opened that of submission and blind imitation (*taqlīd*). No person of sound mind would agree to adopt a doctrine without clear understanding or follow a path without evidence.[12]

From these critical remarks it is evident that al-Shahrastānī disapproved of al-Ḥasan b. al-Ṣabbāḥ's policies both in respect to his armed uprising against the Saljūqs and his restriction of the traditional Ismaʿili teaching activity. The Ismaʿilis were in his view part of the Muslim community, in some respects its core, and should not segregate themselves into a separate community. In spite of his basic espousal of traditional Ismaʿili teaching, he was not prepared to join them in their seclusion. The temporary absence of the Imam, moreover, in his view could not justify the suspension of the religious teaching and reasoning based on the guidance of the past Imams. The teacher, as he saw it, was needed not for his physical presence, but for his teaching which awakened and guided the mind to true knowledge. Restriction of teaching, reasoning and debate rather closed the door to it.

The restriction on theological teaching did not last. Al-Shahrastānī's religious views, dismissed by the 'people of the mountain fortresses' as irrelevant during his time, would later attract their interest. The impact of his thought in the Nizārī community, however, seems to have been limited. His works did not become part of the communal literature and were not quoted. Only Naṣīr al-Dīn al-Ṭūsī, in his autobiographical account about his own path to Ismaʿilism, mentions him prominently. He refers to him as *dāʿī al-duʿāt* and records that his own father's maternal uncle and teacher was a pupil of his. Al-Ṭūsī's father in turn encouraged him to study all disciplines of knowledge and to listen to the discourse of the followers of various schools and doctrines.[13] The title *dāʿī al-duʿāt* here is,

[12] Al-Shahrastānī, *Kitāb al-Milal wa'l-niḥal*, pp. 147–52.

[13] Naṣīr al-Dīn Ṭūsī, *Contemplation and Action: The Spiritual Autobiography of a Muslim Scholar*, ed. and tr. S.J. Badakhchani (London, 1998). Persian text p. 6, transl. p. 26.

no doubt, to be understood as merely honorary. While al-Shahrastānī was not a member of the Ismaʿili *daʿwa*, the passage indicates that his teaching and his works spread Ismaʿili thought and encouraged al-Ṭūsī to join the Nizārī community.

His contemporary Sunni critics also faulted al-Shahrastānī for his pursuit of philosophy. The Khwārizmian Maḥmūd b. Muḥammad b. ʿAbbās b. Arslān, author of a history of Khuwārizm, suggested that his inclination to Ismaʿili 'heresy' (*ilḥād*) was the result of his turning away from the light of the *sharīʿa* and his preoccupation with the darknesses of philosophy. He describes him as going to great lengths in backing and defending the doctrines of the philosophers and adds that he attended several of al-Shahrastānī's preaching sessions where 'there was no word of "God has said", nor "the Messenger of God has said", nor any answer to questions of the *sharīʿa*.'[14] This description, it should be noted, fits the extant *Majlis* of al-Shahrastānī only partly, for this sermon, while dealing with esoteric cosmology rather than religious law, abounds with quotations from the Qurʾan and the hadith of the Prophet.

Ẓahīr al-Dīn al-Bayhaqī, in his supplement to Abū Sulaymān al-Sijistānī's biographies of the philosophers, *Tatimmat Ṣiwān al-ḥikma,* recounts that he criticised al-Shahrastānī for mingling religious exegesis with philosophy (*ḥikma*) and other disciplines in his Qurʾan commentary, and told him that the Qurʾan should be interpreted on the basis of the interpretation of the Companions of the Prophet and the generation following them (*tābiʿūn*). Philosophy, al-Bayhaqī added, must be kept separate from Qurʾan exegesis and, in any case, al-Shahrastānī could not hope to combine religion (*sharīʿa*) and philosophy in a better way than al-Ghazālī. Al-Shahrastānī was filled with anger at this suggestion.[15] With his ironic reference to al-Ghazālī's 'combining' of religion and philosophy, al-Bayhaqī evidently meant that the latter had studied both disciplines but had kept

[14] ʿAbd Allāh al-Rūmī Yāqūt, *Muʿjam al-buldān,* ed. F. Wüstenfeld (Leipzig, 1866–1873), vol. 3, pp. 343–4.

[15] Ẓahīr al-Dīn ʿAlī al-Bayhaqī, *Taʾrīkh ḥukamāʾ al-islām,* ed. Muḥammad Kurd ʿAlī (Damascus, 1365/1946), p. 143.

them strictly apart and in fact distanced himself from philosophy in his religious works. Al-Shahrastānī's angry reaction at the mention of al-Ghazālī as a model for him is significant for his attitude to his celebrated predecessor at the Niẓāmiyya in Baghdad.

THE KITĀB AL-MUṢĀRAʿA

Al-Shahrastānī dedicated his *Kitāb al-Muṣāraʿa* to Sayyid Majd al-Dīn Abu'l-Qāsim ʿAlī b. Jaʿfar al-Mūsawī, amir and *naqīb* (syndic of the ʿAlid nobility) of Tirmidh, a high official in the government of the Saljūq Sultan Sanjar. He mentions that he had earlier presented to the Sayyid his *Kitāb al-Milal wa'l-niḥal,* which had attracted his patron's interest and earned his praise. The *Kitāb al-Milal wa'l-niḥal* had in fact, it is known, been dedicated to al-Shahrastānī's previous patron, Sanjar's vizier Naṣīr al-Dīn Maḥmūd b. Abī Tawba al-Marwazī. When the vizier fell out of favour and was imprisoned in 526/1132, al-Shahrastānī attached himself to Majd al-Dīn al-Mūsawī. He removed the dedication to Naṣīr al-Dīn from the book and presented a copy to his new patron.

Al-Shahrastānī goes on to announce that he now intends to engage in an intellectual wrestling match (*muṣāraʿa*) with Ibn Sīnā (Avicenna), whom he describes as the universally recognised grand master of philosophy of all time, and calls upon Majd al-Dīn to act as a judge between the two contestants in this dispute. This invitation indicates that his patron was no stranger to the philosophical issues involved in the discussion and that al-Shahrastānī was aware of his expert knowledge and views. Al-Shahrastānī had, probably in the time of his employment by Majd al-Dīn, consulted some of the contemporary philosophers, presenting to them his own views and objections to Ibn Sīnā's discourse and asking for their opinions. Thus he exchanged letters with the physician and philosopher Sharaf al-Zamān Muḥammad b. Yūsuf al-Īlāqī (d. 536/1141) on the question of existence and how it is necessitated in the existents, on the relationship between the cogniser and the objects of knowledge and on the absolute knowledge of the Necessary Being, God.[16] He submitted objections to Ibn Sīnā's views by letter to the Qāḍī Zayn al-Dīn ʿUmar b. Sahlān al-Sāwī, a pupil of Īlāqī and expert on logic noted for his *Kitāb al-Baṣāʾir al-Naṣīriyya* which he had dedicated to the vizier Naṣīr al-Dīn al-Marwazī.[17] According to al-Sāwī's extant reply to one of al-Shahrastānī's letters, the objections, though formulated by the latter, had come to him from someone to whom al-Shahrastānī felt deeply obliged.[18] Most likely his patron, the Naqīb Majd al-Dīn al-Mūsawī, is meant. The same objections, in different form, are discussed in the *Muṣāraʿa*. To what extent al-Shahrastānī was influenced by the views of these correspondents must remain the subject of future research.

Al-Shahrastānī remarks that he has chosen some of the most solidly argued statements of Ibn Sīnā in the theological part (*ilāhiyyāt*) of his *Shifāʾ*, in the *Najāt, Ishārāt* and *Taʿlīqāt* for his discussion. He imposes on himself the condition of dealing with his opponent only in his discipline and not to oppose him on mere expressions on whose meaning and reality they both agreed, wishing to be neither a disputatious *kalām* theologian (*mutakallim jadalī*) nor an obstinate sophist. His distancing himself from being a 'disputatious *kalām* theologian' deserves special note. Throughout his book, he does not quote or mention al-Ghazālī's famous refutation of the philosophers, the *Tahāfut al-falāsifa*, even though several of the questions discussed by him had also been treated by al-Ghazālī. Did he disapprove of al-Ghazālī's work because he considered it merely the product of a disputatious *kalām* theologian? This must seem likely in view of the substantial differences in approach and aim between the two books.

Al-Ghazālī's *Tahāfut* falls squarely within the tradition of

[16] See Ādharshab, *Tafsīr al-Shahrastānī,* vol. 1, p. 57. A facsimile edition of the text is provided by Muḥammad Riḍa Jalālī Nāʾīnī, *Dū maktūb* (Tehran, 1369/1990).

[17] See the quotation from ʿImād al-Dīn al-Iṣfahānī's *Taʾrīkh dawlat Āl Saljūq* in Ādharshab, *Tafsīr al-Shahrastānī,* vol. 1, p. 27.

[18] MS Kazan n. 1125, fol. 107.

Ashʿarī theological apologetics and polemics. Its avowed aim was to destroy the basis of philosophy itself, not to correct some views of the philosophers. Although al-Ghazālī insisted that the book was intended only to refute and not to defend any specific religious doctrine and that he would set forth the true doctrines in a separate work, his yardstick of the truth was in fact the Ashʿarī creed. On its basis he chose to refute the philosophers in twenty issues, charging them with infidelity (*kufr*) punishable with death in three of them, and with heretical innovation in the others. In the common style of *kalām* polemics, he pictured the philosophers as maliciously motivated to dupe the public by trickery and obfuscation and their followers as frivolous fools.

Al-Shahrastānī, in contrast, does not question the legitimacy of philosophy as a supreme discipline of wisdom. He proposes to challenge Ibn Sīnā, whom he recognises as the foremost expert in it, on his own ground in specific questions, relying on chosen quotations from his major works. While he sharply criticises some of his views and the contradictions which he perceived in them, he never raises the issue of infidelity or heresy. In all questions he counters Ibn Sīnā's theses, repudiated by him with his own, which, he asserts, were based on the guideline (*miʿyār*) of the prophets.

On the need for such a guideline, there was obviously agreement between al-Ghazālī and al-Shahrastānī. Given this guideline, however, al-Ghazālī saw the use of human reason in religious thought as confined by traditional Ashʿarī interpretation of Qurʾan and hadith, leading him to denounce philosophical inquiry into metaphysics and theology. For al-Shahrastānī, the guideline was rather the solid foundation for sound rational inquiry into the truth. He justified his daring challenge of Ibn Sīnā by assuring his patron Majd al-Dīn that he himself had risen from the depth of blind acceptance (*taqlīd*) in religion to the pinnacle of rational investigation of the truth and submission to it (*taslīm*), as he had drunk a cup from the paradisical wellspring of prophethood.

The basic idea espoused by al-Shahrastānī against Ibn Sīnā

was, as noted, the absolute transcendence of God beyond existence and comprehension by human reason. God, he maintained, was the existentiator of existence (*mūjid al-wujūd*), the giver of both existence and non-existence. God was above all opposites—such as truth and falsehood, unity and multiplicity, knowledge and ignorance, life and death, good and evil, power and impotence—and their sovereign judge (*ḥākim*). As Naṣīr al-Dīn al-Ṭūsī noted in his refutation of the *Muṣāraʿa,* this was the doctrine of the Taʿlīmiyya, the Ismaʿilis, who said: God is neither existent nor non-existent, rather He is the foundation of being and non-being.[19] In one form or another, this view had been upheld by the Persian Ismaʿili writers at least from Muḥammad b. Aḥmad al-Nasafī (d. 332/943) on. Al-Ghazālī denounced it in his *Fayṣal al-tafriqa bayn al-islām wa'l-zandaqa* as unambiguous unbelief.[20] Al-Shahrastānī was certainly aware of the condemnation. His adoption of it clearly reveals his repudiation of Ghazālian orthodoxy.

Al-Shahrastānī did not object to Ibn Sīnā's designation of God as the Necessary Being (*wājib al-wujūd*), but insisted that existence could be predicated of God only equivocally (*bi'l-ishtirāk*), as meaning that He is the giver of existence and its opposite. In his refutation, al-Ṭūsī suggested that the opinion that existence belonged amongst equivocal terms was the doctrine of the Ashʿarī school and of the Muʿtazilī Abu'l-Ḥusayn al-Baṣrī.[21] The ontological basis of the doctrine of these *kalām* theologians, however, was entirely different. For al-Shahrastānī it was a necessary complement to his concept of divine transcendence. Thus he extended the principle of equivocity also to all other descriptions and attributes of God. God is one in the meaning of His giving unity, knowing in the meaning that He gives knowledge, powerful in the meaning that He gives power to the powerful.

19 Naṣīr al-Dīn al-Ṭūsī, *Maṣāriʿ al-muṣāriʿ*, ed. Ḥasan al-Muʿizzī (Qum, 1405/1984), pp. 82–3.

20 Abū Ḥāmid Muḥammad al-Ghazālī, *Fayṣal al-tafriqa bayn al-islām wa'l-zandaqa,* ed. Sulaymān Dunyā (Cairo, 1960), p. 198.

21 Al-Ṭūsī, *Maṣāriʿ*, p. 83.

The *Muṣāraʿa* was initially planned to deal with seven issues of theology. In the first, al-Shahrastānī questions Ibn Sīnā's division of existence into the necessary and the contingent. He argues that Ibn Sīnā's Necessary Existent, God, cannot be part of divisible existence since this would require Him to belong to a species, separated from contingent things by a differentia. In reality existence cannot be predicated of the Necessary Existent in the same way as it is of the contingent things. Only the existence of the latter can be subject to rational division. Al-Shahrastānī then proposes a comprehensive division of contingent beings in contrast to the division set forth by Ibn Sīnā in his *Kitāb al-Najāt.* In the second issue, on the existence of the Necessary Existent, he pursues further his argument on the equivocity of the term existence in relation to God. He suggests that Ibn Sīnā realised that existence could not apply to the necessary and the contingent in the same way, and that he therefore invented the concept of analogous (i.e. ambiguous) terms as distinct from univocal and equivocal terms. Yet Ibn Sīnā's definition of existence as an analogous, rather than univocal, term does not change the fact that existence would apply essentially to both the necessary and the contingent. Existence, al-Shahrastānī insists, can apply to the Necessary Existent only equivocally.

The third issue deals with the unity of the Necessary Existent. Al-Shahrastānī objects to Ibn Sīnā's treatment of the Necessary Existence as a species before proving the unicity of God, and to his thesis that from the One only a single intellect can proceed. He affirms that the reality of God is necessarily known by innate disposition (*fiṭra*) and that all things are equally in immediate relation to God, irrespective of their sequence and ranking in the universe. The fourth issue concerns the knowledge of the Necessary Existent. Al-Shahrastānī objects to Ibn Sīnā's description of God as intellect, intellecting and intelligible and to his assertion that God knows everything only by way of universals. He maintains that the nature of divine knowledge is beyond the comprehension of the human mind and that it relates equally to universals, particulars, and changing times and places. In the fifth issue, al-Shahrastānī deals with the temporality of the world. He rejects Ibn Sīnā's thesis that the world is co-eternal with the Creator and affirms that God is beyond both space and time. Eternal circular motion of the heavenly bodies and infinite time, he seeks to prove, are just as impossible as infinite space.

At the end of the fifth issue, al-Shahrastānī states that adverse circumstances and disasters prevented him from completion of the book as planned and he will confine himself to presenting a number of philosophical problems, doubts and perplexities. The sixth issue had originally been intended to deal with the enumeration of the principles (*mabādiʾ*) of the higher world. It is likely that the seventh issue was to be devoted to the question of the Intellect that is the Giver of Forms, which is now treated briefly at the end of the book. Al-Shahrastānī here agrees with the philosophers about the need for an active Intellect to bring human intellects from potentiality to actuality. He questions, however, why their Active Intellect (*ʿaql faʿʿāl*) should be identified with the Intellect of the lunar sphere, the one closest to earth. Could it not be any of the higher Intellects or even the Necessary Existent? And if closeness to humanity is a consideration, could it not be a human intellect that is active and supported by holy power? Al-Shahrastānī evidently had in mind here the Intellect of the prophets and Imams which, according to Ismaʿili teaching, conveys the spiritual truths emanating from the hierarchy of higher Intellects to the faithful.

The disasters to which al-Shahrastānī alludes have commonly been identified with the crushing defeat of Sultan Sanjar by the Qarā Khiṭāy at Qaṭwān near Samarqand in 536/1141. It is less likely that he was referring to a temporary imprisonment of his patron, the Naqīb Majd al-Dīn, at an earlier date.[22] In 536/1141, the defeated Sultan fled to Tirmidh and then to Balkh, while the Khuwārizm-Shāh seized and sacked his capital, Marw. In the battle al-Shahrastānī's philosophical

[22] See Nāʾīnī, *Dū maktūb*, pp. 23–4.

correspondent al-Īlāqī was killed. It is not known whether al-Shahrastānī was in Tirmidh or in Marw at the time. As Sanjar's reign began to collapse, the intellectual courtly milieu that had encouraged al-Shahrastānī in his philosophical pursuits evidently vanished. He was in no mood to complete his *Muṣāraʿa* as planned.

With its truncated ending, the book probably never had a wide readership. During the time that the Nizārī community was seeking a rapprochement with a broadly conceived Sunnism under the ʿAbbasid caliph al-Nāṣir li-Dīn Allāh, the Sufi Shaykh Shihāb al-Dīn ʿUmar al-Suhrawardī seems to have been attracted to al-Shahrastānī's Ismaʿili thought. In his *Rashf al-naṣāʾiḥ al-īmāniyya wa-kashf faḍāʾiḥ al-yūnāniyya,* written in 621/1224, he polemically denounced both *kalām* theology and Greek-inspired philosophy and adopted some of the terms and concepts of al-Shahrastānī's *Majlis* and *Muṣāraʿa.*[23] It was about the same time that Naṣīr al-Dīn al-Ṭūsī, partly under the influence of al-Shahrastānī's thought, joined the Nizārī Ismaʿili community.

The subjugation of the Ismaʿilis by the Mongol conquerors after the fall of their seat of power at Alamūt in 654/1256 opened a period of severe religious persecution. Al-Ṭūsī now abandoned Ismaʿilism and backed the Twelver Shiʿi community to which he had originally belonged. In order to distance himself from the Ismaʿili teaching he had earlier espoused, he composed a refutation of the *Kitāb al-Muṣāraʿa.* His *Maṣāriʿ al-muṣāriʿ* offered a brilliant and incisive defense of the philosophy of Ibn Sīnā, in which he exposed the inadequacy and flawed logic of al-Shahrastānī's criticism. Yet al-Ṭūsī's own highly polemical attack on al-Shahrastānī, describing him as a mere populist preacher picking his ideas at random from various schools without properly understanding them, fails to do justice

[23] See Angelika Hartmann, 'Ismāʿīlitische Theologie bei sunnitischen ʿUlamāʾ des Mittelalters', in Ludwig Hagemann and Ernst Pulsfort, eds, *Ihr alle aber seid Brüder: Festschrift für A. Th. Khoury zum 60. Geburtstag* (Würzburg-Altenberge, 1990), pp. 190–206; and her 'al-Suhrawardī, Shihāb al-Dīn Abū Ḥafṣ', EI2, vol. 9, pp. 778–82.

to the latter's thought, which rested on a different, but equally coherent philosophical vision with a vital religious impulse.

Al-Ṭūsī's refutation further blunted the potential impact of al-Shahrastānī's book in the Muslim world. It was now mostly read embedded in al-Ṭūsī's work. The latter enjoyed a certain popularity among Twelver Shiʿi students of philosophy, as indicated by the survival of numerous, though badly corrupted, manuscripts of it in Iranian libraries. Mullā Ṣadrā (d. 1050/1640) quoted an argument of al-Shahrastānī from it, siding with al-Ṭūsī's polemical refutation.[24] Among orthodox Sunnis, on the other hand, al-Ṭūsī's defence of Ibn Sīnā's philosophy aroused some sympathy for al-Shahrastānī's work. The Ḥanbalī Ibn Qayyim al-Jawziyya (d. 751/1350) in his *Ighāthat al-lahfān min maṣāyid al-shayṭān* noted with satisfaction that al-Shahrastānī had refuted some of Ibn Sīnā's heresies, which al-Ṭūsī, the 'supporter of atheism' (*naṣīr al-ilḥād*), then attempted to reconfirm.[25] From his description of the contents of the two books, it seems unlikely that he had read them seriously. Al-Ghazālī's *Tahāfut* evidently provided the most persuasive answer to Ibn Sīnā's philosophy from the Sunni point of view. Since in modern times philosophy is no longer so predominantly identified with the Peripatetic tradition, al-Shahrastānī's book may perhaps come to be appreciated as a philosophical response from a broad spiritual perspective.

[24] Muḥammad Ṣadr al-Dīn al-Shīrāzī, *al-Ḥikma al-mutaʿāliya fi'l-asfār al-ʿaqliyya al-arbaʿa* (Beirut, 1981–1990), vol. 6, p. 39.

[25] Ibn Qayyim al-Jawziyya, *Ighāthat al-lahfān min maṣāyid al-shayṭān*, ed. Muḥammad Ḥāmid al-Fiqī (Cairo, 1358/1939), vol. 2, p. 267.

THE EDITION

The present edition of the *Kitāb al-Muṣāraʿa* is based primarily on two manuscripts:

1. The MS A 1103 of the Landesbibliothek of Gotha, on which the previous edition by Suhayr Muḥammad Mukhtār was based. My thanks are due to the authorities of the Gotha Library for providing me with a microfilm of the manuscript. According to the colophon, it was written by Faḍāʾil b. Abiʾl-Ḥasan al-Nāsikh al-Shāfiʿī and completed on 10 Ṣafar 590/ 20–23 February 1194. Several folios are missing, a few are displaced, and in some places words have become unreadable. In general, however, the quality of the text is fair. In the annotation to the edition, the manuscript is identified by the letter *alif.*
2. The MS n.1124, fol. 5b - 98a, of the library of Kazan. This manuscript was noted by Th. Menzel in *Der Islam,* 18 (1928), p. 94. My thanks are due to Dr Nuriya G. Garayeva of Kazan and to the authorities of the library of Kazan for kindly providing me with a microfilm of the manuscript. The copyist of the manuscript is not named, and it is not dated, but appears from the handwriting to be considerably later than the Gotha manuscript. While the text of the book is complete, some folios were evidently displaced at some stage in the transmission. This was not noticed by the next copyist, so that the text abruptly jumps in several places of the manuscript. The proper sequence could be restored by comparison with the Gotha manuscript and the text preserved in al-Ṭūsī's *Maṣāriʿ al-muṣāriʿ*. The manuscript is well preserved and readable, but the quality of the text is generally somewhat inferior to that of the Gotha manuscript. In the annotation, it is identified by the letter *bāʾ*.

Apart from these two manuscripts, the text of the *Kitāb al-Muṣāraʿa* as quoted in al-Ṭūsī's refutation *Maṣāriʿ al-muṣāriʿ* has also been compared in establishing the text of this edition.

Particularly useful in this respect was the Istanbul MS Aya Sofya 2358, which preserves the text of the *Kitāb al-Muṣāraʿa* generally better than the Iranian manuscripts of al-Ṭūsī's work. Since al-Ṭūsī's work is to be re-edited separately, the variants provided by these manuscripts have not been noted in this edition of al-Shahrastānī's book.

The title of the book is given as *Kitāb Muṣāraʿat al-falāsifa* in the Gotha MS. In the Kazan MS it is called *Kitāb al-Muṣāraʿa li'l-Shahrastānī maʿa al-Shaykh al-Raʾīs Abī ʿAlī Ibn Sīnā, raḥimahu'llāh.* In his refutation, al-Ṭūsī states that it is known as *al-Muṣāraʿāt.* For the present edition, the title *Kitāb al-Muṣāraʿa* has been chosen.

Wilferd Madelung

NOTE ON THE TRANSLATION

In translating al-Shahrastānī's text, the aim has been to combine accessibility with accuracy (for example in putting Arabic technical terms into English). In the interests of accessibility, square brackets have been used sparingly. Ellipses have thus sometimes been filled out in the English without this being made explicit. Such cases will be obvious to those who co-ordinate the Arabic with the English. For all that, the translation avoids paraphrasing al-Shahrastānī and tries to mirror his speech and thought closely.

My special thanks to Professor Wilferd Madelung, whose advice and assistance have been indispensable, and with whom it has been an honour to work. My gratitude also to Dr Farhad Daftary, whose support and encouragement made the project and my involvement in it possible.

Toby Mayer

Muḥammad b. ʿAbd al-Karīm b. Aḥmad
al-Shahrastānī

Kitāb al-Muṣāraʿa

In the Name of God, the All-Merciful, the Compassionate

Praise be to God—the praise of those who give thanks! And benediction be upon the Seal of the Prophets, Muḥammad the Chosen One, and on his good family—a benediction whose blessing endures to Doomsday!

When the High Council, the prince, the most illustrious and learned master Majd al-Dīn ['Glory of Religion'], prop of Islam, possessor of authority amongst the *sayyids*,[1] Abu'l-Qāsim ʿAlī b. Jaʿfar al-Mūsawī—may God double his glory and majesty, and lavish his favours and kindness upon him—opened the bazaar of noble deeds, set out on the path to lofty achievements, and revealed the hidden qualities which God (Exalted is He!) had given him and with which He had entrusted him, namely, the two honours of aristocratic nature and pedigree, the two graces of physique and character, the attributes both of knowledge and power, the two sentinels of piety and trustworthiness, and the two shields of intrepidity and courage, besides what he acquired in the way of beauty of virtues and guarding against vices, perfection of knowledge, ultimate wisdom, excellence of morals, beautiful habits, generosity, skill, high-mindedness and eminence of rank, such that were he to compete against all the people of his time with a single one of them, he would have utter superiority and integrity,[2] [then] the least of his servants, Muḥammad b. ʿAbd al-Karīm al-Shahrastānī, came forward to present his paltry wares in the bazaar of his generosity. So he served him by way of a book which he composed 'In Explanation of Religious Denominations and Sects', despite the vacillation of the heart between fear and anxiety. He graciously accepted, and examined it closely, and he succeeded in completely fathoming its meanings and went to great lengths in appreciating his most sincere client. Yet its writer had little to do other than bring all that

[1] *Mālik amr al-sāda.* This refers to Majd al-Dīn's official position as *naqīb al-ashrāf*, syndic of the ʿAlids.

[2] Literally: a pure heart.

had been said together, organise it nicely, and report it well. The depths of the intellect are only plumbed and the worth of a man only becomes clear in the struggle between peers and the combat of heroes. Through trial the cache of what is hidden comes into view and through examination a man comes to be honoured or despised.

There has been agreement that the foremost in the sapiential sciences and the most learned of the age in philosophy is Abū ʿAlī al-Ḥusayn b. ʿAbd Allāh Ibn Sīnā—so no one will follow him in it, even though he destroyed himself,[3] and no one will catch up with him in it, even though he urged on his racehorse. And they are unanimous that whoever arrives at the meaning of what he says and understands the hidden content he has in mind, has won the best arrow,[4] and arrived at the supreme destination. Nay, opposition to him in rejection and confutation and the pursuit of his discourse in denial and contradiction, is a door before which obstacles are thrown up, and which is kept shut by guards and look-outs.

So I desired to fight with him in a wrestling match of heroes, and to clash with him in a battle of men. Therefore, I chose the best and firmest amongst what he says in the Metaphysics of the *Shifāʾ*, the *Najāt*, the *Ishārāt* and the *Taʿlīqāt*, namely, what he demonstrated, investigated and explained. I imposed on myself the condition that I would only deal with him in his craft and would not confront him on any expression on whose meaning and gist we both agreed. Thus I would not be a disputatious theologian, nor a pigheaded sophist. So I would begin by explaining the inconsistency in his actual expressions, in wording and meaning. And I would follow it up by revealing the points of error in the texts of his proofs, materially and formally.

Let the High Council (may God increase it in nobility and elevation!) take up the seat of the judges and arbiters, and let

3 Literally: even though he destroyed blackness.

4 *Al-muʿallā* is the seventh and best arrow in the game of chance called *Maysir*.

him decide with truth and sincerity between the two disputants and contestants. For he is most worthy of judging when appealed to for a decision and most fit to guard over veracity when relied upon. Let him know that I have attained the two extremes of learning[5] and let him not underestimate my rank, 'for a man prevails by means of his heart and his tongue'.[6] Let him realise that I have mounted from the foothills of imitation to the heights of realisation and deliverance, and quenched my thirst at the water-hole of prophecy with a cup whose drink is blended from Tasnīm.[7] He who has dived into the sea's depths does not long for a shore and he who has ascended to the summit of perfection is not scared of a descent.

May the High Council remain in possession of the most fortunate star of destiny, the most lucky auspice, the clearest guidance, the most favourable course, the correctest opinion and direction, the most penetrating thinking and reflection, [and may it remain] within an impregnable refuge, namely God Almighty—and 'There is no power and no strength except through God',[8] the Exalted, the Tremendous!

This 'Wrestling' is in regard to seven issues of metaphysics out of a total of seventy odd issues in logic, physics and metaphysics, in which I throttled him with his own bowstring and threw back at him his arrows in regard to his reasoning. I pushed him back into the depth of his pit and up-ended him on his skull in his hole. 'That is [all] through God's generosity towards us and towards men—but most men are ungrateful'.[9]

[5] A proverbial expression: The two extremes are the beginning and end.

[6] For the meaning of the proverb *fa'l-mar'u bi-aṣgharayhi*, see Edward William Lane, *An Arabic-English Lexicon* (Cambridge, 1984), vol. 1, p. 1692.

[7] According to the Qur'an, a fountain in Paradise from which the blessed drink. Qur'an 83:27.

[8] Prophetic hadith: see Bukhārī, VIII, 108.

[9] Qur'an 12:38.

The First Issue: on the Enumeration of the Subdivisions of Existence.
The Second Issue: on the Existence of the Necessary of Existence.[10]
The Third Issue: on the Unity of the Necessary of Existence.
The Fourth Issue: on the Knowledge of the Necessary of Existence.
The Fifth Issue: on the Incipience of the World.
The Sixth Issue: on the Enumeration of Principles—transformed with the seventh into [a series] of difficult issues and puzzling aporiae.

THE FIRST ISSUE

On the Enumeration of the Subdivisions of Existence

Know that the theologians do not enumerate the subdivisions of existence by a comprehensive division. That is because they say 'The existent subdivides into what has a beginning and what does not have a beginning. What has a beginning subdivides into substance and accident'. By 'substance' they mean something occupying space which prevents what is like it in its definition from being where *it* is. By 'accident' they mean what subsists in something occupying space. They declare impossible the existence of a substance which does not occupy space and the existence of an accident which does not subsist in something occupying space. However, while the first division is correct common to negation and affirmation when the conditions of conflict and opposition are complied within it, through agreement on the meaning of 'priority' essentially, temporally, spatially and by nobility, nevertheless the second division is incorrect and not comprehensive if 'substance' is glossed as

[10] For the metaphrastic translation of *wājib al-wujūd* as 'the Necessary of Existence', see Harry Austryn Wolfson, *Studies in the History of Philosophy and Religion,* eds I. Twersky and G.H. Williams (Cambridge, Mass., 1973), vol. 1, p. 404; also George Hourani, 'Ibn Sīnā on Necessary and Possible Existence', *Philosophical Forum,* 4 (1972), p. 75.

what occupies space, and 'accident' as what subsists in what occupies space; since there is nothing in it which indicates the impossibility of the existence of a *tertium quid* neither occupying space nor subsisting in something occupying space—and the philosophers have affirmed intellectual substances which do *not* occupy space. Moreover, what occupies space is something which has a spatial location, and what receives the occupation of space is not the occupation of space itself, for that by which it receives the occupation of space is matter, and the occupation itself is a form within [the matter]. So in consequence, it is a substance compounded from a matter and a form, and the substance cannot be compounded from two accidents. Therefore they must be two substances *not* occupying space. Thus from what occupies space has emerged something not occupying space, and that is most surprising.

As for the philosophers, they have affirmed intellectual substances which do not occupy space, such as intellects, souls, matters and forms. And they affirm accidents which do not subsist through things occupying space, such as 'motions' in quantity and quality, etc.

Ibn Sīnā presented a division at the beginning of the Metaphysics of the *Najāt*, and claimed that it comprehended all the divisions of existents. So I will report it as it is, then I will explain the different errors involved. He said: 'If two essences come together, then if the essence of each one of them is not fully disunited with the other, such as the situation in respect of a peg and a wall (for though both come together, the inside of the peg is not united with anything of the wall, but rather only its surface joins with it), if then it is *not* like the case of the peg and the wall, each one of them exists *pervasively* with all of its essence in the other. Next, if one of them has a stable condition with the separation of the other, or one of them contributes a meaning by which the thing comes to be attributed by some attribute and the other acquires it, then the stable one and the one which acquires it is called a 'substrate', and the other is called an 'inherer' in it. Next, if the substrate is independent in its subsistence of the inherer in it, we call it a 'subject' for it.

And if it is not independent of it we do not call it a subject, but perhaps we call it matter.'[11]

'Every essence which is not in a subject is a substance, and every essence whose subsistence is in a subject is an accident. So something could be in a *substrate* and despite that be a "substance not in a subject"—if the proximate substrate which it is in, is subsistent through it and is not *self-subsistent.* Then it is a constituent of it and we call it a "form". As for the proof of this, we will give it later. Every substance which is not in a subject must either not be in a substrate at all, or must be in a substrate, which substrate is not independent of it in subsistence. So if it is in a substrate, which substrate is not independent of it in subsisting, we call it a "material form". And if it is not in a substrate at all, then either it is a substrate in itself, containing no composition, or it is not. Then if it is a substrate in itself, we call it "unqualified matter". And if it is not, then either it is composite like our bodies which are compounded of matter and corporeal form, or it is not composite, and we call it a "separate form", like the intellect and the soul. As for if the thing is in a substrate which is a subject—we call it an "accident".'[12]

Shortly before this section he had mentioned that existence is split up into a kind of division between accident and substance, and he mentioned in a chapter after it the proof of the Necessary of Existence, saying: 'We do not doubt that there is existence, and all existence is either necessary or contingent.'[13] I say in rebuttal (and help is from God!):

Are the first two divisions—namely, substance and accident—from the divisions of existence qua unqualified existence, or from the divisions of existence qua contingent existence? If it is the first, then the Necessary of Existence is included in the category of substance, and its counterpart is accident. Then, substance is subdivided into the necessary in itself and the

[11] Ibn Sīnā, *Najāt*, ed. Muḥyi'l-Dīn al-Kurdī (Tehran, 1346 SH/1967), p. 200.

[12] Ibid., pp. 200–1.

[13] Ibid., p. 235.

contingent in itself, and it is implied that substantiality is a genus and necessity is a differentia, so the Necessary of Existence is compounded from a genus and a differentia. This absurd implication is confirmed by his statement in describing substance: it is the existent which is not in a subject. For the Necessary of Existence is an 'existent not in a subject'. And if he gives the excuse for it that substance is the *quiddity* of something such that when it exists its existence is not in a subject[14]—well, that excuse is not what is understood from the description mentioned, explicitly or implicitly. Rather it is only indicated by way of consequence and implication.[15]

If the first two divisions (I mean substance and accident) consist in subdivisions of one of the two divisions, namely the contingent, then it is correct in meaning but incorrect in the expression. However, in explaining one of the divisions, namely substance, he has produced that which includes what is more general and is equal to it. Thus he said 'substance is the existent not in a subject'. And this in itself includes the Necessary of Existence and is equal to It. Then I do not deny that the more general term subdivides into different kinds of division in various ways, as we may say: the existent subdivides in one kind of division into what has a beginning and into what does not have a beginning, and in another kind of division into cause and effect, and in another kind of division into necessary and contingent. But substance and accident are different from that, nay, they consist in subdivisions of the contingent, not subdivisions of existence.

We will come back to existence and whether it is divisible or

[14] See *al-Ishārāt wa'l-tanbīhāt* with Ṭūsī's commentary, ed. Sulaymān Dunyā (Cairo, 1957–1960), vol. 3, pp. 479–80.

[15] Ibn Sīnā's defence is that the Necessary is not a quiddity. So though it is technically true that It is an 'existent not in a subject', It will not be counted as a substance. In that case we would not have to divide substance up between the necessary and the contingent, and we will not produce the absurdity that 'necessary substance' is compounded of the genus 'substance' and the differentia 'necessity'. Instead substance is always contingent in status.

not, God willing. As for his statement, 'If two essences come together, then if the essence of each one of them is not fully disunited with the other', to his statement 'each one of them exists pervasively and fully in the other ...';[16] I say, this proposition is contradictory in various ways, and the consequent does not follow from the premise directly or indirectly. For two accidents are two essences which come together in a substrate, yet each of them is neither fully disunited with the other nor is it pervasively and fully in the other. And the situation in respect to matter and form is different from that, for form is pervasively and fully in matter and matter is not pervasively in form nor united with its surface, so each of them is *not* pervasively and fully in the other. Also the situation in respect to the body and the accident is analogous, for the accident exists pervasively and fully in the body, while the body is not pervasively and fully in the accident, nor united with it by its surface. Likewise the situation in respect to the intellect and soul is that they are two essences in union, but one of them does not unite with the other by its surface, nor is it pervasively and fully in it.

So it is known from that, that union is in various ways and of different kinds, and the union of two bodies is different, and the union of two accidents is different, and the union of matter and form is different, and the union of intellectual substances is different. So why did he present them in a single manner, striking haphazardly? That is not in accordance with logic.

His statement 'Next, if one of them has a stable condition with the separation of the other ...' is a division without a counterpart. Instead, he ought to have said, 'or does not have a stable condition with the separation of the other'. For surely the mention of one of the two divisions does not indicate the other.

Then he changed the expression to his statement 'or one of them contributes a meaning by which the thing comes to be

[16] Al-Shahrastānī typically paraphrases rather than quotes, hence the slight difference in wording.

attributed and the other acquires ...' [This is] a correct division; except that he makes the stable and acquiring thing a substrate, and the unstable and contributive thing an inherer. Consequently he must make form unstable, along with the fact that it is contributive, and matter stable, along with the fact that it acquires. But stability is more appropriate for what contributes than for what acquires.

On the other hand, the substrate may be matter, and it is what is not independent in its subsistence of what inheres in it, namely the form. And it may be a body, and that is what *is* independent in its subsistence of what inheres in it, namely the accident. So the first of the two substrates is stable through the inherer, and the second is stable through itself. So how are they equal in substrate-status?

However, he called the substrate which is independent in its subsistence of the inherer, 'subject', and that which is not independent, 'matter'. 'Subject' is body, since body is independent in its subsistence of the inherer; and therefore he said at the end of the chapter: 'If the thing is in a substrate which is a subject, it is called an "accident".' Thus the meaning of his statement 'Every essence which is not in a subject, is a substance' is: every essence which is not in a *body* is a substance. And it comes down to it being said that 'every essence which is not in a substance, is a substance', but this does not consist in what amounts to an elucidation. Nay! It is more like the discourse of madmen, and most far from the ways of rational men. And if 'subject' has no meaning other than what we have mentioned, let him establish an existence other than a word for it, or a counterpart for it other than itself—and he will find no way to do it!

However, another division is feasible along the lines of his discussion, such that it is said: You have treated matter as a substrate not independent of the inherer, [either] in its subsistence as existent or in its subsistence as a quiddity. But if you say: 'it is a substrate which is not independent of the inherer, in its subsistence as existent'—well, many substances and bodies are not independent of what inheres in them by way of accidents in their subsistence as existent, and despite that the substrate is not matter and the inherer is not form. And if you say: 'it is a substrate which is not independent of the inherer, in the subsistence of its quiddity'—that is not accepted. For matter has a quiddity and reality by itself without form being its constituent part. Were form a constituent part of it, it would be impossible for the idea of it to be inscribed in the mind *without* its constituent part. Also were the form a part of it, matter would be compound and not simple. Thus it has been established that matter needs form in respect of its existence not in respect of its quiddity. However, every substance receptive of an accident shares [this trait], for there are substances which do not dispense with some of the accidents in existence, like being in a place or being in a time, or some of the quantities, or some of the qualities, and position—just as matter does not dispense with form in existence. So what is the difference between the two divisions? This is a doubt we put forth. Where is the escape from it? 'But it is no longer the time to escape!'[17]

As for the divisions of substance which Ibn Sīnā mentions, they are not enumerated through negation and affirmation which are opposites, such that conflict would be apparent in the disjunctive propositions, so no division stands out, nor could a division be added to them. Instead, amongst the divisions there is that for which he has not mentioned a counterpart, so it remains lame; and amongst them is where he mentioned a condition in a division which he did not mention in its counterpart, so it is crooked, such as his statement: 'Every substance not in a subject is either not in a substrate at all or it is in a substrate, which substrate is not independent of it in its subsistence.' But in the disjunctive proposition based on the condition of conflict he ought to have said: Every substance either is not in a substrate at all or is in a substrate. In that case the division would not have been a division of substance but of existence which is more general than it, for accident is included in the second division. So if he took the restriction and

[17] Qur'an 38:3.

condition into account in one of the divisions, then it is necessary that he take them into account in the second division; but if they are not taken into account, the division is invalid and conflict is not apparent in it.

Like that is his statement in respect of the second level: 'If it is not in a substrate at all, then either it is a substrate in itself without composition, or it is not.' It may be that he has somehow abridged here, and he should have said: Either it is a substrate in itself or it is not, and what is a substrate in itself either contains composition or does not, or, what is a substrate in itself must either be simple or compound. Then the simple substrate is prime matter and the compound is the body.

However, this division only applies to a substrate which is not independent of an inherer in subsistence, not to the substrate unqualified. For the unqualified substrate is a substrate for substance and accident together. Prime matter is a simple substrate for form and it is a substance, not a substrate for the accident, and the body is a compound substrate for the accident, not for the substance. And it is wondrous that the body should only be a substrate qua possessor of prime matter, not qua possessor of a form, since substrate-status suggests receptivity and predisposition, and this belongs to prime matter, not to form. Consequently the two divisions come down to a single division.

As for what he said: Whatever is not an inherer nor a substrate must be an intelligible form which is the intellect or the soul—it is pure arbitrariness, since the division does not imply the conceivability of the existence of the two, and he did not establish a proof for their existence, nor are the two similar in substance-status and reality. And the division which he put forward disregarded the divisions of substances, namely, the substances secondary by way of species and tertiary by way of genera. Further he did not take in all the genera of substances, nay, he did not mention a division which exhausts all existents in their species, their individuals, their substances and their accidents, such that by intellectual division the possibility of their existence becomes clear, and by intellectual proof the verification of their existence.

With the help of God (Exalted is He!) we will present a division comprehending [all] that, so that one power of knowledge is distinguished from the other, and one man from the other.

So we say: The existence the meaning of which is inscribed in the intellect and includes the quiddities of all things equally, is susceptible to *intellectual* division. For that which does not consist in univocal terms is not susceptible to division in regard to the [actual] *meaning*. That subdivides by the first division into what is a substrate for an inherer, into what is an inherer in a substrate, and into what subsists by itself not as a substrate nor as an inherer in a substrate. The substrate is that in which the inherer inheres in a pervasive manner, I mean that the inherer is in it in such a manner that it is in all of it. That subdivides: into what is not independent of the inherer in its subsistence, and we mean thereby that what it has by itself is only potentiality and predisposition, and existence occurs for it only through what inheres in it, and it is simple, not compound, and is called prime matter; and into what *is* independent in its subsistence of what inheres in it, and it is called the subject, and the predicate is predicated of it, and that is the body. Since the body is compounded from matter and form, and it is a substance, its two parts are two substances. For the substance cannot be compounded from two accidents, nor can the body be compounded from two intellectual substances.

As for the inherer—it subdivides: into that which its substrate is not independent of in its subsistence, and that is the corporeal form, such as spatiality and conjunction which has no contrary; and into that which its substrate is independent of in its subsistence, and the substrate is not altered by its substitution, such as being in a place, and the conjunction which is the contrary of separation, and it is called an accident. The divisions of accidents are limitless in number by way of negation and affirmation, except that they are limited to the nine categories, and they have been limited in respect of quantity and quality. The substrate includes what is simple and it includes what is compound, and the inherer includes what is a substance and it includes what is an accident. The substrate and inherer together are a particularised individual. Individuals are called primary substances, species are called secondary substances, and genera are called tertiary substances because of their proximity to and remoteness from sense-perception; and if you go in reverse—because of their proximity to and remoteness from the intellect.

As for what is self-subsistent which is neither an inherer nor a substrate, but instead is independent of them both, it must either have a connection with the two of them or not have. What has a connection either has the connection by the emanation of the inherer in the substrate, or the connection of establishing the substrate by the inherer, or the connection of the management of the inherer and the substrate together. What has the connection of the emanation of the inherer upon the substrate is the Active Intellect, the Dispenser of Forms, for the forms and accidents which are incepted in matters and substrates are by way of its emanation and because of it. And what has the connection of the establishment of the substrate by way of the inherer is the universal nature flowing in all the lower corporeal existents, preparing them for the reception of forms and accidents. And what has the connection of the management of the inherer and the substrate together such that they proceed to their perfections from their origins—it must either manage everything, I mean the world as a whole, and its management is a universal not particular management, then it is called universal soul or it must manage the particular bodies, I mean one rather than another. And that subdivides: into things which manage the heavenly bodies which are insusceptible to generation and corruption, then they are called celestial souls, and they are as numerous as the celestial spheres and stars, which are [either] established by observations, or escape the observations of men; and into things which manage the terrestrial bodies which are susceptible to generation and corruption, and they are: [a] the vegetable and animal souls which are corrupted by way of the corruption of the humours, and their management is by a natural subjugation; and [b] the human souls which are *not* corrupted by way of the corruption of the humours, and their management is by an intellectual choice.

As for what does not have a connection with the substrate and the inherer—I mean the things separate from the matters of bodies—wisdom does not rule that they should be idle. Rather they have the connection of the conception of the absolute good in the souls which are the managers by command. So it is necessary for every soul to have an intellect, just as every heavenly sphere has a soul, and it has active, not passive intellections. It is also necessary for the universal soul to have a universal intellect, and the intellect has a universal intellection from which emanates the absolute good upon everything by the medium of the soul, and existence ends up in it, just as existence originated *from* it, as an ordered series connected to the Command of the Creator, Who is exalted and sanctified above His glory falling within the hierarchy of existents or contrariety in beings. For He is the ultimate object of longings and through Him is the obtainment of desires. Intellects are in need of Him for the intellection of universals and particulars, souls are dependent on Him for managing celestial and mundane things, and natures are subject to Him—both simple ones and compound ones. 'Are not the creation and the Command His? Blessed be God, the Lord of the Worlds!'[18] 'He is the Living, there is no god but He! So call upon Him, making religion pure for Him. Praise belongs to God, the Lord of the Worlds!'[19] O God, benefit us by that which You teach us, and teach us that by which You benefit us, by the truth of the Chosen Ones amongst Your servants—upon them be peace!

[18] Qur'an 7:54.
[19] Qur'an 40:65.

THE SECOND ISSUE

On the Existence of the Necessary of Existence

Ibn Sīnā said: 'We do not doubt that there is existence. And it is subdivided into the Necessary in Itself and the necessary by another, which is contingent in consideration of itself.'[20]

'A single thing cannot simultaneously be necessary of existence in itself and by another.'[21]

'Nor can the essence of the Necessary of Existence in Itself have elements which combine, such that the Necessary of Existence is established by them, neither parts of a definition, nor parts of a quantity. Nor do each of the parts of the statement which explains the meaning of Its name signify something which in existence is not the other in itself.'[22]

And he said: 'The Necessary of Existence in Itself is necessary of existence from every aspect. And every necessary of existence in itself is absolute good, absolute perfection and absolute truth.'[23]

And he said: 'Nor can the species of the Necessary of Existence belong to other than Itself, since the existence of the species belongs to It due to Itself.[24] So it cannot be that two necessaries of existence share in the necessity of existence, such that necessity of existence is general for them both as a genus or concomitant, with a generality by equality. Instead Its individuation is because it is simply Necessary of Existence, not because of a factor other than Its individuated essence.'

'Further, every contingent in consideration of its essence possibly exists and possibly does not exist. Thus when existence preponderates over nonexistence, it certainly needs a preponderator. And the preponderator for all the contingents must be *non*-contingent in consideration of itself, but instead it must be necessary in itself, outside the series of contingents.'

20 Compare Ibn Sīnā, *Najāt*, p. 235.
21 Ibn Sīnā, *Najāt*, p. 225.
22 Ibn Sīnā, *Najāt*, pp. 227–8.
23 Compare Ibn Sīnā, *Najāt*, p. 229.
24 Ibn Sīnā, *Najāt*, p. 229.

Rebuttal

We will enumerate the inconsistencies in his argumentation. Then we will set about refuting and invalidating it.

His statement 'The necessary of existence might be by itself and it might be by another' which is a claim of the generality of the necessity of existence belonging to the two divisions, and his statement 'And it cannot be that two necessaries of existence share in the necessity of existence, such that necessity of existence is general for them both, as a genus or a concomitant', are two contradictory propositions. For a meaning which is not general cannot be subdivided and if it is subdivided then it has been made general. Because of this his claim is correct that one of the necessaries is due to itself and the second is due to another. But this is either an essential or a concomitant division, for if there were not an essential or a concomitant generality, then the claim would not be correct.

The Second Inconsistency. His statement 'Each of the parts of the statement which explains the meaning of Its name cannot signify something which in existence is not the other in itself.' Yet the simple statement 'Necessary of Existence in Itself' contains three terms: 'necessary', 'existence' and 'in itself'. Each term signifies a meaning other than the one signified by the next term. On account of this the division is correct such that it be said: 'existence subdivides into a necessary and a contingent, then the necessary subdivides into what is necessary by itself and into what is necessary by another'. Inevitably, each division gives notice of something other than what the next gives notice of, and signifies something which in existence is other than what the next signifies. That is an obvious inconsistency.

It is wondrous that he says: 'The Necessary of Existence does not have quantitative parts, like the body compounded of matter and form, nor parts of a definition, like what is compounded of genus and differentia, nor parts of a generality and a specificity, like colouration and whiteness.' So how did he make existence include the two divisions 'necessity' and 'contingency', then make necessity specific to It? And how did he make necessity of existence include the two divisions 'necessity by itself' and 'necessity by another', then make 'necessity by itself' specific to It? Is that not an unequivocal assertion that there are parts of a generality and a specificity, like colouration and whiteness? Unless he completely shuns these divisions and expressions, so that he says: 'It is some sort of reality which is ineffable.' He has mentioned this in other places in the *Shifā'* and elsewhere, when he had become alert to the like of these absurd implications, except that he contradicted that in saying 'The interpretation of the word for It is that Its existence is necessary by itself'. How extraordinary is something ineffable, the word for which has an explanation! Why did he not say: 'When the discourse comes to God, let them abstain?'[25]

The Third Inconsistency. His statement 'The Necessary of Existence by Itself is necessary of existence from every aspect', and he set about demonstrating it. But since It does not have 'aspects', neither perceptible spatial aspects, nor intelligible relational aspects, how is it that he bothered himself in demonstrating that It is necessary of existence from every aspect? He is like someone who sets about demonstrating that It is necessary of existence in regard to all Its parts and definitions, after explaining that It *has* no part and definition.

Stranger than this is his statement 'Every [*kull*] necessary of existence is absolute good'. We do not understand the meaning of this 'every'. Is it *whichever* individual necessary of existence is absolute good? Then in consequence it is a species or a genus. Or, does he mean thereby that *all* [*kull*] of its essence is absolute good, such that he makes out that it is a whole which has parts? What is that unification even in the expression, and what is this pluralisation even in the meaning?[26]

The Fourth Inconsistency. His statement 'Nor can the species of the Necessary of Existence belong to other than Itself.'

[25] Imāmite hadith. See Muḥammad Bāqir al-Majlisī, *Biḥār al-anwār* (Tehran, 1376–1392/1956–1972), vol. 3, p. 259.

[26] In this ellipsis, al-Shahrastānī scorns the lack of divine unity in Ibn Sīnā's wording, and claims plurality even extends to his meaning.

But how did he consider that it *could* be said 'The species of the Necessary of Existence is constituted by Itself', just as it is said in regard to the sun 'its species is constituted by its individual'? Does he not understand that the negation of many deficiencies from the Real (Exalted is His Majesty!) is a deficiency for Him? As the weavers amongst the literalists and the lowest story-tellers say:[27] 'Neither body, nor substance, nor something shaped, nor measured, nor elongated, nor round, nor square, nor pentagonal, nor obligated, nor put together', and the rabble of humanity respond, 'Glorified is God! Glorified is God!' So Ibn Sīnā set about protracting the chapters in his books with the negation of the like of these attributions from the Necessary of Existence in Itself, prior to proving It. Then he set about proving It by saying that contingents depend on the Necessary of Existence in Itself. So it is as though he grasped It by Its species-status in the mind and established what follows from Its species-status consisting in the negation of these features; then he grasped It by Its individuality such that he proved It on the basis of the contingency in contingents and their dependence on something which is Necessary of Existence in Itself. This is nothing but haphazardness and shooting in utter blindness, and a negation of deficiencies which is an affirmation of deficiencies!

As for the invalidation of what he argued and uttered, we say: in your statement 'we do not doubt that there is existence, and either it is necessary in itself or it is contingent in itself', you have made a counterpart for the Necessary of Existence, namely, the contingent in itself. It is implied by that, that existence includes two divisions which are equal in respect of existence-status, so that it is suited to be a genus or a concomitant tantamount to a genus. And one of the divisions is distinguished by a meaning which is suited to be a differentia or tantamount to a differentia. Thus the essence of the

[27] The weavers were a byword for the lowliest of society, and the professional story-tellers (*qāṣṣa*) were considered an ignorant, popular contrast to the religious scholars (*ʿulamāʾ*).

Necessary of Existence is compounded of a genus and a differentia, or what is tantamount to them by way of concomitants. That contradicts unity and it contradicts absolute independence. For whatever is compounded from two things or from two considerations—a generality and a specificity—is deficient, in need firstly of its constituents for its reality to be realised, and in need secondly of the thing which compounds it for it to existentialise its quiddity.

If Ibn Sīnā says: 'I do not make existence general, inclusive of the two divisions with an equal inclusion, for it belongs to ambiguous not univocal terms. It is more appropriate and primary in the Necessary of Existence, and *not* more appropriate and primary in the contingent. What is amongst ambiguous terms is not suited to be a genus. Rather, univocal terms which include quiddities with an equal inclusion are suited to be a genus. So what you impose as an absurd implication is not implied and what I established is not refuted.'[28] I say: You beg the question in two ways. The first of them is that the division of existence into the necessary in itself and the contingent in itself is *itself* the division of existence into that for which existence is more appropriate and primary, and into that for which it is *not* more appropriate and primary. Existence includes the two of them with an inclusion equal in respect of existence-status. And existence is something essential to the two divisions that are most specific to it, although it is accidental in relation to substance and accident, and the rest of the quiddities.

You have recognised from the definition of the essential that when you make it present in the mind, and you make present what it is essential to, the conceptualisation of what it is essential to is only possible for you through that thing present in the mind. Its existence in the mind is through its existence, not just *with* its existence, and its elimination from the mind is through its elimination, not *with* its elimination. The situation with regard to the Necessary and existence is like that, for the

[28] Compare Ibn Sīnā, *al-Mubāḥathāt*, ed. Muḥsin Bīdārfar (Qum, 1414/1993–4), pp. 218–19.

conceptualisation of the Necessary of Existence is only possible for you through the prior conceptualisation of existence, and when you eliminate existence necessity is eliminated through its elimination. When the man [Ibn Sīnā] had become aware of the like of this absurd implication, he invented for himself a division beyond the univocal, designating it 'the ambiguous'. That is not in the logic of the sages, nor will it protect him from starvation, nor is the absurd implication fended off by it! Even supposing that it is an authentic division, it is not specific to existence. Instead, the like of it applies to 'unity', 'causality', 'truth', and all general concepts consisting in genera and species. Thus it can be said, 'unity is applied to anything single, but it is most appropriate to the First'. 'Cause, truth and origin are applied to other than the Necessary of Existence, but are most appropriate to It.' And 'the term substance is applied to anything which, when it exists, its existence is not in a subject, but it is most appropriate to intellectual substances.' On this basis the division of the univocal would be eliminated and no word would comprise a meaning by equality.

The second way. We say, granted that existence is amongst what is ambiguous, and that it is another division. Is it not the case that existence is common to them both with some sort of generality, and necessity is specific to It with some sort of specificity; and that by which it is general is different from that by which it is particular? Then, It involves the compounding of two aspects by way of two terms, each of which signifies something different from what the second signifies. That negates absolute unity.

If he says 'the meaning of necessity is negative not positive, or relational not existential, so multiplicity is not implied in Its essence', I say our argument is firstly in respect of existence, then in respect of necessity. What do you say in respect of existence and the concept of it in the mind? Is it a general proposition, and an idea which includes the Necessary and the contingent with some sort of inclusivity, or not? If it does include, then there must be particularisation via another idea so that the Necessary is distinguished from the contingent. You cannot say 'the inclusive idea is a negative thing', since how could *existence* not be existential? Necessity is the confirmation of existence, i.e. existence belongs to It by Its essence, and so it follows for It that It is not derived from something else. How then did he take the consequent into account, yet leave out what was essential to It?[29] If necessity were a negative thing, then that to which it stands opposite—namely, contingency—would be an existential thing. Yet we know that you know that existence and affirmation are more appropriate to the Necessary, and nonexistence and negation are more appropriate to the contingent. How, when you have confirmed that existence is more appropriate and primary for the Necessary, and not more appropriate and primary for the contingent, did you forget the category of the ambiguous which you thought up? And even granted that the idea of it is a negative thing, it is not an absolute negation. Instead, it is the 'negation' of something in whose nature it is to be realised and which is suited for distinction, and through it multiplicity occurs. Leave aside what has been said: 'negations and relations do not necessitate multiplicity in the essence'. For they take this proposition as incontestable, but the matter is not like that, in accordance with the detailed analysis which is to come.

As for his statement 'the distinction between existence and necessity by way of generality and specificity is something relational in the mind, not in existence', it is the admission of the evidence for the absurd implication. For the distinction between the idea of being a genus and the idea of being a differentia is [always] only in the mind. So *in existence* there is no 'animal' which is a genus, and 'rational' which is a differentia, instead they are two considerations in the mind, not in the external world. How would a universal thing occur in external existence, there being no universal except in the mind? You know well that colouration and whiteness are two intelligible

[29] Since necessity is the 'confirmation of existence', the existence of the Necessary is not derived from anything else. Ibn Sīnā, allegedly, affirms the latter (=the consequent) but in claiming that necessity is negative in status he would have denied the former (=the antecedent).

considerations in the mind, not in the external world, and that in existence the *colouration* of white is nothing but whiteness.

The man comes back and says: The proliferation of considerations which ensue from the proliferation of terms, generally and specifically, in reality goes back to the proliferation of relations and negations in respect of the Necessary of Existence. For our statement 'It is the origin of existence, its cause, willer, and originator', is the relation to It of existence and [also] of its emanation from It, without anything thereby being incepted for It, or Its essence being multiplied by something. Our statement: It is Necessary of Existence by Its Essence, means, It is an essence from which the need for another is negated. Generality and specificity of existence are one in respect of Him (Exalted is He!), for His necessity *is* His existence, and His individuation does not entail something else which individuates Him, as a concomitant or not as a concomitant. And His unity does not require some other idea which unifies Him, for He is one because He is Necessary of Existence. Our statement 'because He is ...' is not in reality providing [Him] with a cause. Instead the meaning of it is that He is only thus, and this is the meaning of my statement 'the Necessary of Existence is only one from every aspect'. And my statement 'the multiplicity of relations and negations does not necessitate a multiplicity in Its essence', is a proposition accepted by everyone. Surely, our statement 'this body is near to so-and-so, far from so-and-so, [and] does not contain such and such an attribute' does not necessitate a multiplicity in the body's essence, in spite of [the latter's] susceptibility to multiplicity; so what is the state of affairs with an Essence sanctified above the characteristics of multiplicity and change?

I say: Concepts in the mind—general and specific—of general and specific terms, are not inasmuch as they are linguistic terms. Concepts in the mind are only correct due to their correspondence with what is outside the mind. I do not mean by 'correspondence' that the universal in the mind corresponds with a *universal* in the external world—since a universal entity is not to be found in individuals. Rather the universal in the mind corresponds with every single individual amongst what is particular in the external world. As universal humanity in the mind corresponds with every single individual amongst what exists or does not exist. Then, the distinction between one species and another is only by way of essential differentiae, and the distinction between one individual and another is only by way of accidental concomitants.

Since that is proven, it is clear that general existence includes the Necessary and the contingent with some sort of inclusivity. If the inclusivity, however, is by way of equality, it is suited to be a genus, and then there must be an essential differentia, so the essence is compounded of a genus and differentia. If existence is *not* by way of equality, it does not depart from generality and inclusivity, and then there must still be a differentia which is essential or non-essential, so the essence is compounded of something general and something specific. If Its generality is Its very specificity and Its specificity is Its very generality—there is no generality and specificity at all! Then your proposition proves false: 'we do not doubt that there is existence, and it subdivides into necessary and contingent ...' And your positing existence, qua unqualified, as the subject matter of metaphysical science proves false. Moreover, what you mention in the books you have composed proves false, namely 'the concomitants of existence qua existence', and your enumeration of its concomitants qua necessary, not qua existence.

Do you not say: Absence or nonexistence stand opposite It, qua existence, and contingency stands opposite It, qua necessary, not qua existent; Its being one follows for It, qua necessary, and likewise Its being absolutely independent, sanctified above the characteristics of incipience, and Its being an origin for all beings? But his statement 'the multiplicity of negations and relations does not necessitate a multiplicity in the essence' is a proposition which is only uncontested by the commonalty of his companions, and it is *not* apodictic, nor self-evident, nor argued except on the analogy of proximity and distance. And why did he say 'the characterisation of all the relations is the [same as] that of proximity and distance'? If that is conceded to him, then amongst relations there is that which necessitates the multiplicity of accidents, and amongst them there is that which necessitates the multiplicity of considerations. Is not the characterisation of a man's becoming a father when a son occurs to him, an uncle when the son of a brother occurs to him, and an agent when an act occurs through him, *unlike* the characterisation of proximity and distance? It is likewise on the side of negation. For the negation of the cutting of a sword is unlike the negation of the cutting of wool.

Thus negations are various and relations are various. How then can a single characterisation common to them hold true for them? Rather, the difference *itself* between relational ideas and negational concepts necessitates the multiplicity of two considerations in the essence! For you say: This is a relational concept for it, not a negational one, and this is negational, not relational. You say: 'This is a relation from such and such a point of view, and that from such and such a point of view ...', and all that is a relative, mental multiplicity, such that there is understood from each one of them what is not understood from the other, and each term signifies that which is not signified by the other term. So his statement proves false, 'the Necessary of Existence in Itself is not multiple by way of the multiplicity of negations and relations'. We will come back to that in the issue of unity.

The Choice

Our custom is to mention a section at the end of each issue, informing the reader of the cause of error and the mistakes which befell Ibn Sīnā, and pointing out to the student the way of correctness and the truth, through a solid argument which dents the blade and strikes at the joint. And God is the Bestower of success and of help.

I say: These inconsistencies and problems only faced Ibn Sīnā and his associates in philosophy because they made existence general with the generality of genus or the generality of concomitants, and they assumed that since they placed it amongst the ambiguous and removed it from the univocal they escaped safely from these absurd implications. However, nothing will rescue them from them except treating existence and every attribute and term which they apply to Him (Exalted and Sanctified is He!), such as 'unity', 'the One', 'the Truth', 'the Good', 'the Intellect', 'the Intellecting', 'the Intellected', etcetera, by way of *equivocity*, not univocity, nor ambiguity. They are agreed on the fact that the application of 'unity' and 'the one' to Him (Exalted is He!) and to other than Him is by way of pure equivocity. And likewise is 'the truth' and 'the good'—for He is truth in the sense that He makes the truth true and He makes the false false, and He is necessary in His existence in the sense that He necessitates the existence of other than Him, and annihilates, and He is living in the sense that He gives life and death.

Contraries are litigants and variant things are legal appellants, and their Judge is not numbered amongst either of His two appellants, the two litigants before Him. Instead, 'the truth'[30] is applied to the Judge in the sense that He manifests the truth and establishes it, not in the sense that He disputes with one of the two litigants such that He would sometimes be equal to him and at others at variance with him. So existence and nonexistence, necessity and contingency, unity and multiplicity, knowledge and ignorance, life and death, right and wrong, good and bad, power and impotence, are contraries—and exalted be God above contraries and rivals! 'So do not knowingly make rivals for God.'[31] 'And to God belong the most beautiful names, so call upon Him with them. And spurn those who deviate in respect of His names—they will be punished for what they used to do.'[32] O God, benefit us by that which You teach us, and teach us that by which You benefit us, by the truth of the Chosen Ones amongst Your servants—upon them be peace!

[30] Note that the word for 'the truth', *al-ḥaqq*, also means 'right' in a legal sense.

[31] Qur'an 2:22.

[32] Qur'an 7:180.

THE THIRD ISSUE

On the Unity of the Necessary of Existence

Ibn Sīnā said: 'The Necessary of Existence is not predicated of many, nor can the species of the Necessary of Existence belong to other than Itself. For the existence of Its species as such either is entailed by Its species itself, or is entailed by a cause other than Itself. Then if it is entailed by Its species itself, the existence of Its species belongs only to It and if it is due to a cause, It is an effect.'[33]

Then he said: 'And how can the quiddity abstracted from matter belong to *two* essences? Two things are two only either because of the meaning, or because of the subject bearing the meaning, or because of the position and place, or the moment and time, and in general, due to some *cause* or other. And any two things which do not vary by way of the meaning, only vary by way of something other than the meaning.'[34]

Then he said: 'The Necessary of Existence is one in respect of the perfection of Its existence; and one in respect of the fact that Its definition belongs to It [alone]; and one in respect of the fact that It is not divisible, neither by way of quantity, nor by way of principles constituting It, nor by way of the parts of a definition; and one in respect of the fact that Its rank in existence—namely the *necessity* of existence—only belongs to It, and it is impossible for necessity of existence to be shared.'[35] He set about demonstrating that, and was prolix, and the gist of it amounts to his saying: the necessity of existence would either be amongst the concomitants of a self-subsistent quiddity, or would be amongst the constituents of a quiddity which subsists by way of it, or is an expression for that essence Necessary in Itself, with which absolutely nothing else is associated in necessity of existence—and [the latter] is the truth.

Afterwards he said: 'It could not be said 'two necessaries of existence would *not* be associated in anything'—and how—

[33] Ibn Sīnā, *Najāt*, p. 229.

[34] Ibn Sīnā, *Najāt*, pp. 229–30.

[35] Ibn Sīnā, *Najāt*, p. 230.

seeing that they would be associated in the necessity of existence, and associated in being free of a substrate? If the necessity of existence is predicated of the two by way of equivocity, then our argument is not in regard to the *term* ['Necessary of Existence'] but in regard to the meaning on the basis of which the term is predicated univocally such that a general meaning occurs, with the generality of a concomitant or the generality of a genus—and we have explained the absurdity of that.'[36]

Then he set about proving the Necessary of Existence and he demonstrated it, saying: 'We do not doubt that there is existence. And all existence is either necessary or contingent. If it is necessary, then Its existence has proven true, and that is what is aimed at. If it is contingent, then the existence of every contingent goes back to a necessary … .'[37] And he began to substantiate it by way of the division which he mentioned, and he said afterwards: 'Only one emanates from the One, since were two to emanate from It, then it would be from two variant aspects, and were A to emanate from It from the aspect that B emanated from It, A would be B, and this is absurd. Then, that which emanates from It can have various aspects realised for it, since it is *contingent* of existence in consideration of itself, necessary of existence in consideration of that which necessitates it—so it need not be one in every respect, and then it need not be that only one emanates from it, for it possesses considerations and mental aspects. Then insofar as it is contingent in itself a soul or matter emanates from it, and insofar as it is necessary by another an intellect or form emanates from it.'

Evaluation

The rebuttal of him is in respect to the inconsistency in his discussion and defectiveness in his divisions, not in regard to the verdict of the issue, for monotheism is a verdict upon which there is agreement.

[36] Ibn Sīnā, *Najāt*, p. 234.
[37] Ibn Sīnā, *Najāt*, p. 235.

The First Inconsistency. His first statement '"the Necessary of Existence" is not predicated of many', and his statement 'nor can the species of the Necessary of Existence belong to other than Itself'—but 'species' is *only* predicated of many! So how did he apply the term 'species' to the Necessary of Existence? The Necessary of Existence is only predicated of an essence and an existent with which nothing else is associated in name, while species is only predicated of an existent with which something else is associated in name, let alone [in] the description or definition—for they lie above the mere name.

The Second Inconsistency. You took existence qua unqualified and made it the subject of metaphysics, speaking about its concomitants. Next, you placed the Necessary of Existence amongst its divisions and its adjuncts. Then you spoke about the concomitants of the Necessary of Existence qua unqualified, that It is One, that It is Truth, that It is Perfect, that It is a cause, and that It is an origin. Then you spoke in regard to proving the Necessary of Existence and you demonstrated It. Were it not for the fact that you lay necessary existence down as a species, or tantamount to a species, or as something general, or tantamount to something general, you would not mention these differentiae adhering to its status of species. And since Its species does not belong to other than Itself, It has [also] been grasped by Its individuality. Yet the individual, like Zayd, is not sometimes grasped unqualifiedly, so you call attention to its concomitants and adjuncts, and at other times individually, so you call attention to *its* concomitants and adjuncts. For if it is grasped unqualifiedly it departs from being the *individual* Zayd.

The Third Inconsistency. His statement: The Necessary of Existence is one from such and such an aspect, and one from such and such an aspect—and he enumerated seven aspects. I say: He is only one from every aspect if He has no 'aspects' whatsoever. The absolutely one is that which involves no multiplicity, and the multiplicity of these aspects and considerations negates unqualified pure unity. If he says 'This multiplicity comes down to negations and relations, or to aspects and considerations', we have talked about that sufficiently.

The Fourth Inconsistency. He said: 'It cannot be said "two necessaries of existence would *not* be associated in anything"—and how—[seeing that] they would be associated in existence and the necessity of existence, and being free of a substrate?' This admission of his eliminates all his previous words and contradicts them! It is as though he limits the association which precludes unity and occasions duality to association in meaning through univocity alone, and he does not understand that the association in meaning which is general requires differentiation into the meaning which is particular. That is multiplication and compounding, and it is implied unavoidably.

Then we say: Your statement that 'necessity of existence is not predicated of many, nor can the species of the Necessary of Existence belong to other than Itself' contradicts your statement 'existence is predicated of many, and the species of existence can belong to other than itself, and despite that the existence of the Necessary by Itself belongs to nothing other than Itself'. Then why do you not say of the Necessary 'It is predicated of many, and despite that the existence of the Necessary by Itself belongs to nothing other than Itself'? Except that you have explicitly spoken of many!

I say: Amongst substances is that which is distinguished by itself and its reality from the like of it and the opposite of it, without being associated in a genus and differentiated by a differentia, such as the separate intellects, for they do not have something they are associated in, like genus or like matter, nor something through which they are distinguished, like differentia or like form. Despite that they are variant in their realities and distinct in their forms by themselves and nothing else. So why do you not say likewise in regard to two necessaries of existence?

In regard to his statement 'The existence of Its species either is entailed by Its species itself, or is entailed by a cause other than Itself,' it may be said: 'For what would you reproach someone who says "the existence of Its species is not to be supplied with a cause at all, neither by way of the species itself, nor by way of some cause other than itself"—so that the division is useless?' The second division: 'Two things are two only either due to a meaning, or a cause which is the subject bearing the meaning, or due to such and such', is not a comprehensive division. And in his statement 'The Necessary of Existence is one in respect of the perfection of Its existence', he did not explain 'perfection' and did not understand that 'perfection' is a deficiency for Him. One of the sages has said: 'The greatest self-sufficiency is His to whom the creation and the Command belong'—Majestic is our Lord and exalted above being characterised by perfection, *a fortiori* of being characterised by deficiency! For He makes perfect whatever is perfect and makes complete whatever is deficient. Then if Ibn Sīnā meant by 'perfection' that He perfects everything perfect, that is true. However, he is obliged to follow this proposition through for every attribute, even for existence, so that he says: He is 'existent' in the sense that He existentialises every existence, is 'Necessary of Existence' in the sense that He necessitates every existent, is 'knowing' in the sense that He causes whatever is knowing to know, and is 'powerful' in the sense that He empowers whatever is powerful. Yet that is not the man's procedure. Were that the doctrine he espoused he would not have upheld the universality and inclusivity of existence, and he would have judged that existence is amongst purely equivocal terms, as we explained above.

What Ibn Sīnā mentioned—that He is one in respect of the fact that His definition belongs to Him [alone] and one in respect of the fact that He is indivisible—all that is onenesses belonging to each single one of His creatures (Exalted is He!), and their negation from Him and their affirmation for Him is a deficiency. Likewise is his statement 'The necessity of existence is either amongst the concomitants of a quiddity or amongst its constituents', but He has no quiddity such that it could have a concomitant or a constituent. And were He to have a quiddity, either it would be different from existence or it would be existence itself. Both disjuncts are false, for either the quiddity is an associated quiddity like 'animality' for man, horse and donkey, or it is a particular quiddity like 'man'. But there is neither association in the existence of the Necessary of Existence nor particularity.[38] Then why is it that the man uses the term 'quiddity' and 'species-status' on every occasion, while in reality disbelieving it?[39] How—when he does not even affirm quiddities compounded of genera and differentiae for separate intellects, but mentions that they are distinguished by their simple non-compound realities? So how, by mention of quiddity and species-status, did he make as if to affirm the ideas of genus and differentia in respect of the Necessary of Existence?

What he mentioned by way of proof—that It is the support for contingents—is correct, unobjectionable and incontestable, except that he confused the onlooker by mentioning divisions from which It is free, intending to illuminate and explain thereby, but increasing muddle and mystification thereby. And knowledge is a modicum which is added to by the foolish!

In regard to his statement 'only one emanates from the One', it is to be said to him: what is meant by 'emanation' from It? Do you mean existentiation by 'emanation' or do you mean necessitation by it? For existentiation is the bestowal of existence and necessitation is the bestowal of necessity, and the contingent in itself only needs the Necessary in Itself in acquiring *existence*, not necessity. Necessity implies existence and existence does not imply necessity. We will come back to prove this in the issue on the incipience of the world. What he mentioned about the emanation of two different acts only being by way of two different aspects, is a *petitio principii*, only sheer rejection of the counter-thesis and simply ruling it out as fanciful remaining for him. We can establish that in physics,

38 Up to here, al-Shahrastānī has paraphrased Ibn Sīnā's proof for divine unity. Compare *Ishārāt*, vol. 3, pp. 464–9.

39 Perhaps al-Shahrastānī has in mind here Ibn Sīnā's formula, 'His quiddity is His quoddity' (*māhiyyatuhu hiya inniyyatuhu*). In regard to species, al-Shahrastānī began the chapter by quoting Ibn Sīnā, '... nor can the species of the Necessary of Existence belong to other than Itself'.

since heat and cold might emanate from a single thing from a single aspect, however, *into two different substances.* Likewise, whiteness and blackness emanate from the sun into two material substrata, and solidity and liquefaction into two bodies—so what about into intellectual substances?

Next, the like of these aspects do *not* necessitate multiplicity in the essence of the Necessary of Existence. He has admitted the proof of that in different places, reducing them [=the aspects] to negations and relations, and that does not necessitate multiplicity in the essence. He admits the like of that in regard to the First Intellect, for one existent among other existents has emanated from it by each aspect and relation. Next, if only one emanates from the One then it is implied that only two emanate from the two! So if three, or four, or more emanated from it, it would be from different aspects—yet two aspects, not more, have been presupposed for it. Thus the ascription of what is more than two to two aspects is just like the ascription of what is more than one to a single aspect. And the ascription of ten to five is just like the ascription of two to one.

Ibn Sīnā said in the *Najāt* in reply to the like of these absurd implications: 'The First Effect is contingent of existence in itself and necessary of existence through the First; and the necessity of its existence through the First is an intellect, and it intellects its own essence and intellects the First ...' until he says, 'what it has in itself is contingency of existence and what it has from the First is necessity of existence. Then the multiplicity insofar as it intellects its own essence *and* intellects the First, is a multiplicity which is a concomitant of the necessity of its existence from the First. So the multiplicity of these considerations, subsequent to it being contingent of existence in itself, does not have an effect on what it has in itself. This is in contrast to the situation with the Necessary of Existence, for multiplicity *would* have an effect on what It has in Itself, namely unity, in that It is Necessary of Existence.'[40]

I say: Certainly, what it has in consideration of itself is

[40] Compare Ibn Sīnā, *Najāt*, p. 277.

contingency of existence, and contingency of existence is different from *existence*, so it has a 'non-existential' nature. Nonexistence does not existentialise something existent, so no existence is necessitated by it! On the other hand, the necessity of existence which it has is non-essential, but rather is a concomitant—and the concomitant does not bring into existence an essence as an intended existent. So in consequence the intellect does not have what is conducive to emanation from it and existentiation by it. Likewise every contingent has this characterisation, and so there is no existentialiser for beings other than God (Exalted is He!), the Necessary of Existence in Himself. Thus it is necessary for all contingents to be related to Him in the same way, without the mediation of an intellect, a soul and a nature. As for its being an 'intellect', it is a term for its abstraction from matter. Abstraction from matter is simply the negation of matter from it, and how can unqualified negation, or the particular negation of a thing from it be suitable for an intellectual substance which is among the noblest of existents? Therefore, there is no aspect in the intellect conducive to necessitation and origination, and so it is necessary that the universe is directly related to the Necessary of Existence in Itself.

Ibn Sīnā said: 'Contingency has a non-existential nature, so it is conducive to that which has a non-existential nature, namely, matter. And necessity has an existential nature, so it is conducive to that which has an existential nature, namely, form. Inasmuch as it intellects itself in abstraction from matter, it is conducive to an intellect abstracted from matter, or universal soul; also inasmuch as it intellects the First, it is conducive to separate intellects and ruling souls. Then these kinds of conduciveness are not limited by a known number, for the intellect does not determine the limitation of their numbers within a known number. However, astronomical observation has shown that there are nine spheres, and the proof has been established that every sphere has a soul, and every soul an intellect. Thus there are nine separate intellects and nine souls.'

I say: You toil away, you assemblies of philosophers, at

deducing the likes of these tenuous ideas with which even a jurist would not be satisfied in the guesswork of his conjectures, and to which he would not tie any verdict in matters of law—how then the sage who speaks on the highest of sciences, in matters of divinity? Is not 'contingency' a judgement covering all contingents? So if the First Intellect in consideration of its contingency is an originator of matter which has a non-existential nature, then the status of every contingent existent in respect of contingency is the status of the First Intellect, so let it be suited to be an originator of matter! And if the First Intellect in consideration of the necessity of its existence by way of the First is an originator of form which has an existential nature, then every existent which is necessary by another has the same status in respect of 'necessity by the other' as the First Intellect, so let it be suited to be an originator of form! But that is not the case. If the state of affairs were reversed in regard to the hierarchy of beings, such that the First Intellect were last and the compound body first, the situation would not be as far-fetched as he supposed. For the body is multiple simply through form and matter, while the intellect is multiple through necessity and contingency. So form is like necessity and matter is like contingency. And if something can emanate from the Necessary which is contingent in itself and necessary by It, something could also emanate from It which is a matter and a form, without the Necessary being multiplied thereby, just as It is not multiplied by the former.

We say: If the First Intellect were in respect of its contingency to necessitate matter, and in respect of its necessity to necessitate form, then the existent which is after the First Intellect would be a body compounded of matter and form, and the [other] separate intellects would be after *it* in existence. But this contradicts what they set forth in their books regarding the hierarchy of existents.

Sometimes Ibn Sīnā says in some of his *Taʿlīqāt*, 'insofar as the First Intellect intellects its own essence a soul emanates from it, and insofar as it intellects the First an intellect emanates from it'; and sometimes he says in some of his works, 'some forty intellects emanate from Him, which are the "separate intellects"'. His discussion has gone astray in the extreme in this instance. For he was unable to introduce this on the basis of a sound demonstration and a 'straight path'—and whoever takes up knowledge of what is beyond him is stricken by ignorance of what is below it!

We say: If the like of these aspects and considerations which are in the First Intellect were simultaneously to necessitate intellectual existents which are multiple in their identities, without necessitating a multiplicity in the essence of the [First] Intellect, then, intellectual existents which are multiple in their identities can simultaneously emanate from the *Necessary of Existence* via the like of these aspects and considerations, without necessitating a multiplicity in the essence of the Necessary of Existence. So it could be said: 'Insofar as It intellects Itself an intellect emanates from It, and insofar as Its existence is necessary a soul is emitted from It, and insofar as it intellects the First Intellect either a form emanates from It, or a matter and a form ...', and so on by way of arbitrary rulings. For one aspect is indistinguishable from another and one consideration from another.

From another point of view: Since the Necessary of Existence is one from every aspect, and It necessitates a single Intellect from an 'aspect', then let the Intellect also necessitate a single thing from an aspect. For it only necessitates something in consideration of its benefiting from that which necessitates *it*, not in consideration of what it has in itself, so that it follows that existence is arranged from individuals in a continuous sequence, not in unequal quantities and variant individuals. But existence is the opposite of that, so it is incoherent.

From another point of view: Just as many cannot emanate from one, because it would necessitate a multiplicity in the cause, likewise one cannot emanate from one, because it would necessitate a unity in the effect![41] And if it were said 'the

[41] Ibn Sīnā denies that the First Effect is absolutely one in the

multiplicity in the effect is not derived from the cause, but is in consideration of itself—that it is contingent, necessary by another', it may be said: and multiplicity in the *cause* is not in consideration of Its essence but is in consideration of 'relation and negation', and the multiplicity of relations does not necessitate multiplicity in the essence.

And from another point of view we say: Were the Necessary of Existence to intellect two things, it does not follow that it is through two different 'aspects'. Then why, when He originates two things, must it be through two different aspects? Is not His intellection the same as His origination from the point of view of the man, without any difference between [the statements] 'He intellected' and 'He originated'? So if He can intellect two universals He can *originate* two universals. Unless he would cling to this blasphemous innovation and say 'He only intellects one thing, just as He only originates one thing ...'. Thus he would abandon his doctrine that [God] knows things in respect of their universals and their causes. And in that case it would follow for him that He only knows Himself—and that is most blasphemous!

And here is a point of inquiry, namely, in what sense is unity predicated of the Necessary in Itself, of the Intellect, of the Soul and of the rest of the existents? Is it by way of univocity, by way of ambiguity, or by way of equivocity? If it is by way of univocity, allow it to be suited to be a genus, and allow every species to be differentiated by a differentia—and that is composition. If it is by way of ambiguity, allow it to be suited to be something general, and allow every species to be differentiated by a concomitant property—and that too is a composition. If it is by way of equivocity, let him distinguish through essential realities between one unity and another, for two things associated within the term ['unity'] vary through essential concomitant realities and meanings. If the distinction is not evident, the discussion about the unity of the Creator (Praised be He!)

---

manner of the Necessary of Existence. It already involves a relative multiplicity.

is empty talk. So let us make that evident, and mention the divisions of unity such that when we say 'He (Exalted is He!) is one, but not like numerically single things' the unity is unadulterated and absolute. And let us mention the usual section at the ends of the issues, and 'If your neighbours fail you, rely on the master of your house!' May God (Mighty and Majestic!) grant us protection from error and stumbling.

The Correct Choice

Since the starting point of the demonstration establishing the Necessary of Existence in Itself is the division of existence into 'necessary in itself' and 'contingent in itself', and it has become clear that existence belongs to equivocal, not univocal terms, and it has become apparent that the ambiguous is tantamount to the univocal or is a division without meaning—the method of demonstration for Ibn Sīnā and whoever follows him comes apart, because division does not apply to the equivocal. On the other hand, the procedure of the prophets (upon them be peace!) is in accordance with what we will report. So we say: the Creator (Exalted is He!) is too well known for His existence to be pointed to by anything, and the recognition of Him (Exalted is He!) is through innate predisposition. Whoever denies Him has denied himself. Nay! Whoever denies Him has [actually] *confirmed* Him, since He is the absolute Judge. And whoever avers that there is no Judge has made a judgement. So the denial of Him is a confirmation and the negation of Him is an affirmation.

Just as the contingency in all contingents is something essential and the need of the contingent for a preponderator is something necessary, and so it calls for something needed which is *not* contingent, i.e. not in need of other than it—likewise incongruent things when paired and paired things when combined need something absolutely independent to combine them. However, the [status of being] 'absolutely independent' cannot be realised for two since each of the two would be in need as well as needed, in *being two*. So the absolutely independent is the Lord Besought of All, for 'He is God, the One, the Lord Besought of All', and that is mentioned in the 'Sūra of Sincerity'.[42] In accordance with this the starting-point of the summons of the prophets (peace be upon them!) was monotheism, I mean the statement 'No god but God', since the affirmation [of God's existence] was already finished with. Because of this the denial by opponents is confined to monotheism alone: 'This is because when God alone was invoked, you disbelieved';[43] 'When God alone is mentioned, the hearts of those who do not believe in the Hereafter recoil';[44] 'When you mention your Lord in [reciting] the Qur'an, alone, they turn their backs in aversion'.[45] So it is clear that the summons at first was to monotheism, since there is [in fact] no one in the world who denies a creative and wise 'god'. Denial is in regard to monotheism alone, and the proof of monotheism is what we have mentioned amongst the Names in the 'Sūra of Sincerity'.

Next, unity is in accordance with divisions: (1) A unity which is the source and basis of number. As we say, 'one, two ...', number being composed from it, and as the number increases, the relation of one to it diminishes. Unity in this sense is unworthy of the majesty of God (Exalted is He!), since it is not possible for number and the numerable to be composed from Him. (2) A unity which is concomitant to number and the numerable. As we say of every totality, 'it is one', for ten insofar as it is 'ten' is a single totality. And as we say 'one man', 'one horse', 'one inscription'. This unity too is unworthy of the majesty of God (Exalted is He!), since He is not a totality[46] such that the unity of a totality is realised for Him. (3) Like that is the unity of species, the unity of genus, and the unity of the individual which are indicated perceptually and intellectually. Instead, 'unity' is applied to Him (Exalted is He!) and to

[42] Qur'an 112: 1–2.
[43] Qur'an 40:12.
[44] Qur'an 39:45.
[45] Qur'an 17:46.
[46] *Jumla* also suggests 'collection'.

existents purely equivocally. He is one *unlike* the 'ones' mentioned—one such that the two opposites, unity and multiplicity, both emanate from Him, one in the sense that He brings things that are 'one' into existence. He was unique in unicity, then He made it overflow on His creation. Unity and existence belong to Him without an opposite opposing Him or a rival comparing with Him, 'And do not knowingly set up rivals to God!'[47]

As for His origination of beings multiply or His origination of the Intellect singly, since He is single—the absurd implication of both doctrines together has been mentioned. For the existence of a multiplicity through Him and its emanation from Him, necessitates a plurality of aspects and considerations in His essence (Exalted is He!); while the existence of one through one either entails a correlation between the cause and effect, or it entails the oneness in every way of the effect. Both alternatives are false. Rather both alternatives are also correct! For the generality and particularity of the relation is mentioned in the revelation and is accepted by people of intellect. God (Exalted is He!) says, 'There is not one thing in the heavens and the earth but it comes to God as a worshipper'.[48] This is due to the generality of the relation with Him. And He says (the mention of Him is glorious!), 'And the worshippers of the All-Merciful are those who walk gently on the earth'.[49] This is due to the particularity of the relation with Him.

The general can be particularised step by step till it reaches a limit in a single thing which is a 'worshipper', just as the particular can be generalised step by step till it reaches a limit in 'the universe'. The uppermost worshippers of God are His angels 'brought nigh'. The status of the Spirit which rises as a rank, and the angels as a rank,[50] is the status of the universe in company with its parts, or the First Active Intellect in company

[47] Qur'an 2:22.
[48] Qur'an 19:93.
[49] Qur'an 25:63.
[50] This alludes to Qur'an 78:38: 'On a day when the Spirit and the angels stand as a rank ...'

with the separate intellects which direct by the Command. And just as particularity and generality are two things both rational and revealed in regard to 'worship', likewise their status occurs in regard to origination and creation, and in the relation of Lordship to the worshippers as His statement (Exalted is He!): 'the Lord of the worlds, the Lord of Moses and Aaron'.[51]

Furthermore, know that what is mentioned in the divine scriptures, in respect of the generality and particularity of relation, is more worthy of being followed than the proposition of the philosophers, 'only one emanates from the One, and the rest of the existents are related to It by the mediation of that one, in the manner of concomitance'. For the *relation* of that one to It also—if one looks into *its* reality—is in the manner of concomitance, since the existence of that one through It is amongst the concomitants of Its essence. What then is the difference between the two divisions? Why might not the universe be related to It in a single manner without any difference between what emanates from It essentially, without mediation and by primary intention, not by secondary intention, and between what emanates from It contrary to that? The secret of it is that the aspect through which contingents are in need of the Originator is their contingent existence, and existents are equal in regard to this aspect. So there is no difference between what is abstracted from matter and what is associated with matter from the point of view of contingency, nor in respect of contingent existence, and the two divisions are only disparate in rank for *another reason.* So it is appropriate that the First Principle is a principle for everything in a single manner, and the 'intermediaries' are different due to the disparity of levels.

Does not the Intellect, the Dispenser of Forms, emit forms onto the various matters by a single emission, and its essence is not multiplied by their multiplicity, and the relation of them all to it is a single relation, so it is not said: insofar as whiteness emanates from it on a matter, and blackness on a matter, two facets and aspects are incepted for it such that its essence is

[51] Qur'an 7:121–122; 26:48.

multiplied by the multiplicity of the forms which are infinite? The statement about the Necessary of Existence in Itself is like that. If it were said: 'The Active Intellect possesses multiple aspects and considerations, since it is contingent in itself, necessary through that which necessitates it, and it intellects its essence, its cause, and its effect in addition to other aspects of multiplicity—in contrast to the Necessary of Existence in Itself, for *It* is one from every aspect', it may be said: This excuse does not counter the vital aspect of the argument. For were the multiplicity of what emanates to bring about a multiplicity in the essence of the source, then the aspects would be as numerous as the number of what emanates from it, and these aspects would be realised in the essence without limit. We do not doubt that the essence of the Dispenser of Forms does not contain numbers of facets *without limit!* Since there are limited facets in its essence, do there not emanate from the First Intellect limited existents, like the separate intellects and the souls directing the spheres; or else they are limited to three aspects, so three things arise from it: an intellect, a soul, and a matter, in accordance with the divergence in doctrines on this question?

In sum, it is known from that, that the relation of the universe to the Necessary of Existence is in accordance with a single judgement, in which the one and the many, substance and accident, and that which is abstracted from matter and that which is associated with it, are all equal: 'And He is powerful over everything ...!'[52] O God, benefit us by that which You teach us, and teach us that by which You benefit us, by the truth of the Chosen Ones amongst Your servants—upon them be peace!

[52] Qur'an 64:1.

THE FOURTH ISSUE

On the Knowledge of the Necessary of Existence and Its Relationship With the Universal and Particular

Know that the theologians have affirmed that the Creator (Exalted is He!) knows all objects of knowledge, by their method of examining His acts and [the latter's] implication of precision and skill. They claim apodictic knowledge that [for] every precise and skilful act when it is derived from an agent, it must be that its agent is knowledgeable about it in every way. However, this judgement broke down for some of them, since they found agents in empirical experience from which an act is derived in every way, yet its agent does *not* know it in every way.

The philosophers eschew this method, for some of the ancients amongst them held that knowledge is the form of the object of knowledge with the knower, and it is absurd that the First have an essence *and* a form in the essence—for He would either be together with a form, or a possessor of form, and He is exalted above that. Rather this is the description of the First Intellect, since the forms of existents are present with it and inscribed upon it.

Ibn Sīnā said: 'The Necessary of Existence in Itself is an intellect, intellecting and intellected, and It is one in Its essence, not multiplied thereby. As for [the fact] that It is intellected—it is because you know that the nature of existence qua nature of existence is not incapable of being intellected. It only happens accidentally to it not to be intellected when it is in matter and with the accidents of matter, and insofar as it is like that, it is an object of sense perception or of imagination. When existence is in abstraction from this restraining condition, it is existence *and* an intellected quiddity. Everything which in itself is in abstraction from matter and material accidents, insofar as it is abstract, it is an intellect; insofar as it is considered for it that its abstract identity belongs to itself, it is self-intellected; and insofar as it is considered for it that its self has an abstract identity, it is self-intellecting.'[53]

[53] Ibn Sīnā, *Najāt*, pp. 243–4. Also see *al-Shifā': al-Ilāhiyyāt*, ed.

Then he said after that: 'Its being intellected and intellecting *ipso facto* does not necessitate that It is twofold in Itself, nor even twofold in consideration. For the two things are brought about only in that (1) It has an abstract quiddity, [which is] Itself, and (2) Its abstract quiddity belongs to It. So Its being intellecting and intellected does not necessitate multiplicity at all.'[54]

Then he said: 'He is the origin of every existence, so He intellects from Himself that for which He is an origin. He is an origin for the existents which are perfect in themselves, and for the existents which are generable and corruptible, in the first place in their species and by means of that their individuals. It cannot be that He intellects these changeable things together with their change. Instead He intellects each thing in a universal way. No particular thing escapes His notice, and His essence does not change through change in the object of knowledge.'[55]

He further said: 'It cannot be that He knows things through the things themselves,[56] or else His knowledge would be passive. Instead things are known through *Him* and emanate from *Him*. For He cannot bear the trace of anything of what is known by Him or effectuated by Him. Rather, the form of existence is traced on *them* after contingency of existence belonged to them. For the contingency which belongs to all the contingents is as it were their matter, and existence is as it were the form. And the Necessary of Existence is devoid of the nature of contingency and of non-existence, which are the sources of evil.'

Ibrāhīm Madkūr et al.(Cairo, 1960), p. 357.

54 Compare Ibn Sīnā, *Najāt*, p. 245.

55 Ibn Sīnā, *Najāt*, pp. 246–7.

56 Ibn Sīnā, *Najāt*, p. 246.

The Rebuttal of Him by the Inconsistency in His Discussion and the Refutation of His Objective and Aim

The First Inconsistency. His statement: 'Insofar as it is considered that It is abstract It is an intellect, and insofar as it is considered that It is, etc., etc. ...' and he has stipulated three considerations so that he affirmed that It is an intellect, intellecting and intellected. Then he said afterwards that that does *not* necessitate that It is twofold in consideration. So how is it that the last part of his discussion contradicts the first?

The Second Inconsistency. He said: 'He is the origin of every existence, so He intellects from Himself that for which He is an origin.' This gives notice that He originates, *then* He intellects. And after that he said: His intellection and knowledge are active not passive. This gives notice that He intellects, *then* He originates. And he said in some other passage in the *Shifāʾ*: His intellection is His very origination and His origination is His very intellection—so the duality between the intellection and origination is removed. This in wording and sense is a clear inconsistency.

The Third Inconsistency. His statement 'He is the origin of every existence, so He intellects from Himself that for which He is an origin', and his statement 'He intellects Himself by Himself insofar as it is considered for Him that He has an abstract identity'—and he has glossed intellection in one passage as origination, which is a positive entity, and he has glossed intellection in another passage as abstraction, which is a negative entity. This is a dumbfounding incoherence.

As for Refuting Him and Imposing Absurd Implications Upon Him

I say: You stipulated three considerations in the essence of the Necessary of Existence and glossed each consideration with a proper meaning, each of which is not to be understood from the other. That is patent Trinitarianism, and exalted be God above being the third of three! This is not a slander, but the absurd implication of multiplicity in His essence in respect of one consideration and another, just as it attaches to the Christians in respect of one hypostasis and another.

His excuse for multiplicity in consideration, that it does not necessitate two in the essence, is of no avail to him. For the thing through which his excuse is correct such that it negates the two—namely, that the *result* of the two things is that (1) It has an abstract quiddity which is Itself, and that (2) Its abstract quiddity belongs to It—removes the very thing through which there would be a multiplicity of considerations in Its essence [in the first place]. So why is it that he posits them as three considerations and then removes them by this interpretation, just as the Christians lay down the Trinity in divine hypostases, and remove it by way of unification in substantiality, saying 'One in substantiality, Three in hypostases ...'?

In this 'clarification' Ibn Sīnā only added one problem on top of another. For he incorporated the term 'quiddity' in it, so he made out that It has an existence *and* the quiddity of an existence which must be abstract in itself, and its abstraction is its intellection, and its intellection is its [act of] origination. Then if existence, quiddity, abstraction, intellection and origination are synonymous expressions, allow that one of them may stand in the place of another, so that it is said: the abstraction is an intellection and the intellection is an origination, therefore the abstraction is an origination.[57] While if the expressions are distinct, allow that each expression signifies an idea which the other expression does not signify—and that is multiplicity! I say immediately: You are required on the part of some of your companions to establish that the Necessary of Existence is knowing and intellecting, known and intellected. But you did not begin the demonstration of it except by your saying 'It is intelligible of quiddity, for the nature of existence and its subdivisions are not incapable of being intellected'. This is a *petitio principii*, for controversy occurs over it and opposition to it persists.

57 Via hypothetical syllogism.

Those companions *deny* that It is intellected and that It intellects. For intellection is the inscribing of the intellect by the form of the intellected—and the Real is exalted above having form and so being intellected, equally whether the form is corporeal or an incorporeal quiddity. Also He is exalted above intellecting, such that there is both He *and* a form. Rather, He is beyond knowing and being known! And you, you began the proof with the fact that He is knowable in order to establish that He knows, and they objected to you about the more obvious. How then do you argue against them proceeding from the more *obscure* to the more obvious?

Then leave their discourse behind Mount Qāf and return to that which is satisfactory and appropriate![58] You have taken 'existence' by way of generality and univocity as a subject, and have given it a general characterisation as a predicate. But someone who says 'existence applies to the Necessary of Existence and to other than It by way of equivocity, or ambiguity which is tantamount to equivocity', does not concede the generality of this characterisation. This is like someone who characterises *ʿayn* as 'eye'—the generalisation of the characterisation to include the disc of the sun is not conceded to him. And you, though you believe in a kind of generality for existence, you have excluded it in the case of the Necessary of Existence from the rest of existents, with an exclusion more extreme in dissimilarity than the eye and the disc of the sun. So why do you deny that the generality of this characterisation is *not* general for It as for the rest of the existents?

And another thing, namely, that you undertook to prove that It intellects and you embarked on the explanation that it is not impossible that It be intellected. But if it is *not impossible*, it does not become *necessary* that it be intellected as long as no further proof is linked with it. And if it is necessary that It be intellected, it does not follow from that that It intellects. Thus there must be another argument—but we have not heard any

[58] The mythical Qāf mountain was believed to surround the world. See 'Ḳāf', EI2, vol. 4, p. 400.

argument from you other than your proposition, 'It only happens accidentally to it not to be intellected, when it is in matter'. It may be said: What impedes is not limited to presence in matter, but sometimes there may be another impediment. For just as the perceptible is not inscribed on the intellect, qua perceptible, i.e. being in matter, likewise the intelligible is not inscribed on sense perception, qua intelligible, i.e. *not* being in matter![59] Yet He Whose majesty is exalted above being inscribed by anything is also exalted above anything being inscribed by *Him.* And just as something may be imperceptible by force of its hiddenness, likewise it may be imperceptible by force of its obviousness. So the obstacle is not matter or the adjuncts of matter, and his statement proves false: 'The nature of existence qua existent is not incapable of being intellected'. Also the limitation of the obstacles to matter and its adjuncts proves false, and the search reverts anew, and the contest goes on between you and your companions till you come to the universal and the particular.

Perhaps those people persevere in that they say: If He had knowledge, it would not be free of one of two things—either it would be universal or particular. If it were universal, it could not be conceived to be efficient, for that which is brought into being by the universal must *be* universal, just as that which is brought into being by particular knowledge must be particular. Yet there is no universal in individuals at all. So that which occurs through it would not occur in the manner it was produced, and that through which it was produced would not be in the manner it occurs. Then if His knowledge were particular, it would have to be changed by change in the object of knowledge, for the knowledge that Zayd *will* arrive does not remain with the knowledge that he *has* arrived. What is the reply to this problem?

As for us, we say: Concerning your statement that the First qua abstracted from matter is an intellect—abstraction from matter is like affirming transcendence over corporeity and like

[59] Here, the impediment is precisely immateriality.

sublimation above the characteristics of substances and accidents. So why do you say 'when it is not in a matter it must be an intellect, i.e. knowledge and knowing'? And this is because abstraction from matter is a negative attribute, and why should the negation of matter from something necessitate its being knowledge or knowing, an intellect or intellecting? Like the negation of whatever is inappropriate for His majesty, it does not necessitate the *affirmation* of His being Knowing.

Then we say: You affirmed multiple considerations in the Necessary in Itself by His being an intellect, intellecting and intellected, and you affirmed multiple considerations in the First Intellect by its being contingent in itself, necessary by another. It is also an 'intellect' because it is abstracted from matter, and intellecting and intellected by itself since its intellect-status belongs to it essentially and its quiddity does not belong to it through other than it, for what it acquires through other than it is its existence not its quiddity. So if these considerations do not necessitate a multiplicity in the essence of the Necessary of Existence, why do they necessitate multiplicity in the First Intellect—one negation being like another and one relation like another? But if they necessitate multiplicity in the First Intellect, allow that multiplicity is necessitated in the Necessary of Existence. It follows from that, that the multiple individuals may be directly ascribed to the Necessary of Existence through origination and direct production[60] without their emanation from It necessitating a multiplicity, or else they may not be ascribed to the First Intellect just as they may not be ascribed to the Necessary of Existence. This is something to which there is absolutely no reply!

As for his statement 'He is the origin of every existent, so He intellects from Himself that for which He is an origin'—the question about this is: does He intellect then originate, or originate then intellect, or intellect and originate together, or is

[60] *Ibdāʿ* (origination or 'instauration') and *ikhtirāʿ* (direct production) both suggest absolute *creatio ex nihilo*, as against *khalq*, which here means creation of an indirect and qualified kind.

His intellection an origination and His origination an intellection? If he says He intellects then originates, it follows that what is originated is a thing or is the virtuality of a thing such that He originates it, and He is exalted above anything, or the virtuality of anything, being *with* Him! If he says He originates then intellects, it follows that His intellection would be passive, not active. If he says He intellects and originates together, then He does not originate what He intellects and He does not intellect what He originates, and his statement proves false: 'so He intellects from Himself that for which He is an origin'. And if he says His intellection is His origination and His origination is His intellection (and this is the doctrine espoused by the man) various things follow from it, amongst which is that, if the intellection and origination are synonymous, let him say 'He originated Himself', in the sense that He *intellects* Himself! And amongst them is that the intellection may be universal and it may be particular. So let him say 'origination may be universal and it may be particular'. And amongst them is that it invalidates his statement 'He is the origin of every existence, so He intellects from Himself that for which He is an origin', for the implication of it will be 'He intellects every existent, so He intellects that which He is intellecting', and this is an incoherence. Amongst them is also that it invalidates his statement 'He intellects perfect existents in themselves, and generable and corruptible ones through their species and by means of that their individuals'. For the particular 'selves' and individuals are originated, but as for the species, they are intellected and not originated. So were intellection and origination synonymous such that one may take the place of the other, the species qua species would be *originated* in a universal manner, insofar as they are intellected in a universal manner—but that is not the doctrine espoused by the man.

Then he said 'It cannot be that He intellects these changeable things together with their change …' It is to be said: If He can be an origin for perfect existents in themselves, without being multiplied by their multiplicity, then He can intellect changeable things without changing through their change.

Notwithstanding the fact that the doctrine espoused by the man contradicts what he mentions. For according to him He is *not* an origin for perfect existents in themselves together except by the mediation of the First Intellect. So He is an origin for a single thing, and is intellecting a single thing, and by *its* mediation originating and intellecting perfect existents in themselves. Species and individuals are also like that, for He intellects the species and by mediation He intellects individuals. Thus the relation of the perfect existents—which are the separate substances—to the First Intellect, is like the relation of the individuals to the species. However, the species cannot exist in its status of species, and then the individuals exist, but it can be *intellected* in its status of species, and then the individuals are intellected. This is a clear difference between origination and intellection.

In regard to his statement 'Instead He intellects each thing in a universal way and no particular thing escapes His notice ...', I say: since he understood that the knowledge of particulars changes through change in the particulars, and the knowledge of generable and corruptible things is like that, he tried to escape that through running away to the affirmation of the knowledge of universals, particulars then being subsumed under universals by necessary implication and derivation. An example of that is that the knowledge that an individual eclipse will happen at a specific time is not knowledge of what comes to be at the time of the eclipse, nor of what has occurred as an eclipse in the past. Thus it is inevitable that the knowledge changes with the change of the object of knowledge or that there be another knowledge, other than the first knowledge. However, the knowledge that when the moon is in such and such a zodiacal house and the sun is in opposition to it in such and such a house, together with the rest of the causes which make the eclipse necessary, then there must be an eclipse, is 'universal' and unchanging knowledge, and is before the eclipse, during the eclipse and after it in a single manner. So Ibn Sīnā thought that through the like of this example he could escape the absurd implication of changeability. Yet there is no escape, 'it is no longer the moment to flee!'[61]

Let the High Council ponder the absurd implications closely which I present against him, and the claims with which I throttle him, so it understands that all that he depended on are merely plausible claims, not apodictic ones. And plausible propositions do not yield certainty. So I say: you are confronted by the demand to prove that He (Exalted is He!) is knowing, *not* by the method of the speculative theologian, for he infers it from precision and skill in particulars. But you, you do not say 'He knows particulars' except derivatively and by necessary implication, and that is not fit for making the inference from. For in the case of someone who stamps an inscribed seal on wax so that the inscription appears on it, the knowledge of the one who does the stamping is not to be deduced from the beauty of the inscription. Perhaps he does not know the inscription. Instead the inscription has come about through him by necessary implication and derivatively, due to the impression. The one who inscribes is different from the one who stamps, so you are still in the position of being questioned as to *your* method.

We move on from it in the explanation a little, and say: you grant that He is knowing, i.e. an intellect and intellecting, and you say 'you are right'. So we say: Yes, but why do you say 'knowledge is in two ways, universal and particular, and since it cannot be particular it must be universal'? Why do you reprove someone who affirms a kind of knowledge beyond the two divisions? This is like someone saying 'knowledge is either conception or assent', so it is replied: The knowledge of the Necessary of Existence is *neither* conception nor assent. Or else it is said 'knowledge is primary or acquired', so it is replied: With what do you reprove someone who affirms a kind of knowledge neither primary nor acquired? It would be enough for me for the verdict of reason to establish the just claim without giving any example. But I mention the exemplification to safeguard against being blamed for disputation and wrangling.

[61] See Qur'an 38:3.

On the other hand, I move on from it a little and say: Were change in the object of knowledge to necessitate change in the knowledge, then the multiplication of the object of knowledge would necessitate the multiplication of the knowledge. So it would follow that the essence is multiplied by the multiplication of the objects of knowledge, or else the object of His knowledge would become single, so that He would only know one object of knowledge, just as He only originates one intellect; and by its mediation He would know the rest of the objects of knowledge on the basis of concomitance and derivation, just as by its mediation He originates the rest of the existents on the basis of concomitance and derivation. In accordance with this consideration the ruling that He knows universals collapses. Instead He essentially only knows one object of knowledge!

If the existence of the First Intellect is amongst the concomitants of His existence in Himself, and of His intellection of Himself, He is in Himself intellecting Himself alone. The First Effect thus comes to be amongst the concomitants of God in respect of knowledge, just as it is amongst His concomitants in respect of existence—so He only knows Himself alone. See how the rank of knowledge climbs from the particular to the universal, then to the First Intellect, then to the essence of the Necessary of Existence. This is exactly the doctrine of the ancient philosophers: that the First intellects Himself by Himself alone, and He only intellects the First Intellect and the existents subsequent to it *through concomitance*. So He does not intellect universals qua universals, since He would be multiplied by their multiplicity, nor particulars qua particulars since He would be changed by their change. His knowledge is too exalted to be universal or particular, or for Him to know other than His most exalted essence through it.

As for Ibn Sīnā's statement 'It cannot be that He knows things through the things themselves, or else His knowledge would be passive', I say: this issue is between them and the speculative theologians, whether He knows things prior to their coming to be, or with their coming to be, or after it; and whether the knowledge follows the object of knowledge, so that it discovers the object of knowledge as it is, or whether the object of knowledge follows the knowledge; and whether the nonexistent must be a thing such that it may be known and communicated, or cannot be a thing? According to the doctrine espoused by the man, the knowledge of the Necessary of Existence is an active knowledge, by which I mean that it is the cause of the existence of the object of knowledge, and it follows that He does not know the object of knowledge before its coming to be, nor after its coming to be, but His knowledge of it is His very generation of it. It follows from this that He does not know Himself, since He does not generate Himself. Or it follows that His knowledge in relation to things is an active knowledge, and His knowledge of Himself is a passive knowledge. In that case His knowledge of Himself is not the same as Him Himself, and His knowledge of Himself is not the same as His knowledge of things. What a calamity is this confusion on confusion! 'And he for whom God makes no light, is without light.'[62]

The Correct Doctrine

The prophets (upon them be peace!) eschewed these approaches in their methods, and prohibited men from delving into the majesty of God (Mighty and Majestic!), from disputing about Him and discussing His attributes. Their books are full and their words well known to the effect that an atom's weight does not escape His notice on earth nor in heaven,[63] that 'He knows the secret and yet more concealed',[64] that 'He knows what is before them and what is behind them',[65] that 'He is knower of the hidden and manifest',[66] and that 'He knows the traitor of the eyes and what hearts conceal',[67] without

[62] Qur'an 24:40.
[63] Qur'an 34:3; 10:61.
[64] Qur'an 20:7.
[65] Qur'an 20:110.
[66] Qur'an 23:92.
[67] Qur'an 40:19.

a difference between the universal and the particular, nor a distinction between the stable and unchanging, and between the generable and corruptible. On this basis they prescribed acts of worship including supplications and intimate prayers, which show that He hears, sees and responds. And He has the highest of viewpoints, so hearts aim towards Him, hands are raised to Him, glances are lowered for Him, necks bow to His power and His glory, tongues beseech Him for His pardon and His mercy. For one is without need through Him, while He is indispensable, and desire reaches out to Him not away from Him. Requests do not exhaust His treasuries, privileged positions do not alter His judgement, the needs of the needy are not sundered from Him, and the prayers of suppliants do not benefit Him. So this and the likes of it are on account of His knowledge of particulars and universals; indeed His knowledge transcends the two divisions and its compass is higher than the two ways. Rather, amongst His creatures are those who have this attribute—I mean the intellect grasps the universal and sense perception grasps the particular—but His knowledge (Exalted is He!) is beyond both intellect and sense perception: 'Visions do not grasp Him but He grasps visions, and He is the Subtle, the Aware.'[68]

The sages who are the authorities in philosophy have said: the First is not grasped by way of His essence but is only grasped by way of His traces. And each thing that grasps Him does so only in the measure of the trace which is consigned to it and it is endowed with. So each animal praises Him in the measure of what it bears of His workmanship, and of the trace of [His workmanship] which it finds in its nature. And since man's endowment with His works is more ample and his share of His graces more numerous, his cognition is more powerful and his praise more comprehensive. Since the rank of the archangels which are in the highest heaven is [yet] more elevated and exalted, and the graces of workmanship in respect of their substances are more radiant and magnificent, their cognitions are

[68] Qur'an 6:103.

purer. And just as the animal cannot attain the modes of man's cognitions, likewise man cannot attain the modes of the archangels' cognitions. And none of them can attain the mode of the Creator's comprehension of all existents (Exalted is He!), summarily and in their details, their universals and their particulars. Moreover one universal does not distract Him from another, nor one particular from another, and both of them are equal in relation to Him. It ought not to be said 'He knows things before their coming to be or after their coming to be'. For 'before', 'after' and 'with' are temporal characterisations, and His knowledge (Exalted is He!) is not temporal, but times are equal in relation to it. It does not—if Ibn Sīnā deems it universal—depart from being *temporal*, as he believed in regard to the eclipse. Instead, temporal knowledge changes with the change of time, but non-temporal knowledge does not change at all with the change of time. Knowledge might be universal and be in a time! Rather, the universal is inconceivable in regard to Him (Exalted is He!), like the categorical and conditional propositions which he used in regard to the eclipse—I mean '*if* it is so and so, *then* it is so and so'. The knowledge of the Creator (Exalted is He!) is higher than that, so it is not conditional upon propositions like 'if it is so and so, then it is so and so'.

It is amazing that he glosses intellection and knowledge sometimes as abstraction from matter, and sometimes as origination. How can what is abstracted from matter be conceived of as being active? For abstraction is a negation in meaning, i.e. 'it is not in matter'. And if it is active (i.e. necessitating an act and an existent) how can it be universal, when the universal is not actually found in individuals?

Thus it is known from all that, that His knowledge (Exalted is He!) is above the two divisions and higher than the two ways. Its relation to universals and particulars, changing times, and different places, is a single relation: 'Does He not know what He creates? And He is the Subtle, the Aware'.[69]

[69] Qur'an 67:14.

Do we not choose to predicate man and angel with 'speech'[70] by equivocity? Likewise the 'intellect' which belongs to man and angel is by equivocity. For the angels do not intellect things through conceptualisation and assent, by means of definition and syllogism. Instead their intellections are beyond the two divisions—so what is your opinion about a knowledge higher than *all* the divisions? Is it then said 'it is universal or particular'? From the supplication of the Righteous Ones (upon them be peace!) [are the words]: 'O Thou Whom eyes do not see! O Thou of Whom opinions do not conceive! O Thou Whom describers do not describe!' That is, He is higher than sense perception, imagination and intellect. Then they say: 'O Thou Whom as soon as I seek I find! O Thou Whom as soon as I worship I find tranquillity in! O Thou Who, when He knows my loneliness, delights me with His protection! O Thou Who, when something comes between me and seeking refuge, grants me refuge!'

THE FIFTH ISSUE
On the Incipience of the World

The philosophers are of three opinions on this issue. A group of the ancients who were authorities in philosophy from Miletus and Samos arrived at the assertion of the incipience of the world's existents in respect of their principles, simple [bodies] and compounds; just as a party of the Muslims also arrived at it. A group from Athens and the Stoics arrived at the pre-eternity of their principles, consisting in intellect, soul, the separate substances, and simple [bodies], but not the elements and compounds. For the principles are above eternity and time, so temporal incipience does not come about for them, in contrast with compounds, which are below eternity and time, and they denied that motions were sempiternal. The doctrine of a party of the Muslims approximates to their doctrine, with their

70 *Nuṭq* can also mean reason.

assertion of the pre-eternity of the words and letters.[71] The doctrine espoused by Aristotle and whoever followed him amongst his disciples, as well as whoever agrees with him amongst the philosophers of Islam, is that the world is pre-eternal, and circular motions are sempiternal.

We preface the investigation of what Ibn Sīnā said with two preambles. The first of them is in elucidation of the meaning of finitude and infinitude, and which of the divisions necessitates, and which does not necessitate finitude. And the second is in elucidation of the meaning of priority, posteriority and concurrence, and in how many ways they occur.

The First Preamble

They say: Finitude may be perceptual and it may be intellectual. Perceptual finitude only occurs through perceptual delimitation, and that is in accordance with two divisions, spatial and temporal. The spatial division is as the delimitation of a body is determined by another body's delimitation, and they agreed on the fact that a body infinite in extent in all directions or in a single direction is impossible. The temporal division is as the delimitation of a time for a body, is determined by another time. The moderns have said: Infinite times following one another in existence, and likewise infinite motions and moving things following one another in existence, are not impossible.

As for intellectual finitude, it only occurs through intellectual delimitation [i.e. definition], and that is in accordance with two divisions: the formal definition composed of the constituents[72] of the thing; or the descriptive definition composed of the concomitants[73] of the thing (through which it is in opposition and association) and composed of realities through

[71] The reference is to the doctrine of the uncreatedness of the Qur'an, particularly in its more radical Ḥanbalite form.

[72] The elements of the definition, namely, the genus and differentia.

[73] Inseparable accidents, or properties.

which intellectual existents are distinguished *without* being compounded from the constituents of their quiddity, such as the separate substances. And they have agreed on the fact that infinite causes and effects are incapable of actual existence.

The moderns amongst them say: Infinite souls and intellects either simultaneous in existence or following one another are not impossible. The criterion for that is that everything which has a perceptual position,[74] like body, or an intellectual position, such as the cause and the effect, *cannot* comprise what is infinite. While whatever does not have a perceptual position, like circular motions, or an intellectual one, like human souls, is *not* incapable of comprising what is infinite.

The Second Preamble: on Priority, Posteriority and Concurrence

Priority may be temporal, like the priority of the parent to the child; it may be spatial, like the priority of the prayer-leader to the led; it may be by nobility, like the priority of the learned to the ignorant; and it may be essential, like the priority of the cause to the effect. And they have added a fifth sense for it, namely, priority by nature, like the priority of one to two. A sixth sense can be added for it, namely, priority simply by existence, like the priority of the existentialiser to the existentialised.

The enumeration of divisions in what we have mentioned is not something demonstrable, so whoever adds or subtracts when he clarifies the meaning is correct. And just as priority and posteriority come down to these divisions enumerated, likewise concurrence comes down to them, commensurate with them. Thus something may be *with* something else temporally, spatially, in nobility, essentially, naturally and in existence; and

[74] *Al-Waḍʿ*, 'position' (Gk. *to keisthai*), is one of Aristotle's categories. In it are combined the idea of the distribution of the parts of a subject, one to another, and the implication of a wider context within which this occurs. Circular motions have no position in this sense, because as completely self-contained they need no wider context, unlike rectilinear motions.

while it is 'with' something *temporally*, it may be prior to it *essentially*, or vice versa—and likewise in respect of any two divisions.

So Ibn Sīnā said: 'The world exists through the existence of the Creator (Exalted is He!) and is perpetual in existence through His perpetuity. So the Creator (Exalted is He!) is essentially prior to the world, with the priority of the cause to the effect. Nevertheless, the world is perpetual in existence through His perpetuity ...'[75] And he set about proving what he said. He said: 'Pure intellect, which does not deceive, bears witness that the unitary essence, if it is in all its aspects as it was, and there was earlier nothing existing through it, and it is like that now, then there is also nothing existing through it now. But if *now* something comes to exist from it, an intention has occurred in the essence, or a will, or a nature, or a power and capability; or else something analogous to this, which had not been. It also bears witness that what is able both to exist *and* not exist only becomes actual—and it only preponderates for it that it exists—by way of some factor. If this essence, which is the cause, were there without the thing preponderating, then if it preponderates, there must be a preponderating factor. Otherwise its relation with that contingent thing would be as it was before—and no other relation would occur for it—so the matter would be as it was, and the contingency would still be a pure contingency. And if a new relation occurred for it, something would have occurred, and it would have to occur within its essence or outside it, and both of them are absurd.'[76]

He also said: 'How is a time of refraining and a time of engaging distinguishable in non-existence? By what does one time contrast with another? Moreover, the incipient only occurs by way of the inception of a state in the Origin, and that must either be a will or an accident, for otherwise nature does not incept, and compulsion and chance are false. In any case, there must be the incipience of an attribute or state; but if it occurs

[75] Compare Ibn Sīnā, *Najāt*, p. 252, and *Shifā'*: *Ilāhiyyāt*, p. 373.
[76] Ibn Sīnā, *Najāt*, pp. 254–5, and *Shifā'*: *Ilāhiyyāt*, pp. 376–7.

in Its essence, It becomes a substrate for incipients, and if it occurs in a separate substrate, there would be no substrate before the substrate;[77] and if it occurs *not* in a substrate, the argument about that incipient is like the argument about the world.'[78]

Moreover he said: 'The First Reality is an origin for Its acts, and the origin is prior to the act. So by what is It prior, is it by Its essence, or by a time? If It is prior simply by Its essence, that is correct, and we acknowledge it. If It is prior by a time, our argument reverts about that time itself. His existence (Exalted is He!) is eternal, so the times also are eternal. Thus we suppose in these infinite times infinite existents, and all that you impose on us in respect of incipients which are infinite, we impose on you in respect of times which are infinite!'[79]

'Like that is our argument about motions, since whatever is in motion needs a mover, and if the mover is in motion, a regress follows. So there must be an Unmoved Mover, and either It is a body or a soul or an intellect. In short it is necessary that It precedes the thing in motion by Its essence and is parallel to it in its time. This is like the light of the lamp and the rays of the sun, for they converge in time, yet the lamp is "prior" to the light. This is why you say "the lamp exists and so the light exists", but you cannot say "the light exists and so the lamp exists". Likewise you say "my hand moves and so the key moves in my sleeve", but you cannot reverse that.'[80]

77 This ellipsis seems to mean that the substrate postulated for the will or accident, itself would need to be created through a will or accident. So, a will or accident without a substrate follows after all.

78 Compare Ibn Sīnā, *Najāt*, pp. 255–6. This perhaps alludes to the doctrine of the Baṣran Muʿtazila, who held that the divine attribute of will (*irāda*) which because of its temporality cannot inhere in the divine essence, must subsist without any substrate although it is an accident.

79 Compare Ibn Sīnā, *Najāt*, p. 256 and *Shifāʾ*: *Ilāhiyyāt*, p. 379.

80 Compare *Ishārāt*, vol. 3, p. 514 ff.

The Rebuttal of Him

We will speak firstly about the claim and the ruling and we will explain the equivocation in it in respect of the word 'perpetuity' and 'existence'. So long as the point of controversy is not free from kinds of equivocation, the direction of the argumentation is not clear. Thus his statement firstly 'the world is existent through His existence' involves a little confusion, and he ought to say 'the world is existent through His existentiation', so that that gives notice of existential, essential priority. And in his statement 'perpetual in existence through His perpetuity', the term 'perpetuity' is equivocal, for the perpetuity of existence belonging to the Creator (Exalted is He!) is not with the meaning of the perpetuity of existence belonging to the world. Rather, the perpetuity of existence belonging to Him (Exalted is He!) is with the meaning that He is Necessary of Existence by His essence, and the necessary is that which, if its non-existence is hypothesised, an absurdity follows thereby. The perpetuity of existence belonging to the world, however, is with the meaning of the continuousness of time for it, or with the meaning that it is necessary by something else. And were its non-existence hypothesised, an absurdity would *not* follow thereby, for the two do not concomitate in existence, in the beginning and in perpetuity. Thus 'perpetuity' is not with a single meaning in the two existences, but with two meanings different in their reality, and 'existence' is not with a single meaning in the two perpetuities, but with two meanings different in their reality. So the ruling concerning it is abridged, and most of the divergences between scholars arise from the equivocity of terms.

Next, the greatest calamity, which they considered monstrous on the part of Ibn Sīnā, consists of delusive propositions and imaginary premises.[81] Through his bewitchment they were made to imagine 'that they moved rapidly. So Moses conceived a fear in himself. We said "Fear not! Verily, you are the

[81] The doctrine alluded to here as the 'greatest calamity' is that of the eternity of the world.

superior!"'[82] It is exactly the sophism of the Karrāmiyya in regard to 'space',[83] which he carried over to 'time', and 'I am not one to be frightened easily!'[84] Concerning his statement: 'The unitary essence, if it is in all its aspects (*jihāt*) as it was, and there was earlier nothing existing through it, and it is like that now, then there is also nothing existing through it now ...'—we say: You affirm an 'earlier' and a 'now' beyond the world, or you postulate a time, or *two* times, one of which is prior and the other simultaneous. Yet if you postulate it on the basis of the doctrine of the opponent, the opponent does *not* affirm any time whatsoever beyond the world, neither prior (called 'earlier') nor simultaneous (called 'now'), just as he does not affirm any space whatsoever beyond the world, neither void nor full. This is like what the Karrāmite says: 'The unitary essence, if it is on all sides (*jihāt*) as it was, and nothing existed with it, then something existed with it—it must be on some side of it separate from it, by a finite or infinite separation.' Postulating a time for refraining and a time for acting is like postulating an empty space and an occupied space, and you know that since the existence of the Creator (Exalted is He!) is not spatial, neither an empty space nor an occupied space can be ascribed to Him. Likewise, since His existence (Majestic is His sublimity!) is not temporal, an empty time and an occupied time cannot be ascribed to Him such that one of them is called 'refraining from action' and the second 'acting'.

[82] Qur'an 20:66. God here reassures Moses when Pharaoh's magicians made their ropes and staves seem alive.

[83] The Karrāmiyya was a popular Islamic sect in the Iranian regions from the ninth to the thirteenth century CE. It was founded by Abū 'Abd Allāh Muḥammad b. Karrām (d. 869 CE), whose works *'Adhāb al-qabr* and *Kitāb al-Sirr* are only known through citation. His best-known teaching was the spatiality of God—given in interpretation of the verse 'The All-Merciful sat on the Throne' (Qur'an 20:5). Ibn Karrām may also have upheld the eternity of the world in some sense. The two doctrines come together in the discussion here. See 'Karrāmiyya', EI2, vol. 4, p. 667.

[84] The literal meaning of this Arabic proverb is: I am not one for whom worn-out water skins are rattled.

If he then says: 'If you do not affirm a "before" for the world, nor a finite or infinite time, you have in fact ruled the concomitance of the two existences: the existence of the Maker and the existence of the made. Likewise, if you do not affirm a time for refraining from action and a time for acting, you have expressly admitted concomitance', I say: he listened poorly, so he replied poorly! Concomitance in existence and time only follows when the existent is susceptible to time, but we have explained that the world cannot be with Him (Exalted is He!) in time, since it would necessitate that His existence be temporal. So temporal concomitance and combination are absurd, and temporal precedence and priority are also absurd. This is like the Karrāmite's question: 'If you do not affirm a separation—finite or infinite—beyond the world, you have ruled the concomitance of the existences of the Maker and the made', but it does not follow, since His existence (Exalted is He!) is not spatial.

He said: 'When you say "He did not act, then He acted" you have affirmed a time in which you make Him idle from activity, so that you distinguish a time of refraining and a time of engaging for Him. But if you do not affirm a time of idleness and refraining, you have agreed with me about necessitation and concomitance. For I say: the All-Generous cannot be idle from generosity. Thus they are concomitant.' I [Shahrastānī] say: A time of idleness and a time of engagement does not follow from our statement 'He did not act, then He acted', since in expression there is figuration and extended meaning. For in 'He did not act' there is a notification about the past, and in 'then He acted' there is an indication of the future—yet there is no past and future in non-existence. That is just as the opponent says: 'He originated the intellect, then He originated the soul, then matter, then the body'—and that also does not give notification about the past and the sequence of time after it.

In the intellect there is no time before time, nor time with time, just as there is no other world beyond the world, above it, nor alongside the world to the right, nor to the left, nor below the world, underneath. And I only affirm *idleness* from action where the existence of action is conceivable—since action is what has a beginning, while pre-eternity is what does not have a beginning, and the combination of what has a beginning and what has no beginning is absurd. And when you say He is a maker in pre-eternity, you have combined the two sides of the contradiction—I mean the affirmation of having a beginning and the negation of having a beginning! Then would you not say: the Generous cannot be idle from the overflow of generosity *insofar as* [*its*] *existence is conceivable*? But when generosity is not conceivable, that is not called 'declaring idle'. Is it not [the case that] were someone to say: 'If the Maker does not bring into existence a body extending in dimensions infinitely, He is idle from the bestowal of generosity, or His generosity falls short in its perfection', it would be said: If the existence of an infinite body is impossible, the shortcoming devolves on the recipient of the generosity, not on the generosity of the Bestower?

Ibn Sīnā said: 'It is then conceivable for you in the judgement of the intellect to admit that He might have created the world temporally ahead of its time. If that is conceivable but He did *not* create, He was idle from generosity!'[85] I say: Intellectual conceptualisation in regard to time is like intellectual postulation in regard to space—virtually identical. Thus the imagination conceives of and the intellect postulates another world beyond the world, above and beneath, and postulates the volume of the universe as greater and lesser than it actually is—however, on condition that *it be essentially finite*, since the proof is established that an infinite body is impossible. Likewise the intellect postulates a time or an existent temporally prior to the world—however on condition that it be finite, for an infinite time is impossible as we will explain.

He said: 'The body has a natural position, so the hypothesis of infinity in regard to it is impossible, but time has neither a natural position nor an intellectual order, so the hypothesis of infinity in regard to it is conceivable.' I say: This difference

[85] Compare Ibn Sīnā, *Najāt*, p. 257.

between the two forms is ineffective, since the proof which demonstrates the impossibility of the existence of a body infinite in measure, *itself* demonstrates the impossibility of the existence of a period infinite in time and the existence of human souls infinite in number—since the middle term in it is primary things, amongst which is: that the lesser in existing numbers is not equivalent to the greater; and amongst which is that the lesser and the greater are only [found] in respect of finite numbers, and the lesser and greater are inconceivable in regard to what is infinite; and amongst which is that a determinate fraction cannot be realised for something infinite, such as a half, or third, or quarter.

We construct a proof from these premises for each form. Let us consider the argument first in respect of human souls. So we say: If an infinite number of human souls were to enter existence on Sunday, then it would not be possible to increase by a number of souls on Monday. For what is numerically infinite cannot increase in number. Yet it has increased! And the exception of the contradictory of the consequent entails the contradictory of the antecedent.[86]

Another argument[87] is that if souls were infinite on Sunday and they were also infinite on Monday, the lesser would be equivalent to the greater. But if souls vary in number, they must start from a soul with no soul before it. Therefore individuals will be finite, and they must start from an individual with no individual before it. Therefore motions and moving things will be finite, and they must start from a motion with no motion before it. Therefore time which quantifies the motion is finite, and it must start from a time with no time before it. And that is what we wanted to explain.

Another argument is that the existence of everything incepted by some cause depends on the existence of its cause.

[86] That is, contraposition.

[87] *Tarkīb* here translates Greek *sumploke* or *sunthesis,* i.e. the construction of an argument. See Friedrich Wilhelm Zimmermann, *Al-Farabi's Commentary and Short Treatise on Aristotle's* De Interpretatione (London, 1981), p. xxxviii.

Were the existence of that cause dependent on the existence of some other cause, it would lead to regress, and that is absurd because of the dependence. For what depends in its existence on the existence of something, its existence can only occur with that thing already existing. For were every cause to depend on a cause to infinity, this cause in respect of which the hypothesis arises would not occur, because of the dependence of its existence on the existence of what is infinite either *seriatim* or what is in existence *in extenso*—and that is not possible.

Then we transfer this same proof to human individuals, so we say: The existence of this man (and we point to Zayd) has depended on the existence of the sperm from which he was created, and the existence of the sperm depended on the existence of another man from whom it arose. Thus it regresses to infinity, and that is false, as we have all agreed on the absurdity of the existence of infinite causes and effects. However, they apply this rule only to efficient causes, while we enjoin exactly that on them in respect of material causes, the causes being equal in regard to the dependence of effects upon them. When it is thus established that souls and individuals are finite, and they only start from an origin they have, equally whether they are in existence *seriatim* or are simultaneous in existence and not *seriatim*, it is established following that, that circular motions and moving things are finite. Since if they were eternal in motion, the things engendered by these motions would be eternal in existence and infinite, yet it has been established that they are finite. So the time which quantifies the motions must be finite, and this is the goal that we wanted.

We also say: The proof which you mentioned for the impossibility of an infinite distance or an infinite body is that you hypothesise a point on the plane of the infinite body. You posit in your imagination an infinite distance, the beginning of which is this point, and you hypothesise another line parallel with that, which is shorter than it by a cubit. Then you superimpose the point on the point and the line on the line. Then it must either be that the two lines remain infinite or else the smaller falls short. If the two lines remained infinite, *the smaller would be equivalent to the greater.* And if it falls short from the infinite extremity by the measure of a cubit less, *the infinite becomes divisible and finite,* so what is parallel with it becomes finite. Thus it is clear that an infinite body, or distance within a body, is inconceivable.

Then we transfer this same proof to the numbers of human souls and the numbers of circular motions. They only distinguish between the two forms insofar as body has a position, so two lines can be hypothesised within it starting from a point, to infinity, while souls and [circular] motions have no position. It is said: Mere position and the lack of it have no impact on the distinction. For the line hypothesised in the body is imaginary, and anything you suppose in regard to an imaginary line can be supposed in regard to an imaginary number. Thus, hypothesise 'Zayd' and think of him as a point, and hypothesise his ancestors as a straight line [reaching] to infinity, and hypothesise ''Amr' and think of him as a point falling short of Zayd by an ancestor, or two ancestors, or three—and think of his ancestors to infinity, as a line. Then suppose that Zayd and 'Amr are *twins* in existence, and carry through the proof to its conclusion. We showed earlier a kind of order in respect of individuals as there is in respect of causes and effects. The order in respect of causes, souls and individuals is like position in respect of bodies and distances—and the [one] proof is just like the [other] proof, neck and neck.[88]

Then know that [vicious] circularity in respect of sperm and man, eggs and chickens, and seeds and trees, is only interrupted if you specify the start from one of the two sides of the cycle. Otherwise the existence of one of them would depend on the existence of the other, and one of them would not occur without the other. That would lead to neither occurring at all, yet the two *have* occurred. So there is an inevitable break in the cycle at one of the two, and the starting point for human individuals with what is more perfect is more appropriate.

88 Literally: like two racehorses.

Amongst what is argued against Ibn Sīnā is that he mentioned in the *Shifā'* that reasoning from existence to the affirmation of the Necessary of Existence and from the Necessary of Existence to things, is more fitting and noble than reasoning from something other than [existence] to [the affirmation of the Necessary of Existence].[89] Concerning that he said: 'We do not doubt that there is existence, and it is subdivided into "necessary in itself" and into "contingent in itself" ...' and he spoke about the two subdivisions.[90] So I say: If one of the two subdivisions is contingent in relation to its essence, and the contingent is what is neither inevitably existent nor inevitably non-existent, rather the two sides of it (existence and non-existence) are equal in the intellect, then if the aspect of existence preponderates over the aspect of non-existence, it needs a preponderator. Up to this point is the area of agreement, with the self-evidentness of the proof. Then I say: The preponderator must either be an existentialiser or be a necessitater. It is false that it is a necessitater, since the contingent is what fluctuates between existence and non-existence, not what fluctuates between necessity and contingency. Consequently, the preponderator is a preponderator of existence over non-existence, not a preponderator of necessity over contingency, and it is a bestower of existence, not a bestower of necessity. Rather, necessity adheres to the contingent subsequent to its existence *in view of its cause*, while existence is provided it by the existentialiser *in view of its essence*, since the contingent is neither inevitably existent nor non-existent. It may not be said 'the contingent is neither inevitably necessary nor contingent', since that is self-contradictory both in wording and meaning, and the gist of the statement comes down to [the proposition] that the contingent is *not* inevitably contingent! How could that be when contingency is its very quiddity? And the quiddity of the thing is inevitable for it and the essence

[89] *Ishārāt*, vol. 3, pp. 482–3. Al-Shahrastānī perhaps confuses it with *Shifā'*: *Ilāhiyyāt*, p. 27.

[90] Ibn Sīnā, *Najāt*, p. 235.

is not to be parted from *itself.* Thus it is ascertained that the preponderator is an existentialiser, not a necessitater, and the imagined concomitance completely collapses.

A point of inquiry remains as to when the contingent comes into relation with the Necessary, and in how many ways the act is related to the agent, and the subject of power to the powerful? As for when—there is *no* 'when', for no disengagement and engagement, and time of activity and time of inactivity, can be supposed, since the times are alike, and one time is only preferred to another time by reason of a particularising factor. And when the Agent is as He was and nothing is incepted, no particularising factor and preponderator is incepted, whether as His concomitant in existence or whether He precedes it.

According to these people, however, existence only preponderates over non-existence in respect of the contingent in itself through emanation from His essence (Exalted is He!). So they are to be questioned about emanation and necessitation itself. It is said: what is it that entails His being emanative and necessitating? Just as they questioned us about the time of emanation and necessitation. Their reply is that the essence from which something emanates is nobler than an essence from which nothing emanates. It is said to them: This suggests that He acquired perfection through emanation, yet the essentially perfect does not acquire perfection from anything else. They say that emanation from Him derives from His perfection, not that His perfection derives from His emanation. It is said: In that case He is not *essentially* emanative and necessitating, rather the existents emanate from Him and become necessary without His emanating them and His necessitating them. Moreover, this is the characterisation of derivation, and the derivative is always after the source of derivation, in existence—however, it is not ascribed to the source of derivation by intention and essentially, but by derivation and accidentally.

So you have demanded from us a time and cause of origination, and we demand from you a basis and cause of origination! You forced upon us the incipience of an incipient which is *not* due to an incipient entity, and we force upon you the existence of existents derivatively and by accident, not by choice and primary intention—nature and chance being false, without access to His perfection (Exalted is He!).

Rather, we find essentially contingent things have entered existence, I mean one aspect of them has preponderated over the other, and we say: there must be a Preponderator without any contingency in any way, and the relation of contingents to Him (Exalted is He!) is necessary. The kinds of relation are various, and amongst them is emanation and necessitation, and amongst them is nature and natural inclination, and amongst them is purpose and rationale, and amongst them is will and choice, and intention and preference. It is up to you to select the noblest from amongst them. The revealed canons specify the nobility of the relation by way of choice and will, creation, command and dominion, because of the perfection of majesty and honour in this relation, and because of the deficiency and imperfection in the other ways. For in necessitation and emanation there is the analogue of reproduction and generation, while in nature and natural inclination there is the analogue of constraint and need, and in purpose and the demand of the cause[91] is the reality of the need. And God (Exalted is He!) transcends them all: 'Blessed be the name of your Lord, Owner of Majesty and Honour!'[92]

The Correct Choice

We have explained that priority, posteriority and concurrence are of four sorts: priority by time, priority by space, priority by nobility and priority by essence. Priority by nature and priority by existence alone have been added to it. A distinction was made between them and priority by essence in that the priority of one to two is known, and one does not *essentially* bring two about. So it comprises another meaning, namely, priority

[91] *'Illa*, 'cause', can also mean 'disease' or 'imperfection'. The *'illa* causes ('demands') because of its neediness.

[92] Qur'an 55:78.

by nature. Then the priority of the giver of existence to the receiver of existence is also beyond essential causation. And we have explained that the bestower of existence is one thing and the bestower of necessity another—it may be said 'it exists through it, so it is necessary', while it may not be said 'it is necessary through it, so it exists'.

When this principle on priority and posteriority is established, it is clear that all the mentioned senses also apply to concurrence. So we go back and say: The world is not *with* God (Exalted is He!) in time, for the existence of the Creator (Exalted is He!) is not temporal. Then just as His existence (Exalted is He!) does not precede the world's existence in time, likewise it is not with it in time. Neither is the world *with* Him (Exalted is He!) in space, for His existence is not spatial. Then just as He is not above it in space, He is not with it to the right or left in space. Neither is the world *with* God (Exalted is He!) in nobility, for the Necessary of Existence cannot be equated with the possible of existence in nobility. Neither is the world *with* God (Exalted is He!) by essence, according to them because the necessitated is not with the necessitater by essence, and according to us because the existentialised is not with the existentialiser by essence. Neither is the world *with* God (Exalted is He!) by nature, for His existence is not in the manner of number, and 'God was, and nothing was with Him.' The Prophet (upon him be peace!) was asked about the start of this affair, so he said 'God was, and nothing was with Him'.[93] Thus he divulged the secret of the question, set down the very text of the maxim, and cut right through the matter with what dents the blade and strikes at the joint.

So if nothing is with Him in any of the senses of concurrence, He (Exalted is He!) is prior to everything in every sense of priority. And it cannot be said: 'The Necessary of Existence is prior to the contingent of existence by essence, yet is *with* it in some other sense, such as the priority of the lamp to the

93 Prophetic hadith: see Bukhārī, LIX, 1; also Ibn Bābūya, *Kitāb al-Tawḥīd*, ed. Hāshim al-Ḥusaynī al-Ṭihrānī (Beirut, [1387/1967]), p. 67.

light and the motion of the hand to the motion of the ring.' For something might be prior to something by essence, yet be with it in time, like the two examples mentioned, [only] *because their existence is temporal.* But this characterisation is inapplicable in respect of the Creator (Exalted is He!), for He is sanctified above time and He cannot be prior by essence yet parallel in time. Nor can He be parallel in existence, for we have explained that the existentialiser is prior to the existentialised in existence, and because of this they say 'Existence in Him (Exalted is He!) is more appropriate and primary'. So the issue has been unveiled like the morning's dawn, and the occasion of uncertainty is explained. And the dispute reverts to the fact that beginningless incipients, circumscribed by existence *in extenso* or *seriatim* and consecutively, are incapable of existing. We have explained that convincingly.

Amongst the celestial existents are ones separate from materiality, abstracted from matter, hallowed above spatial confines, temporal conditions and corporeal accidents, which have an essential beginning and existential origin, and which the Creator (Exalted is He!) originated by His power absolutely and produced according to His will directly. They are the loci of manifestation for the perfect, pure and untainted Words, and the Words are their sources.[94] What is below them are the stars and moving spheres which are the temples of those spiritual entities. The aeon and time only begin in view of the incipience of movement, and the movement [of the stars and spheres] only begins in view of natural longing and the striving in pursuit of their perfections. So temporal primacy only belongs to moving things, and essential primacy only belongs to the separate substances. And the Lord (Exalted is He!) is the First without any first which was prior to Him, and the Last without any last which will be subsequent to Him. For He is 'the First and the Last', i.e. His existence is *not temporal,* 'and the Outward and the Inward', i.e. His existence is *not spatial.*[95]

[94] 'The perfect words', *al-kalimāt al-tāmmāt,* is Qur'anic. See Qur'an 2:124, 6:115 and 10:82.

[95] The two quotations are from Qur'an 57:3.

Such antonyms coincide in meaning in His case (Exalted is He!), and time and place are twins competing in a single womb, sucking from a single breast, and mollified in a single cradle. So strike down the eternalist with the corporealist and the corporealist with the eternalist, and seek out the religion of God (Exalted is He!) between the extremist and the shortcomer![96] The majesty of God (Exalted is He!) transcends imaginations and intellects, *a fortiori* space and time.

Wherever expression, with its instrument of metaphor, expands in the horizons of thought, wandering in the courts of the One Sought—that whose light is sought becomes obscure, that whose effusion is desired dwindles, the tool becomes blunt, the circumstances go astray, the human intellect comes to naught at it, and the expedient is changed into ineffectuality. Thus there is no recourse—subsequent to these ideas over which the sun of grandeur rises, and which it bakes in the seas' waves and disperses in the ways of the winds—except reliance on the explicit and pure Ḥanīfite Revelation,[97] for it is utterly congenial and in no way distressing. And even though it does not quench to satiety, neither does it leave thirsty!

When I brought the discussion on this issue to this point, and wanted to start on the sixth and seventh issue, I was diverted from their exposition by something the heaviness of which distressed me, and the burden of which weighed heavily on me, consisting in the trials of the time and the blows of misfortune. And to God complaints are addressed and upon Him is reliance in adversity and prosperity! So I confine myself

96 'Seek out the religion of God …' etc. Compare Ibn Qutayba, *'Uyūn al-akhbār*, ed. Aḥmad Zakī al-'Adawī (Cairo, 1343–48/1925–30), vol. 1, pp. 326–7.

97 *Ḥanīf*, pl. *ḥunafā'*, is a Qur'anic term for a follower of primordial monotheism, especially Abraham (e.g. Qur'an 2:135). Islam was seen as reviving this religion predating Judaism. The term probably comes from Syriac *hanpo*, pl. *hanpe*, a pagan. By extension, in Syriac it meant a person of Hellenistic culture, philosophically-minded, thus a monotheist. Then, in Aramaean circles these secondary connotations of *hanpo* overshadowed the meaning 'pagan'. See 'Ḥanīf', EI2, vol. 3, p. 165.

to mentioning the rudiments of these issues consisting in questions, doubts, problems and the deficiencies of intellects, and whoever solves them is worthiest of them, if God (Exalted is He!) wills.

The Deficiencies of Intellects

The sage seeks out the cause for each thing and the reason for each incipient—either an efficient cause, or a material cause, or a final cause, and rarely the formal cause is sought out. Then the first thing asked concerns the enumeration of principles: are they comprehended in a known number, or are they unlimited and infinite? If they are comprehended by a number, then no number is more appropriate than another. Amongst the ancients there is he who says there are four principles—the First, the intellect, soul and matter; amongst them is he who says five, adding nature; amongst them is he who says six, adding void; and amongst them is he who says seven, adding eternity and time.

Ibn Sīnā inclined to [the view] that there are nine, namely the separate intellects. Sometimes he added to that, so that he thereby reached forty odd intellects. And sometimes he would say: 'The separate entities are as numerous as the number of directing souls, and the souls are as numerous as the number of spheres, and perhaps astronomical observation shows that there are nine.' What is it that will free us from this perplexity, and who is it who will save us from this predicament?

A Problem

The separate entities are distinguished by differentiae pertaining to species such as speech for man,[98] or by individual accidents such as shape and form for man, or in some other way such as what he stipulated to the effect that they are distinguished by *essential realities*. This last division is unknown, for

[98] *Nuṭq* could also mean 'reason'. See note 70.

the term 'substantiality' includes them by an essential inclusion, as their genus. So there must be a distinction by way of an essential differentia pertaining to species, and there must be individual peculiar accidents, such that each one can be pointed out through an intellectual indication as this or that. That can only be through bodies which belong to them, such as the spheres. So in consequence they would not be separate, abstracted from matter in every respect, and no difference would occur between them and between human souls. In that case shapes would reside in them, via the states of the motions of the spheres, as they reside in human souls, via the motions of bodies. In general they would depart from being separate in every respect.

Problems

The body is compounded of matter and form, and requires an efficient cause. So what is the cause of the existence of matter, what is the cause in respect to the existence of form, and what is the cause of their compounding together? If the contingency in the essence of the First Intellect is the cause of the existence of matter, then contingency is likewise in every existent other than the Necessary of Existence, so let it be conducive to the existence of matter. However, contingency is a non-existential nature, so it is not conducive to the existence of anything, and the cause in the existence of form is incapable of being the contingency of the thing's existence. Instead it is the 'necessity of its existence by another'. The necessity of existence by another in every existent is through the First Intellect in a single manner, so let it be conducive to every form. In general, everything which they mention in the way of kinds of conduciveness amongst causes, exists amongst effects, so the cause is not more worthy of its status of cause than the effect.

Next: the predisposition in matter is not the same for all matters, but different. So what is the *cause* of the difference in them? For forms only differ due to the difference in the predispositions of matters. Yet prime matter does not differ in predisposition, but is predisposed to receive the form of corporeality alone. As for the size of forms and shapes in regard to smallness and largeness, the less and the more, and particularity and influence—they require causes consistent with them. So what are these causes and what is it that brings about the peculiarity of prime matter to receive the form of the body of the universe in accordance with its size, neither exceeding it nor falling short?

You have sought out the cause of its sphericity, so you said: When the cause is single and the matter single, it is necessary that the body be equivalent in its parts, namely, the shape of the sphere. For there is no angle in the sphere, by which it is distinguished as a quadrangular or triangular or other figure. Then why have you not sought another cause for the *size* of the sphere? And why have you not sought a cause for every celestial sphere—be it a star, or orb [i.e. heaven]—such that the sizes of the magnitudes and bodies are thereby explained? The same statement is to be made about their distances, locations, movements and periods. For [Ptolemy's] *Almagest* only establishes the manner of their existence and does not seek out the cause of their existence, and the Metaphysics includes one of their final causes, but not the efficient or material.[99] The demand confronts them in these issues—the confrontation of the creditor's demand to the procrastinating debtor. And 'If your neighbours fail you, rely on the master of your house!' 'I did not make them witness the creation of the heavens or the earth or their souls ...'[100]

[99] What al-Shahrastānī means by this reference to 'the Metaphysics' (*al-Ilāhiyyāt*) is problematic. It seems that he is referring to the Metaphysics of Ibn Sīnā's *Shifā'*. But in his reply, Ṭūsī rightly points out against al-Shahrastānī that the Metaphysics certainly considers the efficient, material and formal cause of the spheres, in addition to the final, 'to the extent that intellects grasp it'. Ṭūsī, *Maṣāri' al-muṣāri'*, ed. Ḥasan al-Mu'izzī (Qum, 1405/1984), p. 192. Perhaps instead al-Shahrastānī specifically has in mind the limitations of Aristotle's 'Metaphysics' (*Mā ba'd al-ṭabī'a*), in which case he has entitled it misleadingly.

[100] Qur'an 18:51.

A Doubt and a Problem

If whatever is in motion needs a mover, and if that mover is in motion, it also needs a mover, and the proposition regresses till it arrives at an Unmoved Mover. That First Mover must then either be at rest, or it must be neither at rest *nor* in motion! If it is at rest—rest does not bring about motion, which is its opposite. And if it is neither at rest nor in motion, it must be an intellectual substance. So what is it which necessitates in it that it be a mover for other than it—is it a longing which it harbours or a perfection it seeks?

Then after that of necessity: is reaching its perfection possible for it or impossible? If it is possible and it reaches it, then it must cease from moving others, so all the moved things must come to rest. But if it is impossible and it does not reach its perfection at all, then in consequence it is troubled, always afflicted, continuously sorrowful, steadily *increasing* in imperfection, by its motion only growing in longing for its perfection, and by its longing only growing in remoteness from its perfection. If it is said 'it obtains a partial perfection in each motion, so its enjoyment of each partial perfection diverts it from suffering longing for its total perfection', it is replied: but its inability to obtain its total perfection diverts it from the enjoyment of its partial perfection!

Stopping-places of the Intellect

If the body of the universe is a finite sphere, then it has no upper surface, since there is no void nor plenum beyond it such that a surface which is upper would be in evidence for it. Yet if you imagine something which is either a void or plenum, in that case an upper surface is indeed conceivable to you. Then when the sphere moves, two opposite poles are in evidence. So what is it which necessitates the specification of the two poles in the place which they are now in—the parts of the sphere being indistinguishable and equal, and one part no more suitable than another? By this question I simply seek the efficient cause, not the final. Then if the motions of the bodies are spatial, they necessitate the tearing of these bodies, yet they are insusceptible to tearing. If they are positional,[101] positional motions only happen if spatial motion precedes them. Space, like the square, has a position, so if its basis moves towards another, non-quadrangular shape, a motion occurs to it which is in the relation of some of its parts to others, and there must be the motion of transference for some of the parts, so that the relation of the rest of the parts to each other would change. Otherwise the existence of motion within the position would be inconceivable.

A Doubt

'Cause' and 'origin' are said of everything whose existence is complete and through which something else exists. Then, the completeness of its existence may be from itself and it may be from other than it. What is from other than it may be like the part which belongs to that which is its effect, such as the form and matter belonging to the body, or it may not be, like the agent and *telos*—according to the division which Ibn Sīnā mentioned in his books, his aim being to comprehend the causes in four: the matter, form, agent and *telos*. So the doubt about it is that matter's existence is incomplete, yet something else exists through it. Nay, its existence is only brought to completion by form, so that a body comes to exist through the two of them. But how can something else come to exist through something whose *own* existence is incomplete?

Moreover, the division he mentioned does not comprehend all the kinds of cause. Something else other than the kinds which he mentioned might exist, as they consider concerning 'instrument'. And what he mentioned about establishment through [an instrument] is a verbal reservation which does not

[101] 'Positional motion' (*al-ḥaraka al-waḍʿīyya*) designates the self-contained circular motion of the spheres, as opposed to rectilinear motion. See note 74.

preclude the sense of causality and effectuality [for an instrument]. Were it said: 'The agent and *telos* are sufficient in causality, matter being as it were the instrument, and form as it were the form in the agent itself'—whoever adds or subtracts from the division has leeway, and no absurdity follows thereby.

The Proof of Prophecy Through the Faculties and Methods of Intellect

That which transfers material human intellects from potentiality to actuality must be an actual intellect, for they may not by themselves emerge to actuality, and what is potential like them may not transfer them—something incontrovertibly proven. Yet why must that thing which transfers, which is an actual intellect, be specifically single—namely the Active Intellect which is the director of the sphere of the moon, so that it is called the Dispenser of Forms—to the exclusion of the intellects which are the directors of the rest of the spheres, or in association with them? And why might not all the forms be attributed to the First Intellect which is the mediator of the universe, so it would be the 'Active Giver', and its essence would not be multiplied by the multiplicity of the forms, just as the essence of the last intellect is not multiplied thereby? Nay, why might not all the forms be attributed to the Necessary of Existence, the First (Exalted and Hallowed is He!) without His essence being multiplied by the multiplicity of the forms? Blessed be God, the One, the Omnipotent, the Powerful, the Almighty, the Generous, the Giving!

If you seek out something proximate amongst the celestials and you deem the last sphere and its director the most proximate, so that it would be the one which emanates on the matters the forms to which they are predisposed, then why do you take spatial proximity into consideration in regard to *intellectual* substances? Do you not judge that intellectual substances are equal in remoteness and proximity? And do you not believe that the Necessary of Existence is more proximate than everything proximate, so that *He* is the transferer of what is potential to actuality amongst the intellects? 'God is near to those who believe, so He transfers them from the darkness to the light.'[102] Or do you not admit that amongst human intellects there is what is an actual intellect, so it would be the proximate cause, supported through holy power, as you admit the distinction of some intellects through intuitional power? You enjoin a precedence amongst souls and a hierarchy amongst intellects, and precedent and hierarchical things reach a limit in a single one which is the most superior, so they do not regress [to infinity]. 'O Prophet! We have sent you as a witness, a giver of glad news, a warner, a summoner to God by His permission, and as an effulgent lamp.'[103] O God, benefit us by that which You teach us, and teach us that by which You benefit us, by the truth of the Chosen Ones amongst your servants—upon them be peace!

[102] Qur'an 2:257.
[103] Qur'an 33:46.

Bibliography

Ādharshab, Muḥammad ʿAlī. *Tafsīr al-Shahrastānī al-musammā Mafātīḥ al-asrār wa-maṣābīḥ al-abrār.* Vol. 1. Tehran, 1417/1997.

al-Bayhaqī, Ẓahīr al-Dīn ʿAlī. *Taʾrīkh ḥukamāʾ al-islām,* ed. Muḥammad Kurd ʿAlī. Damascus, 1365/1946.

Dānishpazhūh, Muḥammad Taqī. 'Dāʿī al-Duʿāt Tāju'l-Dīn Shahrastāna', in *Nāma-yi Āstān-i Quds,* 7, no. 2 (1346/1968), pp. 71-80; 8, no. 4 (1347/1969), pp. 61–71.

Encyclopaedia of Islam, New edition. Leiden, 1960— .

al-Ghazālī, Abū Ḥāmid Muḥammad. *Fayṣal al-tafriqa bayn al-islām wa'l-zandaqa,* ed., Sulaymān Dunyā. Cairo, 1380/1960.

Gimaret, Daniel, Guy Monnot and Jean Jolivet. *Shahrastani: Livre des religions et des sectes. Vols. 1–2.* Paris–Louvain, 1986–1993.

Guillaume, Alfred. *The Summa Philosophiae of al-Shahrastānī: Kitāb Nihāyat al-iqdām fī ʿilm al-kalām.* London, 1934.

Hartmann, Angelika. 'Ismāʿīlitische Theologie bei sunnitischen ʿUlamāʾ des Mittelalters', in Ludwig Hagemann and Ernst Pulsfort, eds. *Ihr alle aber seid Brüder: Festschrift für A. Th. Khoury zum 60. Gesburtstag.* Würzburg-Altenberge, 1990, pp. 190–206.

—— 'al-Suhrawardī, Shihāb al-Dīn Abū Ḥafṣ', in EI2, vol. 9, pp. 778–82.

Hourani, George. 'Ibn Sīnā on Necessary and Possible Existence', *Philosophical Forum,* 4 (1972), pp. 74–86.

Ibn Bābūya, Abū Jaʿfar Muḥammad b. ʿAlī. *Kitāb al-Tawḥīd,* ed. Hāshim al-Ḥusaynī al-Tihrānī. Beirut, [1387/1967].

Ibn Qayyim al-Jawziyya. *Ighāthat al-lahfān min maṣāyid al-shayṭān,* ed. Muḥammad Ḥāmid al-Fiqī. Cairo, 1358/1939. 2 vols.

Ibn Qutayba, Abū Muḥammad ʿAbd Allāh. *ʿUyūn al-akhbār,* ed. Aḥmad Zakī al-ʿAdawī. Cairo, 1343–8/1925–1930.
Ibn Sīnā, Abū ʿAlī al-Ḥusayn b. ʿAbd Allāh. *al-Ishārāt waʾl-tanbīhāt,* with Ṭūsī's commentary, ed. Sulaymān Dunyā. Cairo, 1377–1380/1957–1960. 3 vols.
—— *al-Mubāḥathāt,* ed. Muḥsin Bīdārfar. Qum, 1414/1993–4.
—— *al-Najāt,* ed. Muḥyiʾl-Dīn al-Kurdī. Tehran, 1346 SH/1967.
—— *al-Shifāʾ: al-Ilāhiyyāt,* ed. Ibrāhīm Madkūr et al. Cairo, 1960.
Lane, Edward William. *An Arabic-English Lexicon.* Cambridge, 1984. 2 vols.
al-Majlisī, Muḥammad Bāqir. *Biḥār al-anwār.* Tehran, 1376–1392/1956–1972.
Monnot, Guy. 'Islam: exégèse coranique', in *Annuaire de l'École des Hautes Études, Section des sciences religieuses,* 90–9 (1981–1991).
—— 'al-Shahrastānī', EI2, vol. 9, pp. 214–16.
Mukhtār, Suhayr Muḥammad, ed. *Kitāb Muṣāraʿat al-falāsifa.* Cairo, 1396/1976.
Nāʾīnī, Muḥammad Riḍā Jalālī. *Sharḥ-i ḥāl wa-āthār-i Ḥujjatuʾl-ḥaqq Abuʾl-Fatḥ Muḥammad b. ʿAbd al-Karīm b. Aḥmad Shahrastānī.* Tehran, 1343 SH/1964.
—— *Dū maktūb.* Tehran, 1369/1990.
Ṣadr al-Dīn al-Shīrāzī, Muḥammad. *al-Ḥikma al-mutaʿāliya fīʾl-asfār al-ʿaqliyya al-arbaʿa.* Beirut, 1402–1411/1981–1990. 9 vols.
al-Shahrastānī, Tāj al-Dīn Muḥammad. *Kitāb al-Milal waʾl-niḥal,* ed. W. Cureton. London, 1842–1846.
—— *Mafātīḥ al-asrār wa-maṣābīḥ al-abrār,* facsim. ed. Tehran, 1409/1989. 2 vols.
Steigerwald, Diane. *ʿAbd al-Karīm Shahrastānī (m. 548/1153), Majlis: Discours sur l'ordre et la création.* Saint-Nicolas, Québec, 1998.
al-Subkī, Tāj al-Dīn Abuʾl-Naṣr. *Ṭabaqāt al-Shāfiʿiyya al-kubrā,* ed. Muḥammad ʿAbd al-Fattāḥ al-Ḥilw and Maḥmūd Muḥammad al-Tanāḥī. Cairo, 1383–96/1964–76. 10 vols.
al-Ṭūsī, Naṣīr al-Dīn Muḥammad. *Maṣāriʿ al-muṣāriʿ,* ed. Ḥasan al-Muʿizzī. Qum, 1405/1984.
—— *Contemplation and Action: The Spiritual Autobiography of a Muslim Scholar,* ed. and tr S.J. Badakhchani. London, 1998.
Wolfson, Harry Austryn. *Studies in the History of Philosophy and Religion,* ed. I. Twersky and G.H. Williams. Cambridge, Mass., 1973. 2 vols.
Yāqūt, b. ʿAbd Allāh al-Rūmī. *Muʿjam al-buldān,* ed. F. Wüstenfeld.

Leipzig, 1866–1873. 6 vols.
Zimmermann, Friedrich Wilhelm. *Al-Farabi's Commentary and Short Treatise on Aristotle's* De Interpretatione. London, 1981.

Index

Aaron 58
Active Intellect (*al-ʿaql al-faʿʿāl*) 12, 31, 57, 59, 97
aeon (*dahr*) 90
ahl al-bayt (Family of the Prophet) 3, 19
ʿAlids 7, 19 n.1
Almagest (Ptolemy) 94
ancients 74
angels 57, 72–3, 74
antonyms 91
Aristotle 75, 76n., 74, 94n., 99
astronomy 51, 92
Athens 74
Avicenna *see* Ibn Sīnā

al-Baṣrī, Abu'l-Ḥusayn 10
al-Bayhaqī, Ẓahīr al-Dīn 6

categorical propositions 73
categories 30, 76 n.74
Christians 63
circularity, vicious 85
cognition 72–3
Command (*al-Amr*) 32, 48, 58
concurrence (*maʿiyya*) 76, 88–90
conditional propositions 73
contingency, contingents 24, 25, 33, 36, 37, 39, 41, 43, 45, 50, 51, 52, 54, 55, 58, 59, 61, 86, 87, 88, 89, 93
contraposition 83 n.86
contraries 43
corporealist (*jismī*) 91

Dispenser of Forms (*al-wāhib li'l-ṣuwar*) 12, 31, 58, 59, 97

eclipse 68,73
efficient cause (agent) 92, 96–7
emanation 45, 49, 50, 52, 53, 57, 58, 59, 87, 88
equivocity 10, 43, 56–7, 74, 79
eternalist (*dahrī*) 91
eternity of the world 77–8, 79
existence, ambiguity (analogy) of 11, 37–8, 43, 55, 64; equivocity of 10, 11, 43, 48, 55, 64; univocity of 11, 43, 64; existentiation 49, 51,

79, 86; existents, division of 22–32 *passim*
extremist (*ghālī*) 91

Fayṣal al-tafriqa bayn al-islām wa'l-zandaqa (al-Ghazālī) 10
figuration *see* metaphor
final cause 92, 96–7
finitude 75–6, 84–5
finitude of space 82, 84
First Intellect (*al-ʿaql al-awwal*) 50, 52, 53, 57, 59, 66, 68, 70, 93, 97
formal cause 92, 96–7
al-Fuṣūl al-arbaʿa (al-Ḥasan b. al-Ṣabbāḥ) 4

genus (*jins*) 34, 36, 37, 38, 41, 42, 45, 47, 49, 54, 56, 93
al-Ghazālī, Abū Ḥāmid Muḥammad 2, 6–7, 8, 9, 14
Giver of Forms *see* Dispenser of Forms
God, absolute transcendence of 3, 9–10, 43, 48; a self-intellecting intellect 60, 62, 63, 64–5, 66; Most Beautiful Names of 43; omniscience of 71–4; unity of 44–59 *passim*
guideline (*miʿyār*) of the prophets 9

Ḥanbalism 74 n.71
Ḥanīfite Revelation 91
al-Ḥasan b. al-Ṣabbāḥ 4
al-Ḥikma al-mutaʿāliya fi'l-asfār al-ʿaqliyya al-arbaʿa (Mullā Ṣadrā) 14
hypothetical syllogism 63

Ibn Karrām, Abū ʿAbd Allāh Muḥammad 80 n.83
Ibn Qayyim al-Jawziyya 14
Ibn Sīnā (Avicenna) 7, 11, 13, 23, 28, 33, 36, 37, 38, 42, 44, 48, 51, 52, 60, 63, 68, 70, 73, 75, 77, 82, 86
Ighāthat al-lahfān min maṣāyid al-shayṭān (Ibn Qayyim al-Jawziyya) 14
ikhtirāʿ (direct production) 66
al-Īlāqī, Sharaf al-Zamān Muḥammad b.Yūsuf 7–8
imams 12, 98
incipience (*ḥidath*) of the world 74–92 *passim*
ineffability 35
infinity 75–6, 82–5
innate disposition (*fiṭra*) 11, 55
instauration *see* origination
al-Ishārāt wa'l-tanbīhāt (Ibn Sīnā) 8, 20, 25 n.14, 49 n.38, 78 n.80, 86 n.89

jurist 52

Karrāmiyya 80, 81
Kitāb al-Milal wa'l-niḥal (al-Shahrastānī) 1, 3, 4
Kitāb al-Najāt (Ibn Sīnā) 8, 11, 20, 23, 24 n.11–n.13 *passim*, 33 n.20–n.24 *passim*, 44 n.33–45 n.37 *passim*, 50, 60 n.53, 61 n.54–n.56 *passim*, 77 n.75–n.76, 78 n.78–n.79, 82 n.85, 86 n.90
Kitāb Nihāyat al-iqdām fī ʿilm al-kalām (al-Shahrastānī) 2, 3n.11, 99

literalists (*ḥashwiyya*) 36
logic 21, 38

Mafātīḥ al-asrār wa-maṣābīḥ al-abrār (al-Shahrastānī) 2
Maḥmūd b. ʿAbbās b. Arslān 6
Majlis (al-Shahrastānī) 2
al-Marwazī, Nāṣir al-Dīn Maḥmūd b. Abī Tawba 7
Maṣāriʿ al-muṣāriʿ (al-Ṭūsī) 13, 15–16, 94 n.99
material cause 92, 96–7
maysir 20 n.4
metaphor 81, 91
metaphysics 21, 46, 52, 94
middle term 83
Miletus 74
Moses 58, 79–80
muʿallā 20 n.4
al-Mubāḥathāt (Ibn Sīnā) 37 n.28
Muḥammad, the Prophet 19, 89, 98
Mullā Ṣadrā 14
al-Mūsawī, Sayyid Majd al-Dīn Abu'l-Qāsim ʿAlī b. Jaʿfar 7, 9, 12, 19
Muʿtazila 78 n.78

al-Nasafī, Muḥammad b.Aḥmad 10
al-Nāṣir li'l-Dīn Allāh 13
natural inclination (*mayl*) 88
Necessary of Existence (*Wājib al-Wujūd*) 22n.,10 *passim*. *Also see* God
negations and relations 38, 39, 40–2, 47, 54, 66
Niẓāmiyya 7
Nizārīs 5, 13

origination (*ibdāʿ*) 57, 58, 62, 63, 66 n.60, 67, 68, 70, 73, 81, 87, 90

particulars 11, 32, 38, 47, 49, 57, 60–74 *passim*
philosophers (*ḥukamāʾ/ falāsifa*) 23, 38, 60, 70, 72, 75, 92
physics 21, 49
position (*waḍʿ*) 76, 82, 96
posteriority (*taʾakhkhur*) 76, 88–90
preponderator (*murajjiḥ*) 33, 55, 77, 86, 87, 88
prime matter (*al-hayūlā/ al-hayūlā al-ūlā*) 24, 29, 93–4
principles 12, 92
priority (*awwaliyya/ taqaddum*) 22, 76, 78, 81, 88–90
prophecy 97–8
prophets 12, 55, 56, 71

Qāf mountain 64
Qarā Khiṭāy 12
Qurʾan, uncreatedness of 74

Rashf al-naṣāʾiḥ al-īmāniyya wa-kashf faḍāʾiḥ al-yūnāniyya (ʿUmar al-Suhrawardī) 13

Saljuqs 5
al-Samʿānī, Abū Saʿd 2
Samos 74
Sanjar, Sultan 7, 12–13
al-Sāwī, Qāḍī Zayn al-Dīn ʿUmar b. Sahlān 8
separate intellects 23, 49, 51, 52, 53, 59, 90, 92, 97, 98
al-Shahrastānī, his criticism of

al-Ḥasan b. al-Ṣabbāḥ 4; Ismāʿīlism of 2; philosophy of 6, 9; Sunnism of 3
al-Shifāʾ (Ibn Sīnā) 8, 20, 35, 60 n.53, 62, 77 n.76, 78 n.79, 86
al-Shīrāzī, Ṣadr al-Dīn *see* Mullā Ṣadrā
shortcomer (*muqaṣṣir*) 91
souls 31–2, 45, 52, 59, 76, 83, 84, 85, 92, 93, 98
species (*nawʿ*) 11, 31, 33, 35, 36, 38, 44, 46, 47, 48, 49, 54, 56, 67, 68, 92, 93
sphere, spheres 90, 92, 94, 95, 97
sphericity 94
Spirit (*al-rūḥ*) 57
Stoics (*aṣḥāb al-riwāq*) 74
storytellers (*qāṣṣa*) 36
al-Suhrawardī, Shihāb al-Dīn ʿUmar 13

Tahāfut al-falāsifa (al-Ghazālī) 8–9, 14
Taʿlīmiyya 10
al-Taʿlīqāt (Ibn Sīnā) 8, 20, 52
taqlīd (blind imitation) 5, 21
Tatimmat Ṣiwān al-ḥikma (al-Bayhaqī) 6
theologians (*mutakallimūn*) 8, 13, 20, 22, 60, 69, 70
Trinitarianism 62–3
al-Ṭūsī, Naṣīr al-Dīn 5–6, 10, 13–14,

unity, types of 48, 56
Universal Intellect (*al-ʿaql al-kullī*) 32
universal nature (*al-ṭabīʿa al-kulliyya*) 31
Universal Soul (*al-nafs al-kulliyya*) 31, 32
universals 11, 32, 39–41, 48, 54, 60–74 *passim*
Unmoved Mover 78, 95

weavers 36
Words, Divine (*al-kalimāt al-tāmma*) 90

Zimmermann, F.W. 83 n. 87
zodiac 68

كتاب المصارعة

كتاب المصارعة

للشيخ الإمام جمال الإسلام طراز الشريعة
محمد بن عبد الكريم الشهرستاني

بسم االله الرحمن الرحيم[١]

الحمد لله حمد الشاكرين، والصلاة على خاتم النبيين محمد المصطفى وعلى آله[٢] الطيبين، صلاة دائمة بركتها إلى يوم الدين.

لما أقام[٣] عالي[٤] مجلس الأمير السيد الأجل العالم[٥] مجدالدين، عمدة الإسلام، مالك[٦] أمر[٧] السادة، أبي القاسم علي بن جعفر الموسوي، ضاعف الله مجده وجلاله[٨] ، وأفاض عليه نعمه وإفضاله، للمكارم سوقها، ونهج إلى المعالي طريقها[٩]، وأظهر مكنون ما جبله الله تعالى عليه، وأودعه فيه من شرفي الحسب والنسب، ولطفي[١٠] الخَلق والخُلق،

١ الرحيم: + رب يسر برحمتك، ا.

٢ وعلي آله: وآله، ب.

٣ أقام: قام، ب.

٤ عالي: -، ب.

٥ الأجل العالم: - ، ب.

٦ مالك: ملك، ا ب.

٧ أمر: الأنام، ب.

٨ مجده وجلاله: جلاله، ب.

٩ طريقها: طرقها، ب.

١٠ لطفي: لطيفتي، ا.

وخلّتي العلم والقدرة، وحارستي الديانة والأمانة[١]، وحاميتي النجدة والشجاعة، سوى ما اكتسبه من بهجة الفضائل، والتوقّي عن الرذائل، وكمال المعرفة، وغاية الحكمة[٢]، ومكارم الأخلاق، ومحاسن الشيم، والجود والبسطة، وعلوّ[٣] الهمة وسموّ الرتبة، ما لو باهى بواحدة منها جميع[٤] أهل زمانه كان له السبق المُبرّ، وخالص السر[٥]، انتدب أصغر خدمه محمد بن عبد الكريم الشهرستاني لعرض بضاعته المزجاة على سوق كرمه، فخدمه بكتاب صنّفه في بيان الملل والنحل، على تردد القلب بين الوجل والخجل[٦]، فأنعم بالقبول، وأمعن[٧] النظر فيه، وبلغ النهاية في اكتناه[٨] معانيه، وبالغ في الثناء على أخلص[٩] مواليه، وما كان للمصنّف فيه كثير تصرّف سوى استيعاب المقالات كلها، وحسن الترتيب، وجودة

١ الأمانة: الإمامة، ا.

٢ الحكمة: مطموس في ا.

٣ علو: مطموس في ا.

٤ جميع: -، ا.

٥ المبر وخالص السر: المبين والحالفة واليسر، ا.

٦ الوجل والخجل: الخجل والوجل، ب.

٧ وأمعن: وانعم: ا.

٨ اكتناه: -، ا.

٩ أخلص: اصغر خلص، ا.

النقل. وإنما يُسبر غور[١] العقل، فتتبين[٢] قيمة الرجل، عند مناجزة الأقران، ومبارزة الشجعان، وبالاختبار، تظهر خبيئة الأسرار، وبالامتحان، يُكرم الرجل أو يهان.

وقد وقع الاتفاق على أن المبرّز في علوم الحكمة، وعلاّمة الدهر في الفلسفة[٣]، أبوعلي الحسين بن عبدالله بن سينا، فلايقفوه فيها قافٍ وإن نقض السواد، ولا يلحقه فيها لاحق وإن ركض الجواد. وأجمعوا على أن من وقف على مضمون كلامه، وعرف مكنون مرامه، فقد فاز بالسهم المعلّى، وبلغ المقصد الأعلى[٤]، بله[٥] الاعتراض عليه ردّاً ورضّا، وتعقّب كلامه إبطالاً ونقضاً، فإن ذلك باب ضُربت دونه الأسداد، وقبضت[٦] عليه الحفظة والأرصاد.

فأردتُ أن أصارعه مصارعة الأبطال، وأنازله منازلة الرجال، فاخترت من كلامه في إلاهيات الشفاء والنجاة والإشارات والتعليقات أحسنه وأمتنه[٧]، وهو ما[٨] برهن عليه وحقّقه وبيّنه، وشرطت على نفسي

١ يسبر غور: يسير غرر، ا.

٢ فتتبين: وتبين، ا.

٣ الفلسفة: العلم، ب.

٤ الأعلى: الأقصى، ا.

٥ بله: يله، ا.

٦ قبضت: قيدت، ب.

٧ أمتنه: مطموس في ا.

٨ وهو ما: وما، ا.

أن لا أفاوضه بغير صنعته، ولا[١] أعانده على لفظ توافقنا على معناه وحقيقته، فلا أكون متكلماً جدلياً، أو معانداً سوفسطائياً، فأبتدئ ببيان[٢] التناقض في فصوص نصوصه لفظاً و معنىً، وأردفه بكشف مواقع الخطأ في متون براهينه مادة وصورة.

فليجلس المجلس العالي، زاده الله علاءً ورفعة، مجلس القضاة والحكام، وليحكم[٣] بين المتناظرَين المتبارزين[٤] بالحق و الصدق، فهو أحرى بالحكم إذا تحوكم إليه، وأحقّ برعاية الصدق إذا عُوّل عليه، ليعلم أني قد بلغت من العلم بأطورَيه[٥]، ولا يستصغر شأني[٦]، فالمرء بأصغريه، ويتحقق أني قد ارتقيت من حضيض التقليد إلي أوج التحقيق والتسليم، وارتويت من مشرع النبوّة بكأسٍ مزاجها من تسنيم، ومن خاض لجّة البحر لم يطمع في شطّ، ومن تعلّى إلى ذروة الكمال لم يخَف مِن حطّ[٧].

لا زال[٨] المجلس العالي على أسعد طالع، وأيمن طائر، وأوضح هدي، وأنجح سعي، وأصوب رأي و تدبير، وأثقب تقدير وتفكير، في حرز حريز، من الله العزيز، ولا حول ولا قوة إلا بالله العلي العظيم.

١ ولا: + علي، ا.

٢ ببيان: في بيان، ا.

٣ وليحكم: ليحكم، ب.

٤ المتبارزين: المتباحثين، ب.

٥ بأطوريه: أطوريه، ب.

٦ شأني: حالي وشاني، ب.

٧ حط: حظ، ا.

٨ زال: ثال، ا.

وهذه المصارعة في سبع مسائل من الإلاهيّات من جملة نيّف وسبعين مسألة في المنطق والطبيعيّات والإلاهيات خنقتُه فيها بوتره[١] ، ورشقتُه بمشاقصه في نظره[٢] ، ورددته في مهوى حُفرته، وأركستُه لأم رأسه في زُبيته[٣]. ذلك من[٤] فضل {اللّهِ عَلَيْنَا وَعَلىَ النَّاسِ ولكِنَّ أَكْثَرَ النَّاسِ لا يَشْكُرُونَ}:

المسألة الأولى في حصر أقسام الوجود ،

المسألة[٥] الثانية في وجود واجب الوجود ،

المسألة[٦] الثالثة في توحيد واجب الوجود ،

المسألة[٧] الرابعة في علم واجب الوجود ،

المسألة[٨] الخامسة في حِدث العالم،

المسألة السادسة في حصر المبادئ ، حُوّلت مع السابعة الي مسائل مشكلة، وشكوك[٩] معضلة.

١ بوتره: بوتده، ا.

٢ في نظره: -، ا.

٣ زبيته: رتبته، ب.

٤ من: -، + (حاشية) لا من، ب.

٥ المسألة: -، ب.

٦ المسألة: -، ب.

٧ المسألة: -، ب.

٨ المسألة: -، ب.

٩ شكوك: شكول، ا.

المسألة الأولى
في حصر أقسام الوجود

اعلم أن المتكّلمين لم يحصروا أقسام الوجود بتقسيم حاصر، وذلك أنهم قالوا: الموجود ينقسم إلى ما له أول وإلى ما لا أول له، وما له أول ينقسم إلى جوهر وعرض. وعنوا بالجوهر المتحيّزَ الذي يمنع مثلَه بحدّه أن يكون بحيث هو، وبالعرض القائمَ بالمتحيّز، وأحالوا وجود جوهر ليس بمتحيّز ووجود[١] عرض ليس بقائم بمتحيّز. لكن[٢] التقسيم الأول صحيح دائر[٣] بين النفي والإثبات إذا روعي فيه شرائط التعاند[٤] والتقابل من الاتفاق على معنى الأولية ذاتاً وزماناً ومكاناً وشرفاً، والتقسيم الثاني غير صحيح ولا حاصر إذا فُسّر الجوهر[٥] بالمتحيّز والعرض بالقائم بالمتحيّز، إذ ليس فيه ما يدل على استحالة وجود قسم ثالث ليس بمتحيّز ولا قائم بمتحيّز، وقد أثبت الفلاسفة جواهر عقلية ليست بمتحيّزة[٦]. ولأن المتحيّز شيء ما، له حيّز، و قابلُ التحيّز غير نفس التحيّز، فما به يقبل التحيّز هو المادة، ونفس التحيّز صورة فيها، فهو إذاً جوهر مركّب من مادة وصورة. والجوهر يستحيل أن يتركب من

١ ووجود: مكرر في ب.

٢ لكنك: لكون، ب.

٣ صحيح دائر: صحيحاً دائراً، ب.

٤ التعاند: التضاد، ب.

٥ الجوهر: والجوهر، ب.

٦ بمتحيزة: + ولا قائمة بمتحيز، ب.

عرضين، فهما إذاً جوهران[١] غير متحيّزين. فقد خرج من المتحيّز ما ليس بمتحيّز، وهذا أعجب[٢].

وأما الفلاسفه فقد أثبتوا جواهر عقلية ليست بمتحيّزات، مثل العقول والنفوس والموادّ والصور، وأثبتوا أعراضاً ليست قائمة بمتحيّزات، مثل الحركات في الكم والكيف وغير ذلك.

وقد أورد ابن[٣] سينا تقسيماً في مبدأ إلاهيّات النجاة، وادعى أنه حاصر لجميع أقسام الموجودات، فأنقلُه على وجهه، ثم أبين وجوه الخطأ فيه. قال: إذا اجتمع ذاتان، ثم لم يكن ذات كل واحد منهما غير مجامع للآخر بأسره، كالحال في الوتد والحائط، فإنهما وإن اجتمعا فداخل الوتد غير مجامع[٤] لشيء من الحائط، بل إنّما يجامعه بسيطه[٥] فقط، فإذا لم يكن كالوتد والحائط[٦]، كان كل واحد منهما يوجد شائعاً بجميع ذاته في الآخر. ثم إن كان أحدهما ثابتاً حاله مع[٧] مفارقة الآخر، أو كان أحدهما مفيداً لمعنى به يصير الشيء موصوفاً [بصفة] والآخر مستفيداً لها، فإن الثابت والمستفيد لذلك يسمّى محلاً، والآخر يسمّى حالاً فيه. ثم إن كان المحل مستغنياً في قوامه عن الحالّ فيه فإنا نسيمه

١ جوهران: + ان، ب.

٢ أعجب: عجب، ب.

٣ ابن: بن، ا.

٤ غير مجامع: مجاورة، ا.

٥ بسيطه: بسطحه، ب.

٦ والحائط: في الحائط، ب.

٧ مع: -، ب.

موضوعاً له. وإن لم يكن مستغنياً عنه لم نسمّه[1] موضوعاً، بل ربّما سميناه هيولى.

وكل ذات لم يكن في موضوع فهو جوهر، وكل ذاتٍ قوامُه في موضوع فهو عرض. فقد[2] يكون الشيء في المحل ويكون مع ذلك جوهراً لا في موضوع إذا كان المحل القريب الذي هو فيه متقوّماً به ليس متقوماً بذاته، ثم هو مقوّماً[3] له، ونسميه صورة. وأما إثباته فقد يأتينا[4] من بعد[5]. وكل جوهر ليس في موضوع فلا يخلو[6] إما أن لا[7] يكون في محل أصلاً، أو يكون في محل لا يستغني في القوام عنه ذلك المحلُ، فإن كان في محل لا يستغني في القوام عنه ذلك المحل[8] فإنا نسيمه صورة مادّيةً، وإن لم يكن في محل أصلاً، فإما أن يكون محلاً بنفسه لا تركيب فيه، أو لا يكون. فإن كان محلاً[9] بنفسه فإنا نسميه الهيولى[10] المطلقة. وإن لم يكن، فإما أن يكون مركّباً مثل أجسامنا المركبة من مادّة

١ نسمه: نسميه، ا.

٢ فقد: وقد، ب.

٣ مقوماً: مقوم، ب.

٤ يأتينا: أثبتناه، ب.

٥ بعد: فعل، ا.

٦ يخلو: يخلوا، ب.

٧ أن لا: لا أن، ا.

٨ فإن كان ... المحل: -، ا.

٩ بنفسه ... محلاً: -، ب.

١٠ الهيولى: هيولى، ا.

ومن صورة جسمية، وإما أن لا يكون، ونحن نسيمه صورة مفارقة كالعقل والنفس. وأما إذا كان الشيء في محل هو[١] موضوع، فإنّا نسيمه عرضاً.

وقد ذكر قُبيل هذا الفصل أنّ الوجود ينقسم نحواً من القسمة إلي جوهر وعرض، وذكر[٢] بعده في فصل إثباتَ واجب الوجود، فقال: لا نشكّ أن وجوداً[٣] ، و كل وجود فإما واجب وإما ممكن. فأقول في الاعتراض وبالله التوفيق:

القسمان الأولان، وهما الجوهر والعرض، أمن[٤] أقسام الوجود من حيث هو وجود مطلق، أم[٥] من أقسام الوجود من حيث هو وجود ممكن؟ فإن كان الأول فواجب الوجود داخل في قسم[٦] الجوهر، وكان قسيمه العرض. ثم ينقسم الجوهر الى واجب لذاته وإلى ممكن لذاته، ويلزم أن تكون الجوهرية جنساً والوجوب فصلاً، فيكون مركباً من جنس وفصل. ويتأكد هذا الإلزام بقوله في رسم الجوهر: إنه الموجود لا في موضوع، فإن واجب الوجود موجود لا في موضوع. وإن اعتذر عنه بأن الجوهر ماهيّة ما[٧] إذا وجد كان وجوده لا في موضوع فذلك الاعتذار غير

١ هو: فهو، ا.

٢ وذكر: ذكر، ب.

٣ وجوداً: + (حاشية) موجوداً، ب.

٤ أمن: من، ا.

٥ أم: أو، ب.

٦ قسم: قسمة، ا ب.

٧ ما: -، ب.

مفهوم من الرسم المذكور مطابقة وتضمّناً، بل مدلول عليه استتباعاً[1] والتزاماً.

وإن كان القسمان الأولان، أعني الجوهر والعرض، من أقسام أحد القسمين، وهوالممكن، فهو صحيح في المعنى، غير صحيح في اللفظ. على أنه قد أتى في شرح أحد القسمين، وهو الجوهر، بما يشمل[2] الأعم ويساويه، فقال: الجوهر هو الموجود لا في موضوع، وهذا بعينه يشمل واجب الوجود ويساويه. ثم إني لا أنكر أن اللفظ العام ينقسم أنحاءً من القسمة من وجوه مختلفة، كما نقول: الموجود ينقسم[3] نحواً من القسمة إلى ما له أول وإلى ما لا أول له[4]، ونحواً من القسمة إلى علة ومعلول[5]، ونحواً[6] من القسمة إلى واجب وممكن، لكن الجوهر والعرض بخلاف ذلك، بل هما من أقسام الممكن، لا من أقسام الوجود.

ونعود[7] إلى الوجود، وأنه هل يقبل القسمة أم لا[8]، إن شاء الله تعالى. وأما قوله: إذا اجتمع ذاتان ثم لم يكن ذات[9] كل واحد منهما غير

١ استتباعاً: استباعاً، ب.

٢ يشمل: شمل، ب.

٣ كما نقول الموجود ينقسم: -، ب.

٤ له: -، ب.

٥ ونحواً من القسمة إلى علة ومعلول: -، ب.

٦ ونحواً: أو نحواً، ب.

٧ ونعود: يعود، ب.

٨ لا: + وسنذكر، ب.

٩ ذات: -، ب.

مجامع للآخر بأسره، إلى قوله: كان كل واحد منهما وجد[١] شائعاً في الآخر بأسره، أقول: هذه القضية منتقضة من وجوه، والتالي لم يلزم المقدّم لزوماً بيناً ولا غير بين. فإن العرضين ذاتان يجتمعان في محل، ثم لا يكون كل واحد منهما غير مجامع[٢] للآخر بأسره ولا شائعاً في الآخر بأسره، والحال في الهيولى والصورة بخلاف ذلك، فإن الصورة شائعة في الهيولى بأسرها والهيولى ليست[٣] شائعة في الصورة ولا مجامعة لها ببسيطها، فلم تكن كل واحدة منهما شائعة في الأخرى بأسرها. والحال في الجسم والعرض كذلك، فإن العرض يوجد شائعاً في الجسم بأسره، والجسم ليس بشائع[٤] في العرض بأسره ولا مجامع له ببسيطه، والحال في العقل والنفس أنهما ذاتان يجتمعان ولا يجامع أحدهما الآخر ببسيطه[٥] ولا يكون شائعاً فيه بأسره.

فعُلم من ذلك[٦] أن الاجتماع على وجوه وأنحاء شتّى، فاجتماع[٧] الجسمين غير، واجتماع العرضين غير، واجتماع الهيولى والصورة غير،

١ وجد: يوجد، ب.

٢ غير مجامع: مجامعاً، ب

٣ والهيولى ليست: وليست الهيولى، ب.

٤ بشائع: شائعاً، ب.

٥ والحال في العقل ... ببسيطه: -، ا.

٦ من ذلك: بذلك، ب.

٧ فاجتماع: واجتماع، ا.

واجتماع الجواهر[١] العقلية غير. فكيف سردها سرداً واحداً رمياً في عماية؟ وليس ذلك على منهاج المنطق.

وقوله: ثم إن كان أحدهما ثابتاً حاله[٢] مع مفارقة الآخر، قسم لا قسيم له، بل حقه أن يقول: أو لا يكون ثابتاً حاله[٣] مع مفارقة الآخر، فإنّ ذكر أحد القسمين لا يدلّ على[٤] الآخر.

ثم غيّر العبارة إلى قوله: أو كان أحدهما مفيداً لمعنى به[٥] يصير الشيء موصوفاً والآخر مستفيداً، تقسيم صحيح، إلا أنه جعل الثابت والمستفيد محلاً وغيرالثابت والمفيد[٦] حالاً، ويلزم عليه أن يجعل الصورة غير الثابت مع أنها مفيدة، والهيولى ثابتة مع أنها مستفيدة، والثبات[٧] بالمفيد[٨] أولى من المستفيد.

على أن المحلّ قد يكون هيولى، وهو ما لا يستغني في قوامه[٩] عن الحالّ فيه، وهو الصورة، وقد يكون جسماً ، وهو ما يستغني في

١ الجواهر: جواهر، ا.

٢ حاله: بحاله، ب.

٣ حاله: بحاله، ب.

٤ على: + ذكره، ب.

٥ به: -، ا.

٦ مفيد: مطموس في ا.

٧ والثبات: والثابت، ا.

٨ بالمفيد: للمفيد بالمفيد، ب.

٩ قوامه: قوله، ب.

قوامه عن الحالّ فيه[١]، وهو العرض. فأحد المحلّين ثابت بالحالّ، والثاني ثابت بذاته، فكيف يستويان في المحلّية؟

على أنه سمّى[٢] المحل الذي يستغني في قوامه عن الحالّ موضوعاً، والذي لا يستغني هيولى، والموضوع هو الجسم، إذ الجسم يستغني في قوامه عن الحالّ، ولذلك[٣] قال في آخر الفصل: إن الشيء إذا كان في محل هو موضوع يسمى عرضاً. فقوله: كل ذات لم يكن في موضوع فهو جوهر، كان معناه: كل ذات لم يكن في جسم فهو جوهر، ويعود إلى أن يقال[٤]: كل ذات لم يكن في جوهر فهو جوهر[٥]، وليس هذا مما يعدّ بياناً[٦]، بل هو بكلام[٧] المجانين أشبه وعن مناهج العقلاء أبعد. وإن لم يكن للموضوع معنى سوى ما ذكرناه، فليحقق له وجوداً غير اللفظ أو قسيماً له غير ذاته، ولا[٨] يجد إليه سبيلاً.

ويتوجه على مساق كلامه تقسيم آخر بأن يقال: إنك جعلت الهيولى محلاً غير مستغنٍ عن الحالّ في قوامه موجوداً أو في قوامه ماهية. فإن قلت: هو محل لا يستغني عن الحالّ في قوامه موجوداً،

١ وهو الصورة ... الحال فيه: -، ا.

٢ سمى: يسمي، ب.

٣ لذلك: كذلك، ا.

٤ يقال: قال، ا.

٥ فهو جوهر: -، ا.

٦ بياناً: ثباتاً، ا.

٧ بكلام: كلام، ب.

٨ ولا: مكرر في ب.

فكثير[١] من الجواهر والأجسام لا يستغني عن الحالّ فيه من الأعراض في قوامه موجوداً، ومع ذلك فالمحلّ لا يكون هيولى، والحالّ لا يكون صورة. وإن قلت: هو محل لا يستغني عن الحالّ في قوام[٢] ماهيته[٣]، فغير مسلّم، فإن الهيولى لها ماهية وحقيقة بذاتها من غير أن تكون الصورة جزأها المقوّم[٤]، ولو كانت الصورة جزءاً مقوماً[٥] لها لاستحال أن يرتسم معناها في الذهن دون جزئها المقوّم، ولو كانت الصورة جزءاً لها[٦] لكانت[٧] الهيولى مركّبة لا بسيطة. فتحقق أن الهيولى محتاجة إلى الصورة في وجودها لا في ماهيتها، وقد[٨] شاركها كل جوهر قابلٍ للعرض، فإن[٩] من الجواهر ما لا يخلو عن بعض الأعراض وجوداً، كالكون في مكان والكون في زمان، وبعض[١٠] الكميات وعن بعض[١١] الكيفيات والوضع، كما[١٢] لا

١ فكثير: فكثر، ا.

٢ قوام: قوامه، ا ب.

٣ ماهيته: وماهيته، ا.

٤ المقوم:المقدم، ا.

٥ مقوماً: -، ا.

٦ لاستحال أن ... جزءاً لها: -، ا.

٧ لكانت: كانت، ا.

٨ وقد: ولو، ب.

٩ فإن: وإن، ا.

١٠ وبعض: وعن بعض، ا.

١١ وعن بعض: وبعض، ب.

١٢ كما: وكما، ا.

تخلو الهيولى عن الصورة وجوداً. فما الفرق بين القسمين؟ وهذا شكّ أوردناه، فما التفصي عنه؟ ولات حين مناص.

وأما أقسام الجوهر التى ذكرها ابن سينا فغير محصورة بالسلب والإيجاب المتقابلين حتى يظهر التعاند في المنفصلات، فلا يشذّ عنها قسم ولا يزاد[١] فيها قسم، بل من الأقسام مالم يذكر له قسيماً فبقي أعرج، ومنها ما ذكر في قسم[٢] شرطاً لم يذكره في قسيمه[٣] فكان أعوج. مثل قوله: وكل جوهر لا في موضوع فإما أن لا يكون في محل أصلاً أو يكون في محل لا[٤] يستغني في القوام عنه ذلك المحل، وكان من حق المنفصلة على شرط التعاند أن يقول: وكل جوهر فإما أن لا يكون في محل أصلاً أو يكون في محل[٥] ، وحينئذ لا يكون التقسيم تقسيماً للجوهر[٦] بل للوجود[٧] الأعمّ منه، فإن العرض يدخل في القسم الثاني. فإن اعتبر القيد والشرط في أحد القسمين فيجب أن يعتبره في القسم الثاني، وإن لم يعتبره[٨] بطل التقسيم ولم يظهر التعاند فيه.

١ يزاد: يزداد، ا.

٢ قسم: قسيم، ب.

٣ قسيمه: قسمه، ا.

٤ لا: -، ا.

٥ محل: + أصلاً، ب.

٦ التقسيم تقسيماً للجوهر: القسيم تقسيم الجوهر، ب.

٧ للوجود: للموجود، ا.

٨ يعتبره: يعتبر، ب.

وكذلك قوله في المرتبة الثانية: وإن لم يكن في محل أصلاً فإما أن يكون محلاً بنفسه لا تركيب فيه أو لا يكون، ولعلّه اقتصر نوع اقتصار ههنا، وكان من حقّه أن يقول: فإما أن يكون محلاً بنفسه أو لا يكون، وما كان محلاً بنفسه فإما أن يكون فيه تركيب[١] أو لا يكون، أو: ما كان محلاً بنفسه فلا يخلو إما أن يكون بسيطاً أو مركباً، ثم المحل البسيط هو الهيولى والمركب هو الجسم.

وهذا التقسيم إنما يرد على محلّ لا يستغني في القوام عن الحالّ، لا على المحل المطلق. فإن المحل المطلق محل للجوهر[٢] والعرض جميعاً، فالهيولى محل بسيط للصورة وهي جوهر، لا محل للعرض، والجسم محل مركّب للعرض لا للجوهر. ومن العجب أن الجسم إنما يكون محلاً بما هو ذو هيولى، لا[٣] بما هو ذو صورة، إذ المحلّية تُشعر بالقبول والاستعداد، وهذا[٤] للهيولى لا للصورة، فإذاً رجع القسمان إلى قسم واحد.

وأما ما قال: إن ما ليس بحالّ ولا محل يجب[٥] أن يكون صورة عقلية هي العقل والنفس، فتحكّم محض، لأن التقسيم لا يقتضي جواز وجودهما ولم يُقم[٦] على وجودهما برهاناً، وليسا[٧] في الجوهرية والحقيقة

١ تركيب: التركيب، ا.

٢ للجوهر: الجوهر، ا.

٣ بما هو ذو هيولى لا: -، ا.

٤ وهذا: ولهذا، ب.

٥ يجب: فيجب، ب.

٦ يقم: يقيم، ا.

متماثلين. وقد[١] أغفل التقسيم الذي أورده[٢] أقساماً من الجواهر[٣]، وهي الجواهر الثانية[٤] من الأنواع والثالثة من الأجناس، ولم[٥] يستوعب جميع أجناس الجواهر، بل لم يذكر تقسيماً يستوفي جميع الموجودات بأنواعها وأشخاصها وجواهرها وأعراضها حتى يتبين بالقسمة العقلية إمكان وجودها[٦] وبالبرهان العقلي تحقُّق[٧] وجودها.

ونحن نورد بتوفيق الله تعالى تقسيماً حاصراً لذلك كله لتمتاز قوّة علم عن قوّة علم[٨] ورجل عن رجل، فنقول: الوجود الذي له معنى يرتسم في العقل ويشمل[٩] ماهيّات الأشياء شمولاً بالسوية، فهو القابل للقسمة العقلية، فإن ما لا يكون من الأسماء المتواطئة لا يقبل التقسيم من حيث المعنى. وذلك ينقسم بالقسمة الأولى إلى ما يكون محلاً لحالّ وإلى ما يكون حالاً في محل وإلى ما يكون قائماً بنفسه ليس بمحل ولا

٧ وليسا: وليس، ا.

١ وقد: فقد، ب.

٢ أورده: أورد، ب.

٣ الجواهر: الجوهر، ا.

٤ الثانية: مطموس في ا.

٥ ولم: ولو، ب.

٦ وجودها: وجوها، ا.

٧ تحقق: تحقيق، ا.

٨ علم: -، ا.

٩ ويشمل: ويشتمل، ب.

حالّ في محل. والمحل ما يحلهّ الحالّ حلول شيوع[١]، أعني أن يكون الحالّ فيه[٢] بحيث[٣] هو بأسره. وذلك ينقسم إلى ما لا[٤] يستغني في قوامه عن الحالّ، ونعني[٥] به أن ما له باعتبار ذاته قوّة واستعداد[٦] فقط، وإنما يحصل له الوجود بالحالّ فيه، وهو بسيط لا مركب، ويسمى الهيولى، وإلى ما يستغني في قوامه عن الحالّ فيه، ويسمى الموضوع[٧]، ويُحمل عليه المحمول[٨] ، وذلك هو الجسم. ولما كان الجسم مركّباً من هيولى وصورة، وهو جوهر، فجزآه جوهران. فإن الجوهر لا يتركب من عرضين، والجسم لايتركب من جوهرين عقليين.

وأما[٩] الحالّ فينقسم إلى ما لا يستغني عنه محلّه في قوامه، وذلك[١٠] هو الصورة الجسمية، مثل التحيّز والاتصال الذي لا ضدّ له، وإلى ما يستغني عنه المحل في قوامه ولا يتبدل المحل باستبداله، مثل

١ شيوع: مسروع، ا.

٢ فيه: -، ب.

٣ بحيث: نميث، ا.

٤ لا: -، ا.

٥ ونعني: ويعني، ا.

٦ واستعداد : واستعداداً، ب.

٧ الموضوع: موضوعاً، ب.

٨ المحمول: المحلول، ا.

٩ وأما : فأما ، ا.

١٠ وذلك: -، ب.

الكون في المكان[١] والاتصال الذي هو ضدّ الانفصال، ويسمى عرضاً. وأقسام الأعراض غير محصورة بالنفي والإثبات في عدد، إلا أنها حُصرت بالمقولات التسع، وقد حصرت في الكم والكيف. والمحل منه ما هو بسيط ومنه ما هو مركب، والحالّ[٢] منه ما هو جوهر ومنه ما هو عرض. والمحل والحالّ معاً شخص معيّن. وتسمّى الأشخاص الجواهرَ الأولى[٣] ، والأنواع الجواهر الثانية، والأجناس الجواهر الثالثة لقربها وبُعدها من الحسّ[٤]، وإن عكست فلقربها وبعدها من العقل.

وأما القائم بنفسه الذي ليس بحالّ ولا محل، بل هو المستغني عنهما[٥] ، فلا يخلو إما أن يكون له تعلق بهما أو لا يكون. وما له تعلق فإما أن يكون له تعلق إفاضة الحالّ في المحل أو تعلق إقامة المحل بالحالّ أو تعلق[٦] تدبير الحالّ والمحل معاً. فما له تعلق إفاضة الحالّ على المحلّ فهو العقل الفعّال الواهب للصّور، فإن الصور والأعراض[٧] التي تحدث في الموادّ والمحالّ من فيضه وسببه. وما له تعلق إقامة المحل بالحال فهو الطبيعة الكليّة السارية في جميع الموجودات السفلية الجسمانية المعِدّة

١ المكان: مكان، ا.

٢ والحال: + فيه، ب.

٣ الأولى: الأول، ا.

٤ الحس: الجنس، ب.

٥ عنهما: عنها، ا.

٦ تعلق: + بين، ا.

٧ والأعراض: والأعرض، ب.

لها في قبول الصور والأعراض. وما له تعلق تدبير[١] الحالّ والمحل معاً[٢] حتى تتوجه[٣] إلى كمالاتها من مبادئها فلا يخلو إما أن يكون مدبراً للكل[٤]، أعني العالم بأسره، وتدبيره تدبير كلي لا جزئي، فيسمى النفس الكلية، وإما أن يكون مُدبّراً للأجسام الجزئية[٥]، أعني بعضها دون بعض، وذلك ينقسم إلي مدبّرات الأجرام السماوية التي لا تقبل الكون والفساد، فتسمى[٦] النفوس الفلكية[٧]، وهى متعددة بعدد[٨] الأفلاك والأنجم التي قامت عليها الأرصاد، أو فاتت أرصاد العباد، وإلى مدبرات الأجسام الأرضية التي تقبل[٩] الكون والفساد، وذلك هي النفوس النباتية والحيوانيّة، وهي فاسدة بفساد المزاج، وتدبيرها تسخير طبيعي، والنفوس[١٠] الإنسانية التي لا تفسد بفساد المزاج، وتدبيرها تخيير[١١] عقلي.

١ تدبير: + بين، ا.

٢ معاً: جميعاً، ب.

٣ تتوجه: يتوجه، ا ب.

٤ للكل: للمحل، ا.

٥ الجزئية: الجزفة، ا.

٦ فتسمى: فيسمى، ا ب.

٧ الفلكية: الملكية، ا.

٨ بعدد: تعدد، ا.

٩ تقبل: + التي تحت، ا.

١٠ والنفوس: أو النفوس، ا.

١١ طبيعة ... تخيير: –، ب.

وأما ما لا تعلق له بالمحل والحال[١]، أعني المفارقات لموادّ الأجسام، فلا تقتضي الحكمة أن تكون عاطلة، بل لها تعلق تصوّر[٢] الخير المطلق في النفوس التي هي المدبّرات أمراً، فيجب أن يكون لكل نفسٍ عقل كما لكل فلك نفس، ويكون[٣] لها تعقلات فعلية لا انفعالية، ويجب أن يكون للنفس الكلية عقل كلي، ويكون له تعقل كلي[٤] يفيض[٥] منه[٦] الخير المطلق على الكل بواسطة النفس، وينتهي إليه الوجود كما ابتدأ منه الوجود، سلسلة مترتبة متّصلة بأمرالبارئ تعالى وتقدس عن[٧] أن يكون جلاله تحت[٨] الترتيب في الموجودات أو التضادّ في الكائنات، فهو منتهى مطلب الحاجات، ومن عنده نيل الطلبات، فالعقول محتاجة إليه لتعقل كليات أو جزئيات، والنفوس مفتقرة إليه لتدبّر سماويات أو أرضيات، والطبائع مسخرة[٩] له بسائط[١٠] ومركبات. {أَلاَ لَهُ الْخَلْقُ وَالأَمْرُ تَبَارَكَ اللَّهُ رَبُّ الْعَالَمِينَ} (٧ الأعراف ٥٤) {هُوَ الْحَيُّ لاَ إِلَهَ إِلاَّ هُوَ

١ بالمحل والحال: بالحال والمحل، ا.

٢ تصور: بصورة، ب.

٣ ويكون: وويكون، ب.

٤ كلي: -، ب.

٥ يفيض: تفيض، ا.

٦ منه: -، ا.

٧ عن: -، ب.

٨ تحت: نحب، ا.

٩ مسخرة: مسخرات، ا.

١٠ بسائط: بساط، ب.

فَادْعُوهُ مُخْلِصِينَ لَهُ الدِّينَ} (٤٠ غافر ٦٥)، الحمد لله ربّ العالمين، اللهم انفعنا بما علّمتنا وعلّمنا ما تنفعنا[1] به، بحق المصطفين من عبادك عليهم السلام.

١ تنفعنا: ينفعنا، ا.

المسألة الثانية
في وجود[١] واجب الوجود

قال ابن سينا: لا نشك[٢] أن وجوداً، وإنه ينقسم إلى واجب لذاته وواجب لغيره[٣] ممكنٍ باعتبار ذاته. ولا يجوز أن يكون شيء واحد واجب الوجود بذاته وبغيره معاً، ولا[٤] يجوز أن يكون لذات واجب الوجود بذاته مبادئ تجتمع[٥] فيتقوم منها واجب الوجود، لا أجزاء حدّ، ولا أجزاء كميّة، ولا تكون[٦] أجزاء القول الشارح لمعنى اسمه يدلّ كل واحد منها[٧] على شيء هو في الوجود غير الآخر بذاته. وقال: واجب الوجود بذاته هو واجب الوجود من جميع جهاته، وكل[٨] واجب الوجود بذاته فإنه خير محض وكمال محض وحقّ محض. وقال: ولا[٩] يجوز أن يكون نوع واجب

١ وجود: وجوب، ب.

٢ نشك: شك، ب.

٣ لغيره: بغيره، ب.

٤ ولا: فلا، ا.

٥ تجتمع: تجمع، ا.

٦ تكون: يكون، ا ب.

٧ منها: منهما، ا.

٨ وكل: فكل، ا.

٩ ولا: فلا، ب.

الوجود لغير ذاته، لأن وجود نوعه له لعينه[١]، فلا يجوز أن يشترك واجبا[٢] الوجود في وجوب الوجود حتى يكون وجوب الوجود عاماً لهما جنساً أو لازماً عموماً بالسوية، بل تعيّنه لأنه واجب الوجود فقط لا لأمر غير ذاته المتعين. ثم إن كل ممكن باعتبار ذاته ممكن أن يوجد وممكن أن لا يوجد، فإذا ترجّح الوجود على العدم احتاج الى مرجّح لا محالة، والمرجّح لجميع الممكنات يجب أن يكون غير ممكن باعتبار ذاته، بل واجباً بذاته خارجاً عن سلسلة الممكنات.

الاعتراض

نعد[٣] المناقضات في كلامه، ثم نشتغل بالنقض والإبطال.

قوله: واجب الوجود قد يكون بذاته وقد يكون بغيره، قول بعموم وجوب الوجود للقسمين، وقوله: ولا يجوز أن يشترك واجبا[٤] الوجود في وجوب الوجود حتى يكون وجوب الوجود عامّاً لهما جنساً أو لازماً، قضيّتان متناقضتان. فإن المعنى إذا لم يعمّ لم ينقسم، وإذا قُسم فقد عمّ[٥]، ولهذا صحّ اعتذاره أن أحد الواجبين لذاته والثاني لغيره، وهذا فصل ذاتي أو لازم، فلولا عموم ذاتي أو لازم لما صحّ الاعتذار.

١ لعينه: بعينه، ب.

٢ واجبا: واجب، ب.

٣ نعد: بعد، ا ب.

٤ واجبا: واجب، ب.

٥ عمم: عم، ب.

التناقض الثاني

قوله: لا يجوز أن تكون[١] أجزاء القول الشارح لمعنى اسمه يدلّ كل واحد منها[٢] على شيء غير[٣] الآخر بذاته في الوجود، ومطلق قوله: واجب الوجود بذاته، مشتمل على ثلاثة ألفاظ: واجب ووجود وبذاته، ويدلّ كل لفظ على معنى غير ما يدلّ عليه اللفظ الثانى. وعن هذا صحّت القسمة بأن يقال: الوجود ينقسم إلى واجب وإلى ممكن، ثم الواجب ينقسم إلى ما يكون واجباً بذاته[٤] وإلى واجب بغيره[٥]. ولا محالة يفيد كل قسم غير ما يفيده القسم الثاني ويدلّ على شيء هو في الوجود غيرُ ما يدلّ عليه الثاني، وذلك تناقض ظاهر.

ومن العجب أنه يقول: ليس لواجب الوجود أجزاء كمية كالجسم المركب من هيولى وصورة، ولا أجزاء حدّ كالمركب من جنس وفصل، ولا أجزاء عموم وخصوص كاللونية[٦] والبياضية، فكيف جعل الوجود شاملاً لقسمي الوجوب والإمكان، ثم جعل الوجوب خاصّاً به؟ وكيف[٧] جعل وجوب الوجود شاملاً لقسمي الوجوب بذاته والوجوب بغيره، ثم جعل الوجوب بذاته خاصّاً به؟ أليس ذلك قولاً صريحاً بأجزاء عموم وخصوص

١ تكون: يكون، ا ب.

٢ منها: منهما، ا.

٣ غير: دون، ا.

٤ بذاته: لذاته، ب.

٥ بغيره: لغيره، ا.

٦ اللونية: الليونية، ا.

٧ وكيف: فكيف، ا.

كاللونية والبياضية؟ اللهم إلا أن يُعرض عن هذه التقسيمات والبيانات كلها إعراضاً كلياً، فيقول[١]: هو حقيقة ما عديم الاسم[٢]. وقد ذكر هذا في مواضع أخر من الشفاء وغيره، إذ قد تنبّه بمثل هذه الإلزامات، إلا أنه ناقض ذلك بأن قال: شرح اسمه أنه يجب وجوده بذاته، فيا لله[٣] من عديم اسم له شرح اسم. فهلاّ قال: إذا بلغ الكلام إلى الله فأمسكوا؟

التناقض الثالث

قوله: واجب الوجود بذاته واجب الوجود من جميع جهاته، وأخذ يبرهن عليه، فإذا لم يكن له جهات، لا جهات مكانية حسية[٤] ولا جهات اعتبارية عقلية، فكيف أتعب نفسه في البرهان على أنه واجب الوجود من جميع الجهات؟ وهو كمن أخذ يبرهن علي أنه واجب الوجود من جميع الأجزاء والحدود بعد[٥] أن بين[٦] أنه لا جزء له[٧] ولا حدّ.

١ فيقول: فقول، ب.

٢ الاسم: للاسم، ا.

٣ لله: له، ب.

٤ حسية: حيثية، ا.

٥ بعد: -، ا.

٦ بين: -، ا.

٧ له: -، ا.

وأعجب من هذا قوله: وكل واجب الوجود فهو خير محض، ولا ندري[١] ما معنى هذا الكل، أيّ واحد من واجب الوجود فهو خير محض، فهو إذاً نوع أو جنس، أو يعنى به[٢] أن كل ذاته خير محض حتى يوهم[٣] أنه كلّ ذو أجزاء؟ فما ذلك التوحيد حتى في اللفظ، وما هذا[٤] التكثير حتى في المعنى؟

التناقض الرابع[٥]

قوله: ولا يجوز أن يكون نوع واجب الوجود لغير ذاته، فكيف استجاز أن يقال: نوع واجب الوجود في ذاته، كما يقال في الشمس[٦]: إن نوعها في شخصها؟ أما عرف أن نفي كثير من النقائص عن الحق جلّ جلاله نقص له؟ كما يقوله[٧] الحاكة من الحشوية[٨] والداصة[٩] من القاصّة[١٠]: نه

١ ندري: يدري، ا ب.

٢ به: -، ا.

٣ يوهم: توهم، ا.

٤ هذا: هو، ا.

٥ الرابع: والرابع، ا.

٦ الشمس: -، ا.

٧ يقوله: نقوله، ا.

٨ الحشوية: + والكرامية، ب.

٩ والداصة: والراصة، ب.

١٠ القاصة: + والقاص من العامة الفارسية، ب.

جسم نه[١] جوهر نه مشكّل نه مقدر نه مطول[٢] نه مدور نه مربع[٣] نه مخمس[٤] نهمكلف[٥] نه مؤلف، ويقول الهمج من الناس: سبحان الله، سبحان الله. فأخذ ابن سينا[٦] يطوّل الفصول في كتبه بنفي أمثال هذه الصفات عن واجب الوجود بذاته قبل إثباته، ثم أخذ في إثباته بأن قال[٧]: الممكنات تستند إلي واجب الوجود لذاته، فكأنه أخذه بنوعيته[٨] فى الذهن وقرر ما يلزم نوعيّته من نفي[٩] هذه السمات، ثم أخذه[١٠] بعينيّته[١١] حتى أثبته بدليل الإمكان في الممكنات واستنادها إلى واحد هو واجب الوجود بذاته.

١ نه: ونه، ب.

٢ مطول: + نه مربع، ب.

٣ مربع: مرتفع، ا؛ -، ب.

٤ نه مخمس: - ،ا ب ، والإضافة عن مصارع المصارع.

٥ مكلف: مكيف، ب.

٦ ابن سينا: بني شينا، ا.

٧ قال: -، ا.

٨ كأنه أخذه بنوعيته: مطموس في ا.

٩ نفي: -، ا ب.

١٠ أخذه: -، ا ب.

١١ بعينيته: بعينه + (حاشية) خ بتعينه، ب.

وما هو إلا خبط[١] عشواء، ورمي في عماية عمياء، ونفي نقائص هو[٢] إثبات نقائص.

وأما[٣] إبطال ما استدلّ به وأطلقه، فنقول:

قولك: لا نشك أن وجوداً، وإنه إما واجب لذاته وإما[٤] ممكن بذاته[٥]، فقد جعلت[٦] لواجب الوجود قسيماً[٧]، وهو الممكن بذاته. ويلزم على ذلك أن يكون الوجود[٨] شاملاً للقسمين شمولاً بالسوية[٩] من حيث الوجودية، فيصلح أن يكون جنساً أو لازماً في حكم الجنس، ويخصّ[١٠] أحد القسمين بمعنى يصلح أن يكون فصلاً أو في حكم الفصل، فتتركب ذات واجب الوجود من جنس وفصل، أو ما في حكمهما من اللوازم. وذلك ينافي الوحدة وينافي الاستغناء المطلق، فإن المركب من معنيين أو

١ خبط: + في، ب.

٢ هو: هي، ا.

٣ وأما: أما، ب.

٤ وإما: او، ب.

٥ بذاته: لذاته، ب.

٦ جعلت: جعل، ب.

٧ قسيماً: قسما، ا.

٨ الوجود: -، ا ب.

٩ بالسوية: بالقسمة، ا.

١٠ ويخص: ونخص، ا.

من اعتبارين عمومٍ وخصوص فقيرٌ[١] محتاج إلى مقوماته أولاً حتى تتحقق حقيقته، وإلي مركّب[٢] ثانياً حتى يوُجِد[٣] ماهيته.

فإن[٤] قال ابن سينا: إني لا أجعل الوجود عاماً[٥] شاملاً[٦] للقسمين شمولاً بالسوية، فإنه من الأسماء المشككة[٧] دون المتواطئة، وهو في واجب الوجود أولى وأول، وفي الممكن[٨] لا أولى ولا أول، وما كان من الأسماء[٩] المشككة لم يصلح أن يكون جنساً، بل الأسماء المتواطئة التي تشمل[١٠] الماهيات شمولاً[١١] بالسوية تصلح أن تكون جنساً، فلم يلزم ما ألزمتَه ولم ينتقض ما أبرمتُه، قلت: صادرت على المطلوب الأول من وجهين، أحدهما أن انقسام الوجود[١٢] إلى الواجب بذاته والممكن بذاته هو

١ فقير: فغير، ا؛ فهو، ب.

٢ مركب: تركب، ب.

٣ يوجد: توجد، ا.

٤ فإن: -، ا ب.

٥ عاماً: عللا، ا؛ علما، ب.

٦ شاملاً: كاملا، ا.

٧ المشككة: المشكلة، ا.

٨ الممكن: ممكن الوجود، ا.

٩ الأسماء: -، ا.

١٠ تشمل: تشتمل جميع، ب.

١١ شمولاً: + لا، ا.

١٢ الوجود: + ينقسم، ا.

بعينه[١] انقسام الوجود إلى ما هو أولى به وأول له[٢] وإلى ما هو لا[٣] أولى به[٤] ولا أول له. والوجود شامل لهما شمولاً بالسوية من حيث الوجودية، والوجود أمر ذاتي للقسمين الأخصّين[٥] به، وإن كان[٦] عرضياً بالنسبة إلى الجوهر والعرض وسائر الماهيات.

وقد عرفت[٧] من تعريف الذاتي أنك إذا[٨] أحضرته في الذهن وأحضرت ما هو ذاتي له لم يكمنك تصوّرُ ما هو ذاتي له إلا بذلك الحاضر في الذهن، وكان[٩] وجوده في الذهن بوجوده لا عند وجوده، وارتفاعُه عن الذهن بارتفاعه لا عند ارتفاعه[١٠]، والحال[١١] في الواجب والوجود كذلك، فإنك لا يمكنك تصوّرُ واجب الوجود إلا بسبق تصوّر الوجود، وإذا رفعتَ

١ بعينه: + عين، ب.

٢ له: -، ب.

٣ هو لا: لا هو، ا.

٤ به: -، ب.

٥ الأخصين: الأخفين، ا؛ أخصين، ب.

٦ كان: -، ا.

٧ عرفت: عرفته، ا.

٨ إذا: إذ، ب.

٩ وكان: فكان، ب.

١٠ لا عند ارتفاعه: -، ا.

١١ والحال: والحالة، ا.

الوجود ارتفع الوجوب بارتفاعه. والرجل لما فطن[١] لمثل هذا الإلزام وضع لنفسه قسماً وراء المتواطئة سماه المشككة، وليس في منطق الحكماء ذلك، ولا يغنيه[٢] من جوع[٣]، ولا الإلزام عنه مدفوع[٤]. وهب[٥] أنه قسْم محقق، فليس يختص ذلك بالوجود، بل يجري مثلُه في الوحدة والعلّية والحق[٦] وجميع العمومات[٧] من الأجناس والأنواع، فيقال: الوحدة تطلق[٨] على كل واحد، وهي بالأول أولى، والعلة والحق[٩] والمبدأ[١٠] تطلق[١١] على غير واجب الوجود وهي[١٢] به أولى، واسم الجوهر يطلق على كل ما إذا وجد[١٣]

١ لما فطن: لما تفطن، ا؛ قد فطن، ب.

٢ يغنيه: بعينه، ب.

٣ من جوع: مرجوع، ا.

٤ مدفوع: مرفوع، ب.

٥ وهب: من هنا سقط النص من نسخة ا حتى: والوجه الثاني.

٦ والعلية والحق: واحق والعلة، ب.

٧ العمومات: العامات، ب.

٨ تطلق: مطلق، ب.

٩ والحق: واحق، ب.

١٠ والمبدأ: فالمبدأ، ب.

١١ تطلق: مطلق، ب.

١٢ وهي: وهو، ب.

١٣ إذا وجد: -، ب.

كان وجوده لا في موضوع وهو بالجواهر العقلية أولى، وعلى هذا فينتفي[١] قسم المتواطئة، فلا يشمل لفظٌ ما معنى بالسوية[٢].

والوجه الثاني، نقول: هب أن الوجود من المشككة، وهو[٣] قسم آخر، أليس أن الوجود يعمهما عموماً ما والوجوب يخصّه خصوصاً ما، وما به عمّ غير ما به خصّ؟ ففيه تركب[٤] وجهين بلفظين يدلّ كل واحد منهما على غير ما يدلّ عليه الثاني، وذلك ينافي الوحدة المحضة.

فإن[٥] قال: معنى الوجوب أمر سلبي لا إيجابي أو أمر[٦] اعتباري لا وجودي، فلا يلزم التكثّر في ذاته، قُلتُ: كلامنا أولاً في الوجود، ثم في الوجوب، فما تقول في الوجود ومفهومه في الذهن؟ أهو قضية عامّة ومعنى يشمل الواجب والممكن شمولاً ما أم لا؟ فإن شمل فلا بدّ من خصوص معنى أخر حتى[٧] يمتاز الواجب عن الممكن، فلا يمكنك أن تقول: إن المعنى الذي شمل أمر[٨] سلبي، إذ الوجود كيف لا[٩] يكون وجودياً[١٠]

١ فينتفي: فيبقى، ب.

٢ لفظ ما معنى بالسوية: لفظه بمعنى السوية، ب.

٣ وهو: وهم، ا.

٤ تركب: تركيب من، ب.

٥ فإن: -، ب.

٦ أمر: -، ا.

٧ حتى: -، ا.

٨ أمر: + عام، ب.

٩ لا: لأن، ب.

١٠ وجودياً: + والوجود ذاتي الوجود، ب.

والوجوب تأكيد الوجود، أي الوجود له[1] بذاته، ويلزمه أنه غير مستفاد عن[2] غيره، فكيف اعتبر اللازم وترك ما هو ذاتي له؟ ولو كان الوجوب أمراً سلبياً لكان الذي يقابله، وهو الإمكان، أمراً وجودياً، ونحن نعلم أنك تعلم أن الوجود والإثبات أولى بالواجب، والعدم والسلب أولى بالممكن، كيف وقد قررت[3] أن الوجود أولى وأول بالواجب، ولا أولى ولا أول بالممكن، فكيف نسيت المشككة التي ابتدعتها[4]؟ وهب أن[5] معناه أمر سلبي فليس سلباً مطلقاً، بل سلب شيء من شأنه أن يتحقق، وهو يصلح للتمييز وبه يحصل التكثّر. ودع ما قيل: إن السلوب والإضافات لا توجب تكثّراً[6] في الذات، فإنهم أخذوا القضية مسلّمة، وليس الأمر كذلك على ما سيأتي تفصيله.

وأما قوله: إن التمييز[7] بين الوجود والوجوب بالعموم والخصوص أمر اعتباري في الذهن، لا في الوجود، فتسليمُ[8] ظاهر الإلزام، فإن التمايز[9] بين معنى الجنسية ومعنى الفصلية لا يكون إلا في الذهن، فليس

١ الوجود له: له الوجود، ب.

٢ عن: من، ب.

٣ قررت: قدرت، ا.

٤ ابتدعتها: ابدعتها، ب.

٥ أن: بأن، ب.

٦ تكثراً: تكثيرا، ب.

٧ التمييز: التميز، ا.

٨ فتسليم: فتسليمه، ب.

٩ التمايز: التماييز، ا.

في الوجود حيوان هو جنس وناطق هو فصل، بل هما اعتباران في الذهن، لا في الخارج. وكيف يحصل أمر كلّي في الوجود، ولا كلّي إلا في الذهن؟ وأنت تعرف أن اللونية و البياضية اعتباران عقليان في الذهن، لا في الخارج، وألاّ في الوجود لونية البياض غير بياضيته.

عاد الرجل وقال: تعدُّد الاعتبارات الناشئة من تعدد الألفاظ عموماً وخصوصاً يرجع في الحقيقة إلى تعدد الإضافات والسلوب في حق واجب الوجود، فإن قولنا: هو مبدأ[١] الوجود وعلته ومريده ومُبدعه، هو إضافة الوجود إليه وصدوره عنه من غير أن يحدث له منه شيء أو تتكثر ذاته بشيء، وقولنا: إنه واجب الوجود بذاته، أي هو ذات مسلوب عنه[٢] الحاجة إلى الغير، وعموم الوجود وخصوصه في حقه تعالى واحد، فإن وجوبه وجوده، وتعيّنه لا يقتضي معنى آخر يعيّنه لازماً أو غير لازم، ووحدته لا تستدعي معنى آخر يوحّده، فهو واحد لأنه واجب الوجود، وقولنا[٣]: لأنه، ليس تعليلاً في الحقيقة، بل المعنى فيه أنه ليس إلا كذلك، وهذا معنى قولي: إن واجب الوجود لا يكون إلا واحداً من كل وجه، وقولي: إن كثرة الإضافات والسلوب لا توجب كثرة في ذاته، قضية مسلّمة عند الكل. فإن قولنا: هذا الجسم قريب من كذا، بعيد من كذا، ليس فيه صفة كذا وكذا، لا يوجب تكثّراً في ذات الجسم[٤] مع كونه قابلاً للتكثّر[٥]، فكيف الحال بذات مقدّس عن سمات التكثّر والتغيّر[٦]؟

١ مبدأ: مبتدأ، ا.

٢ ذات مسلوب عنه: مسلوب عنه ذات، ب.

٣ وقولنا: وقوله، ا.

٤ ذات الجسم: ذاته أي في الجسم، ب.

٥ للتكثر: للتكثير، ب.

قلت: الألفاظ العامّة والخاصّة مفهوماتها في الذهن عامة وخاصّة لا من حيث كونها ألفاظاً في اللسان، والمفهومات[١] في الذهن إنما[٢] تكون صحيحة لمطابقتها ما هو في[٣] الخارج عن الذهن. ولا أعني بالمطابقة أن يكون الكلّي في الذهن يطابق كلّياً في الخارج إذ ليس في الأعيان أمر كلّي، بل[٤] الكلّي في الذهن يطابق كلّ واحد واحد من الجزئي في الخارج، كالإنسانية العامّة في الذهن تطابق كلّ شخص شخص مما وجد[٥] ومما لم يوجد. ثم التمييز بين نوع ونوع إنما يكون بالفصول الذاتية، والتمييز بين شخص وشخص إنما يكون باللوازم العرضية.

وإذ[٦] تحقّق ذلك فبيّن[٧] أن الوجود العامّ شمل[٨] الواجب والممكن شمولاً ما. فإن كان الشمول بالسوية صلح أن يكون جنساً، فلا بد من فصل ذاتي، فتركب الذات من جنس وفصل، وإن لم يكن بالسوية لم يخرج عن العموم والشمول، فلا بدّ أيضاً من فصل ذاتي أو غير ذاتي،

٦ التكثر والتغير: التغير والتكثر، ب.

١ والمفهومات: فالمفهومات، ب.

٢ إنما: وإنما، ب.

٣ في: -، ا ب.

٤ بل: بلى، ا.

٥ وجد: يوجد، ا.

٦ وإذ: وإذا ثبت، ب.

٧ فبين: تبين، ب.

٨ شمل: يشمل، ب.

فتركّب[١] الذات[٢] من عامّ وخاصّ، وإن كان عمومه عين خصوصه وخصوصه عين عمومه لم يكن عموم وخصوص أصلاً، فبطل قولك: لا نشك أن وجوداً، وإنه ينقسم إلى واجب وممكن[٣]، وبطل[٤] وضعك الوجود مطلقاً موضوعاً للعلم الإلهي[٥]، وبطل ذكرك[٦] في الكتب التي صنفتها : لوازم الوجود من حيث هو وجود، وتعديدك لوازمه من حيث هو واجب لا من حيث هو وجود.

ألست تقول: إن العدم أو اللاوجود[٧] يقابله من حيث هو وجود، وإن[٨] الإمكان يقابله من حيث هو واجب لا من حيث هو موجود[٩]، وكونه واحداً يلزمه من حيث هو واجب، وكذلك كونه غنياً على الإطلاق مقدّساً عن[١٠] سمات الحدوث، وكونه مبدأ للكائنات[١١] كلها. وقوله: إن كثرة السلوب والإضافات لا توجب كثرة في الذات، قضية يسلّمها عامة

١ فتركب: فركب، ا.

٢ من جنس ... فتركب الذات: -، ب.

٣ وممكن: وإلى ممكن، ب.

٤ وبطل: فبطل، ب.

٥ الإلهي: اللالهي، ا.

٦ ذكرك: قولك، ب.

٧ اللاوجود: ان لا وجود، ا.

٨ وإن: فإن، ا.

٩ موجود: وجود موجود، ا؛ وجود، ثم أضيف: موجود، ب.

١٠ عن: على، ا.

١١ للكائنات: الكائنات، م.

أصحابه، وليست هي يقينية ولا بيّنة بنفسها ولا[١] مدلولاً عليها إلا بمثال القرب والبعد. ولِم قال: إن جميع الإضافات حكمها حكم القرب والبعد؟ وإن سُلّم له ذلك فإن من الإضافات ما يوجب كثرة الأعراض ومنها ما يوجب كثرة الاعتبارات. أليس صيرورة[٢] الرجل أباً إذا حصل له ولد، وعمّاً[٣] إذا حصل له[٤] ابن أخ، وفاعلاً حين[٥] يحصل منه فعل، ليس حكمه[٦] حكم القرب والبعد؟ وكذلك في جانب السلب، فإن سلب القطع من السيف ليس[٧] كسلب القطع من الصوف.

فالسلوب[٨] مختلفة والإضافات[٩] مختلفة، فكيف يصحّ عليها حكم واحد يعمّها؟ بل نفس الفرق[١٠] بين المعاني الإضافية والمعاني السلبية أوجب كثرة[١١] اعتبارين[١٢] في الذات، فإنك تقول: هذا معنى إضافي له لا

١ ولا: لا، ا ب.

٢ صيرورة: صورة، ا.

٣ وعما: مطموس في ا.

٤ ولد ... حصل له: -، ب.

٥ حين: حتى، ا.

٦ حكمه: مطموس في ا.

٧ ليس: وليس، ا.

٨ فالسلوب: والسلوب، ا ب.

٩ والإضافات: والإضاف، ب.

١٠ الفرق: المعرف، ب.

١١ أوجب كثرة: مكرر في ب.

سلبي، وهذا سلبي لا إضافي، وتقول: هذا[١] إضافة من وجه[٢] كذا وهذا من وجه كذا[٣]. وكل ذلك كثرة اعتبارية عقلية[٤]، يفهم من كلّ واحد ما لا يفهم من الآخر، ويدلّ كلّ لفظ على غير ما يدل عليه اللفظ الآخر، فبطل قوله[٥]: إن واجب الوجود بذاته لا يتكثر بكثرة السلوب والإضافات، وسنعود[٦] إلى ذلك في مسألة التوحيد.

المختار[٧]

عادتنا[٨] أن نذكر في آخر كلّ مسألة فصلاً يُطلع الناظر على مثار الغلط والخطاء الذي عرض لابن سينا وينبّه[٩] الطالب على وجه الصواب والحق بكلام متين يفلّ[١٠] الحدّ ويصيب المَفْصِل، والله الموفق والمعين.

١٢ اعتبارين: الاعتبارات، ب.

١ هذا: هذه، ا ب.

٢ وجه: وجهه، ب.

٣ وهذا من وجه كذا: -، ب.

٤ عقلية: -، ب.

٥ قوله: قولك، ب.

٦ وسنعود: ونعود، ب.

٧ المختار: والمختار، ب.

٨ عادتنا: من عادتنا، ب.

٩ ينبه: بينه، ب.

١٠ يفل: مطموس في ا؛ يعد، ب.

أقول: إنما توجهت هذه المناقضات والمطالبات على ابن سينا وشركائه في الحكمة[١] لأنهم وضعوا الوجود عامّاً عموم الجنس أو عموم اللوازم، وظنّوا أنهم لما وضعوه من[٢] المشككة وأخرجوه من المتواطئة خلصوا نجياً من هذه الإلزامات، ولا يخلصهم عنها إلا وضع الوجود وكلّ صفة ولفظ يطلقون عليه تعالى وتقدس من الوحدة والواحد والحق والخير والعقل والعاقل والمعقول[٣] وغيرها بالاشتراك، لا بالتواطؤ ولا بالتشكيك، وقد توافقوا على أن إطلاق الوحدة والواحد عليه[٤] تعالى وعلى غيره بالاشتراك المحض، وكذلك الحق والخير، فهو حق بمعنى أنه يُحق الحق ويبطل الباطل، وواجب[٥] وجوده بمعنى أنه يوجب وجود[٦] غيره ويعدم، وحيّ[٧] بمعنى أنه يُحيي[٨] ويميت.

والمتضادات متخاصمات والمختلفات متحاكمات، والحاكم عليها لا يكون في عداد[٩] أحد المتحاكمين إليه المتخاصمين عنده، لكنه يطلَق

١ الحكمة: الحطمة، ا.

٢ وضعوه من: وضعوا، ا.

٣ والعقل والعاقل والمعقول: والعاقل والعقل والعقول، ب.

٤ عليه: -، ا.

٥ وواجب: وواجبه، ب.

٦ وجود: وجوده، ا.

٧ وحي: وحتى، ا؛ وهي، ب.

٨ يحيي: يويحيى، ب.

٩ عداد: أعداد، ب.

الحق على الحاكم بمعنى أنه يُظهر الحق ويحقّه[١]، لا بمعنى أنه يخاصم أحد المتخاصمين فيساويه تارةً[٢] ويباينه أخرى. فالوجود والعدم، والوجوب والإمكان، والوحدة[٣] والكثرة، والعلم والجهل، والحياة والموت، والحق والباطل، والخير والشرّ، والقدرة والعجز، متضادات، وتعالى الله عن الأضداد والأنداد. {فَلاَ[٤] تَجْعَلُوا للّٰه أَنْدَاداً وَأَنْتُمْ تَعْلَمُونَ} (٢ البقرة ٢٢) {وَللّٰه الْأَسْمَاءُ الْحُسْنَى فَادْعُوهُ بِهَا. وَذَرُوا[٥] الَّذِينَ يُلْحِدُونَ فِي أَسْمَائِهِ سَيُجْزَوْنَ[٦] مَا كَانُوا يَعْمَلُونَ} (٧ الأعراف ١٨٠). اللّهم انفعنا بما علّمتنا وعلّمنا ما تنفعنا به[٧] بحقّ المصطفين[٨] من عبادك عليهم السلام[٩].

١ يحقه: يخفيه، ا.

٢ تارة: تبارة، ا.

٣ والوحدة: والواحدة، ب.

٤ فلا: ولا، ب.

٥ وذروا: وذر، ب.

٦ سيجزون: يسخرون، ا.

٧ به: -، ب.

٨ المصطفين: الصالحين، ب.

٩ عليهم السلام: -، ب؛ اللهم ... السلام: -، ا.

المسألة الثالثة
في توحيد واجب الوجود

قال ابن سينا: إن واجب الوجود لا يقال[١] على كثيرين[٢]، ولا يجوز أن يكون نوع واجب الوجود لغير ذاته. فإن وجود نوعه بعينه إما أن يقتضيه ذات نوعه أو تقتضيه علة غير ذاته، فإن كان يقتضيه ذات نوعه فوجود نوعه لا يكون إلاّ له، وإن كان لعلة فهو معلول.

ثم[٣] قال: وكيف يمكن أن تكون الماهية المجرّدة عن المادة لذاتين؟ والشيئان إنما يكونان[٤] اثنين[٥] إمّا بسبب المعنى، وإما بسبب الحامل للمعنى، وإمّا بسبب الوضع والمكان، أو الوقت[٦] والزمان، وبالجملة لعلة[٧]

١ يقال: يقابل، ا.

٢ كثيرين: -، ب.

٣ ثم: -، ا.

٤ يكونان: يكون، ب.

٥ اثنين: اثنان، ا.

٦ أو الوقت: والوقت، ب.

٧ لعلة: العلة، ب.

من العلل، وكلّ اثنين لا يختلفان[١] بالمعنى فإنما[٢] يختلفان بشيء غير[٣] المعنى.

ثم قال: واجب الوجود واحد من جهة تمامية وجوده، وواحد من جهة أنّ حدّه له، وواحد من جهة أنه لا ينقسم، لا[٤] بالكم ولا بالمبادئ المقوّمة له، ولا بأجزاء الحدّ، وواحد من جهة أن[٥] مرتبته في الوجود، وهو وجوب الوجود، ليس إلا له، ولا يجوز أن يكون وجوب الوجود مشتركاً فيه. وأخذ في البرهان عليه وطوّل، و حاصله يؤول[٦] إلى أن يقول: وجوب الوجود إما أن يكون من لوازم ماهية متقومة بذاتها، وإما أن يكون من مقومات ماهية تتقوم به، وإما أن يكون عبارة عن تلك الذات الواجبة بعينها لا يشاركها غيرها في وجوب الوجود البتة، وهو الحق.

وقال بعده: ولا يجوز أن يقال: إن واجبي الوجود لا يشتركان في شيء، وكيف، وهما مشتركان[٧] في وجوب الوجود ومشتركان[٨] في البراءة عن[٩] الموضوع؟ فإن كان وجوب الوجود يقال عليهما بالاشتراك فكلامنا

١ يختلفان: يختقان، ب.

٢ فإنما: وإنما، ا.

٣ غير: عن، ا.

٤ لا: -، ا.

٥ أن: انه، ب.

٦ يؤول: يول، ب.

٧ مشتركان: يشتركان، ا ب.

٨ ومشتركان: ويشتركان، ب.

٩ عن: من، ا.

ليس في الاسم، بل[١] في معنى ما يقال[٢] عليه الاسم قولاً بالتواطؤ حتى يحصل[٣] معنى عام عمومَ لازم أو عموم[٤] جنس، وقد بيّنا استحالة ذلك.

ثم أخذ في إثبات واجب الوجود وبرهن عليه، فقال: لا نشك أن وجوداً، وكل[٥] وجود فإما واجب وإما ممكن، فإن كان واجباً فقد صحّ وجوده، وهو المطلوب، وإن كان ممكناً فكل ممكن ينتهي[٦] وجوده إلى واجب. وشرع في تحقيقه بالتقسيم الذي ذكره، وقال بعده: الواحد لا يصدر عنه إلا الواحد، إذ لو صدر عنه اثنان فعن حيثيتين مختلفتين[٧]، فإنه لو صدر عنه ا من حيث صدر عنه ب كان ا ب، وهذا محال. ثم الصادر عنه فيجوز أن يتحقق له أحياث مختلفة، إذ هو ممكن الوجود باعتبار ذاته واجب الوجود باعتبار موجبه، فليس[٨] يلزم أن يكون واحداً من كل وجه، فليس يلزم أن يصدر عنه واحد، فهو ذو اعتبارات وجهات عقلية، فمن حيث هو ممكن بذاته يصدر عنه نفس أو هيولى، ومن حيث هو واجب بغيره[٩] يصدر عنه عقل أو صورة.

١ بل: -، ب.

٢ يقال: يقابل، ب.

٣ يحصل: حصل، ب.

٤ أو عموم: وعموم، ا.

٥ وكل: وان كل، ب.

٦ ينتهي: فينتهي، ب.

٧ مختلفتين: مختلفين، ب.

٨ فليس: وليس، ب.

الفصل

الاعتـراض عليـه من جـهـة التناقض في كـلامـه والخلل في أقسامه، لا في حكم المسألة، فإن التوحيد حكم متفق عليه.

فالتناقض الأول

قوله الأول: إنّ واجب الوجود لا يقال على كثيرين، وقوله: ولا[١] يجوز أن يكون نوع واجب الوجود لغير ذاته، فالنوع لا يقال إلاّ على كثيرين، فكيف أطلق لفظ النوع على واجب الوجود؟ وواجب الوجود[٢] لا يقال إلا على ذات وموجود لا يشاركه في الاسم غيره، والنوع لا يقال إلا على موجود يشاركه في الاسم غيره[٣]، دع الرسم والحدّ، فإنهما فوق الاسم المجرّد.

التناقض الثاني

إنك[٤] أخذت الوجود مطلقاً وجعلته موضوع العلم الإلهي[٥] وتكلمت في لوازمه، ثم جعلت واجب الوجود من أقسامه ولواحقه، ثم

٩ بغيره: بغير، ب.

١ ولا: لا، ب.

٢ وواجب الوجود: -، ا؛ + لغير، ب.

٣ والنوع ... غيره: -، ا.

٤ إنك: + إذا، ب.

٥ الإلهي: التي، ب.

تكلمت في لوازم واجب الوجود مطلقاً بأنه واحد، وأنه[١] حقّ، وأنه تام[٢]، وأنه علة وأنه مبدأ[٣]. ثم تكلمت في إثبات واجب الوجود وبرهنت عليه، فلولا أنك وضعته[٤] نوعاً أو في حكم نوع، أو عاماً أو في حكم عام، وإلا لما ذكرت هذه الفصول أخذاً[٥] بنوعيته. وإذ[٦] لم يكن نوعه لغير ذاته[٧] فقد أخذ[٨] بعينيته. فالعين مثل زيد لا[٩] يؤخذ تارة بإطلاق فتذكر لوازمه ولواحقه، وتارة بعين فتذكر لوازمه ولواحقه، فإنه إذا أخذ[١٠] بإطلاق خرج عن أن يكون زيداً[١١] عيناً.

١ واحد وأنه: -، ا.

٢ حق وأنه تام: -، ب.

٣ وأنه مبدأ: ومبدأ، ا.

٤ وضعته: وضعة، ب.

٥ أخذاً: أخذ، ب.

٦ وإذ: وإذا، ب.

٧ ذاته: + فهو واحد بعينه كالعين مثل زيد، ب.

٨ أخذ: أخذه، ا ب.

٩ لا: -، ب.

١٠ أخذ: أخذه، ب.

١١ زيداً: زيد، ا.

التناقض الثالث

قوله: واجب الوجود واحد من جهة كذا، وواحد[١] من جهة كذا، وعدّد[٢] سبعة أوجه، أقول: إنما يكون واحداً[٣] من كل وجه إذا لم يكن له وجوه البتّة، فالواحد[٤] المطلق ما لا كثرة فيه، وكثرة هذه الوجوه والاعتبارت تنافي الوحدة المطلقة الخالصة. فإن[٥] قال: إن هذه الكثرة ترجع إلى السلوب والإضافات، أو إلى الوجوه والاعتبارات، فقد تكلمنا على ذلك[٦] بما فيه مقنع.

التناقض الرابع

قال: ولا يمكن أن يقال: إن واجبي الوجود لا يشتركان في شيء، فكيف، وهما يشتركان في الوجود ووجوب الوجود والبراءة عن الموضوع؟ وهذا الاعتراف منه يرفع جميع كلماته السابقة ويناقضها، فكأنه قصر[٧] الاشتراك[٨] المانع من الوحدة الجالب[٩] للاثنينية على الاشتراك

١ وواحد: ووا، ب.

٢ وعدد: وعد، ب.

٣ واحداً: واحد، ب

٤ فالواحد: والواحد، ا.

٥ فإن: وإن، ا.

٦ على ذلك: عليه، ا.

٧ قصر: قصد، ب.

٨ الاشتراك: لاشتراك، ب.

في المعنى[١] بالتـواطؤ فـقط، ولـم يعلم أن الاشـتـراك في المعنى الذي يعمّ يستدعي انفصالاً في المعنى الذي يخص، وذلك هو التكثر[٢] والتركب، وهو لازم لا محيص[٣] عنه.

ثم نقول: قولك بأن[٤] وجوب[٥] الوجود لا يقال على كثيرين، ولا يجـوز أن يكون[٦] نوع واجب[٧] الوجـود لغـيـر ذاته، مناقض لقـولك: إن[٨] الوجود يقال على كثيرين، ويجوز أن يكون نوع الوجود لغير ذاته، ومع[٩] ذلك وجود[١٠] الواجب لذاته لا لشيء آخر غير ذاته. فهلا قلت في الواجب: إنه يقال على كثيرين، ومع ذلك وجود الواجب لذاته لا لشيء آخر غير ذاته؟ على أنك قد صرحت بالقول على كثيرين. وأقول: من الجواهر ما

٩ الجالب: الواجب، ا.

١ المعنى: + المسمى، ب.

٢ التكثر: الكثرة، ب.

٣ محيص: مخلص، ا.

٤ بأن: ان، ا.

٥ وجوب: واجب، ب.

٦ يكون: يلون، ا.

٧ واجب: مكرر في ب.

٨ إن: بأن، ا.

٩ ومع: ومنع، ا.

١٠ وجود: وجوب، ا.

يتمايز[١] بذاته وحقيقته[٢] عن مثله أو خلافه من غير أن يشترك في جنس وينفصل[٣] بفصل، كالعقول المفارقة، فإنه ليس لها شيء[٤] تشترك فيه كالجنس أو كالمادة وشيء[٥] تتمايز به كالفصل أو كالصورة، ومع[٦] ذلك هي متباينة الحقايق متمايزة الصور[٧] بذاتها لا بشيء آخر، فهلا قلت في واجبي الوجود كذلك؟

وقوله: إن[٨] وجود نوعه إما أن تقتضيه ذات نوعه أو تقتضيه علة[٩] غير ذاته، يقال: ما أنكرت على من قال: وجود نوعه غير معلل أصلاً، لا بذات نوعه ولا بعلة غير ذاته، فيكون التقسيم عاطلاً؟ والتقسيم الثاني: إن الشيئين إنما يكونان اثنين لمعنى أو لسبب هو حامل المعنى أو لكذا وكذا، تقسيم غير حاصر. وقوله: إن واجب الوجود واحد من جهة تمامية وجوده، ولم يفسر التماميّة ولم يعلم أن التمامية نقص له، وقد قال بعض الحكماء: الغنى الأكبر لمن له الخلق والأمر، جلّ ربّنا وتعالى عن أن يوصف بالتمام فضلاً عن أن يوصف بالنقص، فهو متمّم

١ يتمايز: يمتاز، ا.

٢ وحقيقته: وحقيقه، ب.

٣ وينفصل: ويفصل، ب.

٤ شيء: شيئاً، ا.

٥ وشيء: أو شيء، ب.

٦ ومع: مع، ب.

٧ الصور: مطموس في ا.

٨ وقوله إن: مطموس في ا.

٩ علة: لا يوجد النص التالي في نسخة ا لسقوط بعض ورقات منها.

كل تامّ، ومكمل كل ناقص. فإن عنى بالتمامية أنه المتمم لكل تام فهو صحيح، لكنه يجب أن يطرد هذه القضية في كل صفة حتى في الوجود، فيقول: هو موجود بمعنى أنه موجد كل وجود، وواجب الوجود بمعنى أنه موجِب كل موجود، وعالم بمعنى أنه معلّم كل عالم، وقادر بمعنى أنه مقدِّر كل قادر، وليس ذلك بمنهاج الرجل. ولو كان ذلك مذهبه لما قضى بعمومية الوجود وبشموله ولحكم بأن الوجود من الأسماء المشتركة المحضة كما بيّناه قبلُ.

وما ذكر أنه واحد من جهة أن حدّه له، وواحد من جهة أنه لا ينقسم، كل ذلك وحدات[1] لواحد واحد من مخلوقاته تعالى، وسلبها عنه[2] وإيجابها له نقص. وكذلك قوله: وجوب[3] الوجود إما أن يكون من لوازم ماهية، أو من مقوماتها، فلا ماهية له حتى يكون لها لازم[4] أو مقوّم، ولوكانت له ماهية فإما أن تكون غير الوجود أو نفس الوجود، وكلا القسمين باطل. والماهية إما أن تكون ماهية مشتركة كالحيوانية للإنسان والفرس والحمار، أو ماهية خاصة كالإنسان، ولا اشتراك في وجود واجب الوجود ولا خصوص. فما بال الرجل يستعمل لفظ الماهية والنوعية في كل وِرْد وصدر، و هو لا يعتقدها[5] حقيقة؟ كيف، ولم يقرر للمفارقات ماهيات مركبة من أجناس وفصول، بل ذكر تمايزها بحقائقها البسيطة

١ وحدات: واحدات، ب.

٢ عنه: + تعالى، ب.

٣ وجوب: واجب، ب.

٤ لازم: لا لزم، ب.

٥ لا يعتقدها: ما لا يعتقده ما، ب.

غير المركبة، فكيف أوهم في حق واجب الوجود بالماهية والنوعية إثباتَ الجنسية والفصلية؟

وما ذكر من البرهان على أنه مستند[١] الممكنات فهو صحيح لا بأس به ولا اعتراض عليه، غير أنه خلّط[٢] على الناظر بذكر أقسام هو مستغنٍ عنها، أراد بها الكشف والبيان، فزاد بها اللبس والتعمية. والعلم نقطة كثّرها الجهال[٣].

وأما قوله: إن الواحد لا يصدر عنه إلا الواحد، يقال له: ما المعني بالصدور[٤] عنه؟ أتعني بالصدور الإيجاد، أم تعني به الإيجاب؟ فإن الإيجاد إعطاء الوجود والإيجاب إعطاء الوجوب، والممكن بذاته فإنما يحتاج إلى الواجب بذاته في استفادة الوجود لا الوجوب، والوجوب يلزم الوجود، والوجود لا يلزم الوجوب، وسنعود الى تقرير ذلك في مسألة حدث العالم[٥]. وما ذكر أن صدور الفعلين المختلفين إنما يكون من وجهين مختلفين، مصادرة على المطلوب[٦]، ولا يبقى له إلا إنكار[٧] محض واستبعاد صرف. وأمكننا تقرير ذلك في الطبيعيات[٨]، إذ قد تصدر حرارة

١ مستند: يستند، ب.

٢ خلط: خبط، ب.

٣ والعلم نقطة كثرها الجهال: -، ب.

٤ بالصدور: بالصور، ب.

٥ العالم: + إن شاء الله تعالى، ب.

٦ المطلوب: + الأول، ب.

٧ إلا إنكار: الإنكار، ب.

٨ الطبيعيات: طبيعيات، ب.

وبرودة من شيء واحد من[١] وجه واحد، ولكن في جوهرين مختلفين، وكذلك يصدر بياض وسواد من الشمس في مادّتين[٢]، وجمود وذوب في جسمين[٣]، فكيف في الجواهر العقلية؟

ثم مثلُ هذه الوجوه لم توجب تكثراً في ذات واجب الوجود، فإنه قد اعترف بتقرير[٤] ذلك في مواضع، ورجع بها إلى السلوب والإضافات، وذلك لا يوجب تكثراً في الذات. واعترف بمثل ذلك في العقل الأول، وقد صدر عنه بكل وجه واعتبارٍ موجود من الموجودات. ثم إن[٥] لم يصدر من الواحد إلا واحد فيلزم أن لا يصدر عن الاثنين إلا اثنان[٦]. فإنه إن صدر عنه ثلاثة أو أربعة أو أكثر فعن وجوه مختلفة، وقد فُرض له وجهان لا غير، فنسبة الزائد إلى وجهين[٧] كنسبة الزائد إلى[٨] وجه واحد، ونسبة العشرة إلى الخمسة كنسبة الاثنين إلى الواحد.

قال ابن سينا في[٩] النجاة جواباً عن أمثال هذه الإلزامات: المعلول الأول ممكن الوجود بذاته واجب الوجود بالأول، ووجوب وجوده به عقل،

١ من: -، ب.

٢ مادتين: مايتين، ب.

٣ جسمين: الجسمين، ب.

٤ بتقرير: يتقدم، ب.

٥ إن: -، ب.

٦ اثنان: الاثنان، ب.

٧ إلى وجهين: على الوجهين، ب.

٨ إلى: على، ب.

٩ في: + كتاب، ب.

وهو يعقل ذاته ويعقل الأول، إلى أن يقول: ما له بذاته[١] إمكان الوجود وما له من الأول وجوب الوجود، ثم كثرة أن يعقل ذاته ويعقل الأول كثرة لازمة لوجوب وجوده عن الأول. فكثرة هذه الاعتبارات بعد أن كان ممكن الوجود بذاته[٢] لم تؤثر فيما هو له بذاته بخلاف حال واجب الوجود، فإن الكثرة تؤثر فيما هو له بذاته، وهو التوحيد، بأنه واجب الوجود.

قلتُ: بلى ما له باعتبار ذاته إمكان الوجود، وإمكان الوجود[٣] غير الوجود، فله طبيعة عدمية، والعدم لا يوجد موجوداً، فلا يجب به وجود. ووجوب الوجود له غير ذاتي، بل هو لازم، واللازم لا يوجد ذاتاً موجوداً مقصوداً، فليس للعقل[٤] إذاً ما يناسب الصدور عنه والإيجاد به. وكذلك كل ممكن فله هذا الحكم، فلا موجد للكائنات إلا الله تعالى الواجب وجوده بذاته، فيجب أن تُنسب الممكنات كلها إليه نسبة واحدة لا بتوسط عقل ونفس وطبيعة. وأما كونه عقلاً فعبارة عن تجرده عن المادة، والتجرد عن المادة[٥] نفي المادة عنه. والنفي المطلق أو نفي شيء عنه كيف يناسب جوهراً عقلياً هو من أشرف الموجودات؟ فإذاً ليس في العقل وجه ما يناسب الإيجاب والإبداع، فوجب أن يضاف الكل إلى واجب الوجود بذاته.

١ بذاته: من ذاته، ب.

٢ واجب الوجود بالأول ... بذاته: الجملة مكررة في ب.

٣ وإمكان الوجود: -، ب.

٤ للعقل: العقل، ب.

٥ والتجرد عن المادة: -، ب.

قال ابن سينا: الإمكان له طبيعة عدمية[١]، فيناسب ما له طبيعة عدمية[٢]، وهو الهيولى، والوجوب[٣] له طبيعة وجودية، فيناسب ما له طبيعة وجودية، وهو الصورة، وبما[٤] يعقل ذاته مجرّداً عن المادة يناسب عقلاً مجرداً عن المادة أو نفساً كلية، وبما يعقل الأول عقولاً مفارقة ونفوساً مدبّرة. ثم هذه المناسبات لا تنحصر في عدد معلوم، فالعقل لا يقضي[٥] بانحصار أعدادها في عدد معلوم، لكن الرصد قد دل على أن الأفلاك تسعة، وقام الدليل على أن لكل فلك نفساً ولكل نفس عقلاً، فالعقول المفارقة تسعة والنفوس تسع.

قلت: تعبتم معاشر الحكماء في استنباط أمثال هذه المعاني الرقيقة التي لا يرتضيها الفقيه لنفسه في مظانّ المظنونات ولا يربط بها حكماً شرعياً في الشرعيات، فكيف الحكيم الذي يتكلم في أعلى علوم الإلاهيات؟ أليس الإمكان قضية شاملة لجميع[٦] الممكنات؟ فإن كان العقل الأول باعتبار إمكانه مبدعاً للهيولى التي لها طبيعة عدمية، فكل موجود ممكن حاله في الإمكان حال العقل الأول، فليصلح مبدعاً للهيولى. وإن كان العقل باعتبار وجوب وجوده[٧] بالأول مبدعاً للصورة التي لها طبيعة وجودية، فكل موجود واجب بغيره حاله في الوجوب بالغير حال العقل الأول، فليصلح مبدعاً للصورة، وليس الأمر كذلك.

١ عدمية: وعدمية، ب.

٢ عدمية: وعدمية، ب.

٣ والوجوب: والواجب، ب.

٤ وبما: وما، ب.

٥ يقضي: يقتضي، ب.

٦ لجميع: بجميع، ب.

ولو عكس الأمر في ترتيب الكائنات حتى يكون العقل الأول آخراً والجسم المركب أولاً لم[١] يكن الأمر بذلك المستبعد الذي قدّره، فإن الجسم إنما يتكثر بالصورة والهيولى[٢]، والعقل يتكثر بالوجوب والإمكان، فالصورة كالوجوب والهيولى كالإمكان، وإذا جاز أن يصدر عن الواجب[٣] شيء هو ممكن بذاته وواجب به جاز أن يصدر عنه شيء هو هيولى وصورة ولا يتكثر[٤] الواجب به كما لم يتكثر بذلك.

نقول: لو كان العقل الأول من حيث إمكانه موجباً للهيولى ومن حيث وجوبه موجباً للصورة لكان الموجود الذي بعد العقل الأول هو الجسم المركب من مادّة وصورة، ولكانت المفارقات بعده في الوجود، وهذا خلاف ما أوردوه[٥] في كتبهم من ترتيب الموجودات.

وربما يقول ابن سينا في بعض تعاليقه: إن العقل الأول بما يعقل ذاته يصدر عنه نفس، وبما يعقل الأولَ يصدر عنه عقل، وربما يقول في بعض مصنّفاته: إنه يصدر عنه نيف وأربعون عقلاً هي المفارقات. وقد تخبط كلامه في هذا الموضع غاية[٦] التخبط، فلم يمكنه أن

٧ وجوده: وجوه، ب.

١ لم: -، ب.

٢ بالصورة والهيولى: بالهيولى والصورة، ب.

٣ الواجب: الوجب، ب.

٤ يتكثر: يتكر، ب.

٥ أوردوه: أورده، ب.

٦ غاية: غايط، ب.

يورد ذلك بناء على برهان قويم، وصراط مستقيم، ومن تعاطى علم مافوقه ابتُلي بجهل[1] ما تحته.

ونقول: مثل هذه الوجوه والاعتبارات التي في العقل الأول لو أوجبت موجودات عقلية معاً متكثرة بأعيانها ولم توجب كثرة في ذات العقل لجاز أن يصدر عن واجب الوجود بمثل هذه الوجوه والاعتبارات موجودات عقلية معاً متكثرة بأعيانها فلا توجب كثرة في ذات واجب الوجود، حتى يقال: بأن يعقل ذاته صدر عنه عقل، وبأن وجب وجوده فاضت عنه نفس، وبأن يعقل العقل الأول صدر عنه إما صورة، وإما هيولى وصورة، إلى غير ذلك من التحكمات، فلا يمتاز[2] وجه عن وجه واعتبار عن اعتبار.

وبوجه آخر، إذا كان واجب الوجود واحداً من كل وجه وأوجب[3] عقلاً واحداً من وجه فليوجب العقل أيضاً واحداً من وجه، فإنه إنما يوجب باعتبار[4] استفادته من موجبه، لا باعتبار ما له بذاته، حتى يلزم أن يترتب الوجود من آحاد متسلسلة، لا في أعدادٍ متفاوتة وأعيان مختلفة، والوجود بخلاف ذلك، فهو خلف.

١ بجهل: بحمل، ب.

٢ فلا يمتاز: فلاعتبار، ب.

٣ وأوجب: وواجب، ب.

٤ باعتبار: اعتبار، ب.

وبوجه آخر، كما لا يجوز أن يصدر الكثير عن الواحد لأنه[١] يوجب كثرة في الموجِب كذلك لا يجوز أن يصدر الواحد عن الواحد[٢] لأنه يوجب وحدة في الموجَب. فإن قيل: الكثرة[٣] في الموجَب[٤] لم تكن مستفادة من الموجِب، بل من حيث ذاته أنه ممكن واجب بالغير، قيل: والكثرة في الموجِب لم تكن باعتبار ذاته، بل كانت[٥] باعتبار الإضافة و السلب، وكثرة الإضافات لا توجب الكثرة في الذات.

وبوجه آخر نقول: لو عقل واجب الوجود اثنين[٦] لم يلزم أن يكون عن جهتين مختلفتين، فلِمَ إذا أبدع اثنين وجب أن يكون عن جهتين مختلفتين؟ أليس عقله إبداعه عند الرجل، ولا فرق بين عَقَلَ وأبدَعَ؟ فإذا جاز أن يعقل اثنين كليين[٧] جاز أن يبدع اثنين كليين، إلا أن يلتزم هذا[٨] البديعَ الشنيع فيقول: لا يعقل إلا واحداً كما لا يبدع إلا واحداً[٩]، فيترك

١ لأنه: لا، ب.

٢ الواحد: الكثير، ب.

٣ الكثرة: للكثرة، ب.

٤ في الموجب: -، ب.

٥ كانت: كان، ب.

٦ اثنين: ذاتين اثنين، ب.

٧ اثنين كليين: كليين اثنين، ب.

٨ هذا: من هذا، ب.

٩ واحداً: واحد، ب.

مذهبه أنه[1] يعقل الأشياء من حيث كلياتها وأسبابها، وحينئذ يلزمه أن لا يعقل إلا ذاته، وذلك أشنع.

وههنا موضع بحث، وهو أن الوحدة[2] تطلق على الواجب بذاته وعلى العقل وعلى النفس وعلى سائر الموجودات بأي معنى؟ أبالتواطؤ[3]، أم بالتشكيك، أم بالاشتراك[4]؟ فإن كان بالتواطؤ فليصلح جنساً ولينفصل كل نوع بفصل، وذلك هو التركيب. وإن كان بالتشكيك فليصلح عامّاً ولينفصل كل نوع[5] بخاصّ لازم، وهو أيضاً تركيب. وإن كان بالاشتراك فليميز بين وحدة ووحدة بالحقائق الذاتية، فإن المشتركَين في الاسم يتباينان بالحقائق والمعاني[6] الذاتية واللازمة، وإذا لم يتبين التمايز كان الكلام في وحدة البارئ سبحانه لغواً. فلنبين ذلك ولنذكر أقسام الوحدة حتى إذا قلنا: إنه تعالى واحد لا كالآحاد، كان التوحيد صرفاً خالصاً. فلنذكر الفصل المعهود في أواخر المسائل، وإذا أعيتك جاراتك فعوّلي على ذي بيتك، أعاذنا الله عز وجل من الخطأ والزلل[7].

١ أنه: ان، ب.

٢ الوحدة: الواحدة، ب.

٣ أبالتواطؤ: بالتواطو، ب.

٤ بالتشكيك أم بالاشتراك: بالاشتراك ام بالتشكيك، ب.

٥ بفصل ... كل نوع: -، ب.

٦ والمعاني: والمعنى، ب.

٧ الخطأ والزلل: الذلل والخطل، ب.

المختار[١] الحق

إذا كان مصدر البرهان على إثبات واجب الوجود بذاته هو انقسام الوجود إلى واجب لذاته[٢] وممكن[٣] لذاته، وتبين أن الوجود من الأسماء المشتركة لا المتواطئة، وظهر أن المشككة في حكم المتواطئة أو قسم لا معنى له، انحسم طريق البرهان على ابن سينا ومن[٤] تابعه، إذ التقسيم لا يرد على المشتركة. ثم منهاج الأنبياء عليهم السلام على ما نحن نقرره، فنقول: البارئ تعالى أعرف من أن يُدل على وجوده بشيء، فالمعرفة به تعالى فطرة، ومن أنكره فقد أنكر نفسه، بل من أنكره فقد أقرّ به، إذ هو الحاكم المطلق، ومن أنكر أن لا حاكم فقد حكم، فكان إنكاره إقراراً ونفيه إثباتاً.

وكما[٥] أن الإمكان في الممكنات كلها أمر ذاتي لها واحتياج الممكن إلى مرجّح أمر ضروري، فيستدعي محتاجاً إليه غير ممكن، أي غير محتاج إلى غيره[٦]، كذلك[٧] المتنافرات[٨] إذا ازدوجت، والمزدوجات إذا

١ المختار: والمختار، ب.

٢ لذاته: بذاته، ب.

٣ وممكن: وممكناً، ب.

٤ ومن: -، ب.

٥ وكما: او كما، ب.

٦ غيره: غير، ب.

٧ كذلك: ذلك، ب.

٨ المتنافرات: المنفردات، ب.

اجتمعت، احتاجت إلى جامع[١] غني على[٢] الإطلاق، والغني المطلق لا يتحقق في اثنين، لأن كل واحد منهما محتاج ومحتاج إليه في أن يكونا اثنين. فالغني[٣] المطلق هو الصمد، فهو الله الأحد الصمد، وذلك مذكور في سورة[٤] الإخلاص، وعن هذا كان افتتاح دعوة الأنبياء عليهم السلام بالتوحيد، أعني قول: لا إله إلاّ الله، إذ الإثبات كان مفروغاً عنه، ولهذا كان الإنكار من الخصماء مقصوراً على التوحيد فقط، {ذَلِكُمْ بِأَنَّهُ إِذَا دُعِيَ اللَّهُ وَحْدَهُ كَفَرْتُمْ[٥]} (٤٠ غافر ١٢). {وَإِذَا ذُكِرَ اللَّهُ وَحْدَهُ اشْمَأَزَّتْ قُلُوبُ الَّذِينَ لاَ يُؤْمِنُونَ بِالآخِرَةِ} (٣٩ الزمر ٤٥)، {وَإِذَا ذَكَرْتَ رَبَّكَ فِي الْقُرْآنِ وَحْدَهُ وَلَوْاْ عَلَى أَدْبَارِهِمْ نُفُوراً} (١٧ الإسراء ٤٦). فظهر أن الدعوة أولاً[٦] كانت إلى التوحيد، إذ لا منكر في العالم للإله[٧] الصانع الحكيم، إنما الإنكار في التوحيد فقط، والبرهان على التوحيد ما ذكرناه من أسامي سورة الإخلاص.

ثم الوحدة على أقسام، وحدة هي مصدر العدد ومبدؤه، كما نقول: واحد، اثنان، والعدد متركب منها، وحيثما زاد العدد تنقص

١ جامع: صانع، ب.

٢ على: عن، ب.

٣ فالغني: فالمعنى، ب.

٤ سورة: صورة، ب.

٥ كفرتم: وان يشرك به تؤمنوا، ب.

٦ أولاً: -، ب.

٧ للإله: إلا عرف أن له، ب.

نسبة الواحد إليه[١]. والوحدة بهذا المعنى لا تليق بجلال الله تعالى، إذ لا يجوز أن يتركب منه العدد والمعدود، ووحدة هي ملازمة للعدد والمعدود، كما نقول في كل جملة: إنها واحدة، فإن العشرة من حيث أنها عشرة جملة واحدة، وكما نقول: إنسان واحد، فرس واحد، ونقش واحد، وهذه الوحدة أيضاً لا تليق بجلال الله تعالى، فليس هو جملة حتى[٢] تتحقق له وحدة الجملة، وكذلك وحدة النوع، ووحدة الجنس، ووحدة العين المشار إليها حسّاً وعقلاً. بل الوحدة تطلق عليه تعالى وعلى الموجودات بالاشتراك المحض، وهو واحد لا كالآحاد[٣] المذكورة، واحد يصدر عنه الوحدة والكثرة المتقابلتان، واحد[٤] بمعنى أنه يوجد الآحاد، فتفرّد بالوحدانية، ثم أفاضها على خلقه، والوحدة والوجود له من غير ضد يضادّه أو نِدّ يماثله[٥] {فَلاَ تَجْعَلُوا لِلَّهِ[٦] أَنْدَاداً وَأَنْتُمْ تَعْلَمُونَ} (٢ البقرة ٢٢).

وأما إبداعه للكائنات متكثرة أو إبداعه للعقل بواحده وهو واحد فقد ورد الإلزام على المذهبين[٧] جميعاً، فإن وجود الكثرة عنه وصدورها منه يوجب تكثر وجوه واعتبارات في ذاته تعالى، ووجود الواحد عن

١ الواحد إليه: الوحدانية، ب.

٢ حتى: -، ب.

٣ كالآحاد: ما الآحاد، ب.

٤ واحد: فهو واحد، ب.

٥ يماثله: يماثلثه، ب.

٦ لله: الله، ب.

٧ المذهبين: مذهبين، ب.

الواحد[١] يقتضي مناسبة بين الموجِب والموجَب، أو يقتضي اتحاد الموجَب[٢] من كل وجه، وكلا[٣] الوجهين باطل، بل وكلا الوجهين صحيح، فإن عموم الإضافة وخصوصها مذكور[٤] في التنزيل، ومقبول عند أهل العقول. قال الله تعالى: {إِنْ كُلُّ مَنْ فِي السَّمَاوَاتِ وَالأَرْضِ إِلاَّ آتِي الرَّحْمَنِ عَبْداً} (١٩ مريم ٩٣) وهذا لعموم[٥] الإضافة[٦] إليه، و قال عزّ[٧] ذكره: {وَعِبَادُ الرَّحْمَنِ الَّذِينَ يَمْشُونَ عَلَى الأَرْضِ هَوْناً} (٢٥ الفرقان ٦٣) وهذا لخصوص[٨] الإضافة إليه.

وقد يتخصص العامّ درجة درجة[٩] إلى أن ينتهي إلى واحد يكون عبداً، كما يعمّ الخاصّ درجة فدرجة إلى أن ينتهي إلى[١٠] الكل. فعباد الله العلّيون ملائكته المقرّبون، وحكم الروح الذي يقوم صفّاً والملائكة صفّاً حكم الكل مع الأجزاء، أو العقل[١١] الأول الفعال[١٢] مع المفارقات المُدبّرات

١ الواحد: الوحدة، ب.

٢ الموجب: الموجب والموجب، ب.

٣ وكلا: وكلى، ب.

٤ مذكور: مذكورة، ب.

٥ لعموم: للعموم، ب.

٦ الإضافة: للإضافة، ب.

٧ عز: عن، ب.

٨ لخصوص: الخصوص، ب.

٩ درجة: -، ب.

١٠ واحد ... إلى: -، ب.

١١ أو العقل: والعقل، ب.

أمراً. وكما أن[١] الخصوص والعموم[٢] معقولان ومسموعان في العبودية، كذلك يجري حكمهما[٣] في الإبداع والخلق وإضافة الربوبية إلى العباد كقوله تعالى: {رَبِّ الْعَالَمِينَ رَبِّ مُوسَى وَهَارُونَ} (٧ الأعراف ١٢١-١٢٢).

ثم اعلم أن ما ورد في الكتب الإلهية من عموم النسبة وخصوصها فهو أحق أن يتبع من قول الفلاسفة[٤]: إن الواحد لا يصدر عنه إلا واحد وسائر الموجودات تضاف إليه بتوسط ذلك الواحد على طريق اللزوم، فإن نسبة ذلك الواحد إليه[٥] أيضاً إذا فُتش عن حقيقتها[٦] كانت نسبته على طريق اللزوم، فوجود ذلك الواحد عنه من لوازم ذاته، فما الفرق بين القسمين؟ ولِمَ[٧] لا يجوز أن يضاف الكل إليه على وتيرة واحدة، من غير فرق بين ما صدر عنه بالذات[٨] من غير توسط وبالقصد الأول، لا بالقصد الثاني، وبين ما صدر عنه على خلاف ذلك؟ والسرّ فيه أن الجهة التي تحتاج بها الممكنات إلى المبدع هي وجودها الممكن، والموجودات في

١٢ الفعال: -، ب.

١ وكما أن: وكان، ب.

٢ الخصوص والعموم: العموم والخصوص، ب.

٣ حكمهما: حكمها، ب.

٤ الفلاسفة: + والحكماء، ب.

٥ إليه: -، ب.

٦ حقيقتها: حقيقها، ب.

٧ ولم: ولو، ب.

٨ بالذات: باللذات، ب.

هذه الجهة على السواء، فلا فرق بين المجرّد عن المادة وبين الملابس للمادة في جهة الإمكان، ولا في الوجود الممكن، وإنما يتفاضل القسمان من[١] وجه آخر، فينبغي أن يكون المبدأ الأول مبدأ للكل على نمط واحد، والمتوسطات في البين[٢] لتفاضل الدرجات.

أليس العقل الواهب للصور يفيض الصور على الموادّ المختلفة إفاضة واحدة، ولا تتكثر ذاته[٣] بتكثرها، وتكون نسبة جميعها[٤] إليه نسبة واحدة، ولا يقال: إنه من حيث أنه يصدر عنه بياض في مادة وسواد في مادة فيحدث له حيثيتان وجهتان حتى تتكثر ذاته بتكثر الصور التي لا نهاية لها؟ كذلك القول في واجب الوجود لذاته. وإن قيل: إن العقل الفعّال ذو وجوه واعتبارات لأنه ممكن في ذاته واجب بالموجب ويعقل ذاته وعلته ومعلوله، إلى غير ذلك من وجوه التكثر، بخلاف واجب الوجود لذاته، فإنه واحد من كل وجه، قيل: هذا الاعتذار ليس[٥] يدفع[٦] وجه الإلزام، فإن كثرة الصادر لو أوجبت كثرة في ذات المصدر لتعددت[٧] الوجوه تعدّد الصادر عنه، ولكانت تلك الوجوه محققة في ذاته بلا

١ من: -، ب.

٢ البين: المبين، ب.

٣ ذاته: -، ب.

٤ جميعها: جميعا، ب.

٥ ليس: وليس، ب.

٦ يدفع: دفع، ب.

٧ لتعددت: لقدد، ب.

نهاية، ولا نشك أن[١] ذات واهب الصور لم يشتمل على أعداد[٢] من الأحياث بلا[٣] نهاية. أليس العقل الأول، لما كانت في ذاته أحياث[٤] محصورة، صدرت عنه[٥] موجودات محصورة، مثل العقول المفارقة والنفوس المدبرة للأفلاك، أو كانت محصورة في ثلاثة أوجه، فحدثت عنها ثلاثة، عقل ونفس وهيولى، على اختلاف المذاهب في هذه المسألة؟

وبالجملة، عُلم من ذلك أن نسبة[٦] الكل إلى واجب الوجود على قضية واحدة، يستوي فيها الواحد والكثير، والجوهر والعرض، والمجرد عن المادّة والملابس لها: {وَهُوَ عَلَى كُلِّ شَيْءٍ قَدِيرٌ}. اللّهم انفعنا بما علّمتنا وعلّمنا ما تنفعنا به بحق المصطفين من عبادك عليهم السلام[٧].

١ أن: في ان، ب.

٢ أعداد: من هنا يستأنف نص نسخة ا.

٣ بلا: بلي، ا.

٤ أحياث: واجبات، ا.

٥ عنه: -، ب.

٦ نسبة: تشبه، ا.

٧ الهم ... السلام: -، ب.

المسألة الرابعة
في علم واجب الوجود وتعلّقه بالكلي والجزئي

اعلم أن المتكلمين[١] قد أثبتوا كون البارئ تعالى عالماً بجميع المعلومات بطريقهم[٢] من النظر في أفعاله واشتمالها على الإحكام والإتقان، وادعوا علم الضرورة في أن كل فعل محكم متقن انتسب إلى فاعل فيجب أن يكون فاعله عالماً به من كل وجه. وانتقض هذا الحكم على بعضهم، إذ[٣] وجدوا الفاعلين في الشاهد قد انتسب إليهم الفعل من كل وجه ولم يكن فاعله عالماً به من كل وجه.

والفلاسفة[٤] تنكبوا[٥] هذه الطريقة، فبعض القدماء منهم صار[٦] إلى أن العلم صورة المعلوم عند العالم، ويستحيل أن يكون للأول[٧] ذات

١ اعلم أن المتكلمين: المتكلمون، ب.

٢ بطريقهم: بطريق هم، ب.

٣ إذ: إذا، ب.

٤ والفلاسفة: + والحكماء، ب.

٥ تنكبوا: ينكتوا، ا.

٦ صار: صاروا، ا.

٧ للأول: الأول، ا.

وصورة في الذات فيكون هو وصورة أو ذو صورة[١]، ويتعالى عن ذلك، بل هذا صفة العقل الأول، إذ صور الموجودات حاضرة عنده مرتسمة[٢] فيه.

وقال ابن سينا: واجب الوجود بذاته عقل وعاقل ومعقول، وهو واحد في ذاته لا يتكثر به. أما أنه معقول فلأنك تعرف أن طبيعة الوجود بما هي طبيعة الوجود غير ممتنع عليها أن تُعقل، وإنما يعرض لها أن لا تعقل إذا كانت في المادة ومع عوارض المادة، فإنها من حيث هي كذلك محسوسة أو متخيلة، والوجود[٣] إذا جُرِّد عن هذا العائق[٤] كان وجوداً وماهية معقولة، وكل ما هو بذاته مجرّد عن المادة والعوارض المادية فبما هو مجرّد هو عقل، وبما يعتبر له أن هويته المجرّدة لذاته فهو معقول لذاته، وبما يعتبر له أن ذاته له هوية[٥] مجرّدة فهو عاقل لذاته.

ثم قال بعد ذلك: إن نفس كونه معقولاً وعاقلاً لا يوجب أن يكون اثنين في الذات، ولا اثنين في الاعتبار، فإنه ليس يحصّل[٦] الأمرين إلا أنه له ماهية مجرّدة ذاتهُ وأن ماهيته[٧] المجرّدة له، فكونه عاقلاً ومعقولاً لا يوجب كثرة البتة.

١ أو ذو صورة: -، ب.

٢ مرتسمة: من تسمية، ب.

٣ والوجود: فالوجود، ب.

٤ هذا العائق: هذه العلائق، ب.

٥ هوية: هويته، ا.

٦ يحصل: تحصيل، ا.

٧ وأن ماهيته: وماهيته، ب.

ثم قال: هو مبدأ كل وجود[١]، فيعقل من ذاته ما هو مبدأ له. وهو مبدأ للموجودات التامة[٢] بأعيانها والموجودات الكائنة الفاسدة بأنواعها[٣] أولاً، وبتوسط ذلك أشخاصِها، ولا يجوز أن يكون عاقلاً لهذه المتغيرات مع تغيرها، بل يعقل كل شيء على وجه كلي، ولا يعزب[٤] عنه شيء جزئي ولا تتغير ذاته بتغير المعلوم[٥].

وقال[٦]: ولا يجوز أن يعلم الأشياء من الأشياء، وإلا كان علمه انفعالياً، بل الأشياء تعلم منه وتصدر عنه[٧]. فلا[٨] يجوز أن يرتسم بشيء من معلوماته ومعلولاته، بل يرتسم فيها صورة الوجود بعد أن كان لها[٩] إمكان الوجود. فالإمكان لجميع الممكنات كالمادة لها، والوجود

١ وجود: موجود، ب.

٢ التامة: + القائمة، ب.

٣ بأنواعها: بأعيانها، ب.

٤ يعزب: يعذب، ب.

٥ ولا تتغير ... المعلوم، -، ا.

٦ وقال: -، ا؛ ثم قال، ب.

٧ عنه: + ولا تتغير ذاته بتغير المعلوم وقال، ا.

٨ فلا: ولا، ا.

٩ لها: -، ا.

كالصورة، وواجب الوجود بريء[١] عن طبيعة الإمكان والعدم اللذان[٢] هما منبعا الشر[٣].

الاعتراض عليه بالتناقض في كلامه والنقض لمقصوده ومرامه

التناقض الأول

قوله: فبما يعتبر أنه مجرد [هو] عقل، وبما يعتبر أنه كذا وكذا، فقد نصّ على اعتبارت ثلاث، حتى أثبت كونه عقلاً وعاقلاً ومعقولاً، ثم قال بعد ذلك: إنه لا يوجب ذلك أن يكون[٤] اثنين في الاعتبار، فكيف ناقض آخر كلامه أوله؟

التناقض الثاني

قال: هو مبدأ كل وجود، فيعقل من ذاته ما هو مبدأ له، وهذا يشعر بأنه أبدع ثم عقل، وقال[٥] بعده: عقله وعلمه فعلي لا انفعالي، وهذا يشعر بأنه عقل ثم أبدع. وقال في موضع آخر[٦] من كتاب الشفاء:

١ بريء: يرى، ب.

٢ اللذان: اللذين، ب.

٣ الشر: + والله أعلم، ا.

٤ أن يكون: -، ا ب.

٥ وقال: فقال، ا.

٦ موضع آخر: بعض مواضع أخر، ب.

عقله عين[١] إبداعه وإبداعه عين عقله، فترتفع[٢] الاثنينية بين العقل والإبداع، وهذا في اللفظ والمعنى تناقض ظاهر.

التناقض الثالث

قوله: هو[٣] مبدأ كل وجود، فيعقل من ذاته ما هو مبدأ له، وقوله: يعقل ذاته لذاته بما يعتبر له أن له هوية مجرّدة[٤]، فقد فسر العقل بالإبداع في موضع[٥]، وهو أمر إيجابي[٦]، وفسر العقل بالتجريد في موضع، وهو أمر سلبي[٧]، وهذا تهافت لا يهتدى[٨] إليه.

١ عين: غير، ب.

٢ فترتفع: فرفع، ب.

٣ هو: -، ب.

٤ بما يعتبر ... مجردة: -، ا.

٥ في موضع: -، ب.

٦ وهو أمر إيجابي، -، ا.

٧ وهو أمر سلبي: -، ا.

٨ يهتدى: يهذي، ب.

أما النقض والإلزام عليه

أقول[١]: نصصتَ[٢] على اعتبارات ثلاث في ذات واجب الوجود، وفسرت كل اعتبار بمعنى صحيح لا يفهم أحدها من الآخر، وذلك تثليث[٣] صريح، وتعالى[٤] الله[٥] أن يكون ثالث ثلاثة. وليس هذا تشنيعاً بل إلزام التكثر في ذاته من حيث الاعتبار والاعتبار، كما لزم النصارى من حيث الأقنوم والأقنوم.

ولا يغنيه اعتذاره عن كثرة الاعتبار بأن[٦] ذلك لا يوجب اثنين[٧] في الذات، لأن ما به صح اعتذاره حتى نفى الاثنين وهو أن[٨] تحصيل الأمرين، أنه له ماهية مجردة ذاته وأن ماهيته[٩] المجردة له، يرفع[١٠] ما به كثرة الاعتبارات في ذاته[١١]، فما باله وضعها ثلاث اعتبارات ثم رفعها

١ أقول: أقو، ب.

٢ نصصت: نصبت، ب.

٣ تثليث: تثبيت، آ؛ بثلث، ب.

٤ وتعالى: تعالى، ب.

٥ الله: -، ا؛ + عن، ب.

٦ الاعتبار بأن: الاعتبارات، ا.

٧ اثنين: الاثنين، ب.

٨ أن: -، ا.

٩ ماهيته: ماهية، ب.

١٠ يرفع: يدفع، ب.

١١ في ذاته: بذاته، ا.

بهذا التفسير، كالنصارى يضعون التثليث في الأقانيم ويرفعونه بالتوحيد في الجوهرية[١]، ويقولون: واحد بالجوهرية[٢] ثلاثة[٣] بالأقنومية؟

وما زاد ابن سينا في هذا[٤] البيان إلا إشكالاً على إشكال، فإنه أدرج لفظ الماهية فيه، فأوهم[٥] أن له وجوداً وماهية وجود أوجبت أن تكون مجرّدة لذاتها، وتجردها[٦] تعقلها، وتعقلها[٧] إبداعها، فإن كان الوجود والماهية والتجريد والتعقل والإبداع عبارات مترادفة فليقم بعضها مقام بعض حتى يقال: إن التجريد تعقل والتعقل إبداع فالتجريد إبداع. وإن كانت العبارات متباينة فلتدل[٨] كل عبارة على معنى لا تدل عليه العبارة الأخرى، وذلك تكثر. وأقول من رأس: أنت مطالَب من جهة بعض أصحابك بإثبات كون واجب الوجود عالماً عاقلاً ومعلوماً ومعقولاً، وما شرعت في البرهان عليه إلا بقولك: هو معقول الماهية، فإن طبيعة الوجود وأقسامه[٩] لا يمتنع عليها أن تعقل، وهذه مصادرة على المطلوب، فإن

١ الجوهرية: الجوهر، ا.

٢ بالجوهرية: بالجوهر، ا.

٣ ثلاثة: ثلاث، ب.

٤ هذا: هذه، ب.

٥ فأوهم: وأوهم، ب.

٦ وتجردها: وتجرها، ب.

٧ تعقلها وتعقلها: تعلقها وتعلقها، ا ب.

٨ فلتدل: فليدد، ب.

٩ أقسامه: أقسامها، ا ب.

النزاع واقع فيه والخلاف قائم عليه[١].

وأولئك الأصحاب يمنعون أن يُعقل وأن[٢] يَعقل، فإن التعقل[٣] ارتسام العقل[٤] بصورة المعقول، وتعالى الحق أن يكون ذا صورة فيُعقل، سواء كانت الصورة جسمانية أو ماهية غير جسمانية، وتعالى[٥] أن يَعقل حتى يكون هو وصورة[٦]، بل هو فوق[٧] أن يَعلم ويُعلم[٨]. وأنت ابتدأت البرهان بأن يُعلم حتى تثبت[٩] أن يَعلم، وهم ناقشوك في الأظهر، فكيف تستدل عليهم[١٠] بالأخفى على الأظهر؟

ثم دع كلامهم خلف قاف، وارجع إلى ما هو شافٍ كافٍ. إنك أخذت الوجود بالعموم والتواطؤ موضوعاً[١١] وحكمت عليه حكماً عاماً محمولاً، فمن قال: إن الوجود يطلق على واجب الوجود وعلى غيره

١ عليه: عليك، ا.

٢ وأن: + لا، ب.

٣ التعقل: العقل، ب.

٤ العقل: للعقل، ب.

٥ وتعالى: فتعالى، ا ب.

٦ وصورة: صورة، ا ب.

٧ فوق: فرق، ا.

٨ ويعلم: -، ب.

٩ حتى تثبت: سبب، ب.

١٠ عليهم: -، ا.

١١ موضوعاً: مطبوعاً، ب.

بالاشتراك أو بالتشكيك الذي هو في حكم الاشتراك، لا يسلم[١] عموم هذا الحكم. هذا كمن حكم على العين بأنها باصرة لا يسلّم[٢] له تعميم الحكم في قرص الشمس. وأنت، وإن[٣] اعتقدت في الوجود نوع عموم، فقد أخرجته في حق واجب الوجود عن سائر الموجودات إخراجاً أبعد تبايناً[٤] من الباصرة وقرص الشمس. فما أنكرت أن هذا الحكم لا يعمه عمومه[٥] سائر الموجودات؟

وشيء آخر، وهو أنك انتصبت لإثبات أن يَعقل، وتصديت لبيان أنه لا يمتنع أن يُعقل، وإذا لا يمتنع[٦] لا يجب أن[٧] يُعقل ما لم يقرن[٨] به دليل آخر. وإذا وجب أن يُعقل لا يلزم منه أن يَعقل. فلا بد من دليل آخر[٩]، وما سمعنا[١٠] منك دليلاً إلا قولك: وإنما يعرض لها أن لا تُعقل إذا كانت في المادة. قيل: وليس العارض مقصوراً على الكون في المادة، بل ربّما يكون عارض آخر، وكما أن المحسوس لا يرتسم في العقل من حيث

١ يسلم: نسلم، ا.

٢ يسلم: نسلم، ا.

٣ وإن: −، ا.

٤ تبايناً: بياناً، ب.

٥ عمومه: عموم، ا؛ عموماً، ب.

٦ يمتنع: يمنع، ا.

٧ أن: + لا، ب.

٨ يقرن: يقترن، ب.

٩ وإذا وجب ... آخر: −، ا.

١٠ وما سمعنا: وسمعنا، ا.

هو محسوس، أي في[١] مادة، كذلك المعقول لا يرتسم في الحس[٢] من حيث[٣] هو معقول، أي لا في مادة، فمن يتعالى جلاله عن الارتسام بشيء يتعالى أيضاً[٤] عن ارتسام شيء به. وكما لا يدرَك الشيء لشدة خفائه كذلك[٥] لا يدرَك لشدة ظهوره. فلم يكن المانع هو المادة أو علائق المادة، فبطل[٦] قوله: إن طبيعة الوجود بما هو موجود[٧] لا يمتنع عليها أن تُعقل، وبطل حصر[٨] الموانع في المادة وعلائقها، وعاد الطلب جَذَعاً، والدست[٩] قائم[١٠] بينك وبين أصحابك إلى أن تصل ألى الكلي والجزئي.

وربما تمسك أولئك القوم بأن قالوا: لو كان له علم لم يخل من أحد أمرين[١١]، إما أن يكون كلّياً أو جزئياً، ولو كان كلياً لما تُصور أن

١ في: -، ب.

٢ الحس: الحبس، ب.

٣ حيث: -، ا.

٤ أيضاً: -، ب.

٥ كذلك: -، ا.

٦ فبطل: فيبطل، ا.

٧ موجود: وجود، ب.

٨ حصر: حصول، ب.

٩ والدست: والرست، ب.

١٠ قائم: قائماً، ا ب.

١١ وربما ... أمرين: -، ا.

يكون فعلياً، فإن[1] المكوِّن بالكلي[2] يجب أن يكون كلياً، كما أن المكون[3] بالعلم الجزئي يجب أن يكون جزئياً، ولا كلي في الأعيان البتة، فما به حدث[4] لم يحدث[5] على الوجه الذي أحدث به، وما أحدث به لم يكن على الوجه الذي حدث[6]. وإن كان علمه[7] جزئياً[8] وجب أن يتغير بتغير[9] المعلوم، فإن العلم بأن سيقدم زيد لا يبقي مع العلم بأن قد[10] قدم، فما الجواب عن هذا[11] الشك؟

ونحن نقول[12]: قولك بأن الأول بما هو مجرد عن المادة عقل، فالتجريد عن المادة كالتنزيه عن الجسمية وكالتقديس عن سمات الجواهر والأعراض، فلِم قلت: إنه اذا لم يكن في مادة وجب أن يكون عقلاً، أي علماً وعالماً؟ وهذا لأن التجريد عن المادة صفة سلبية، فسلب المادة عن

١ فإن: مطموس في ا.

٢ بالكلي: الكلي، ا.

٣ بالكلي ... المكون: -، ا.

٤ به حدث: حدث به، ب.

٥ يحدث: مطموس في ا.

٦ به وما أحدث ... حدث: -، ب.

٧ علمه: علة، ب.

٨ جزئياً: + حديثاً، ب.

٩ بتغير: -، ب.

١٠ قد: -، ا.

١١ هذا: هذه، ب.

الشيء لمَ أوجب كونه علماً أو عالماً[١]، عقلاً أو عاقلاً؟ وهو كسلب ما لا يليق بجلاله[٢] لا[٣] يوجب إثبات كونه عالماً.

ثم نقول: أثبتَّ اعتبارت في الواجب بذاته[٤] من كونه عقلاً وعاقلاً ومعقولاً، وأثبتَّ اعتبارات في العقل الأول من كونه ممكناً بذاته واجباً بغيره، وهو أيضاً عقل لأنه مجرد عن المادّة، وعاقل ومعقول لذاته لأن عقليته[٥] له ذاتية وماهيته له لا من غيره، فالذي اكتسب من غيره[٦] وجوده لا ماهيته[٧]، فإن كانت[٨] تلك الاعتبارات لا توجب كثرة في ذات واجب الوجود، فلم أوجبت الكثرة[٩] في العقل الأول، والسلب كالسلب والإضافة كالإضافة؟ وإن أوجبت الكثرةَ في العقل الأول فلتوجب في واجب الوجود. ويلزم على ذلك أن تضاف الأعيان الكثيرة إلى واجب الوجود إبداعاً واختراعاً، ولا يوجب صدورها عنه كثرة، أو لا تضاف إلى العقل الأول كما لا تضاف إلى واجب الوجود، وهذا مما لا جواب عنه قطعاً.

١٢ نقول: + له، ا.

١ علماً أو عالماً: عالماً أو علماً، ب.

٢ بجلاله: بخلاله، ب.

٣ لا: + لم، ب.

٤ بذاته: لذاته، ب.

٥ عقليته: عقليه، ب.

٦ فالذي ... غيره: هو، ب.

٧ ماهيته: ماهية، ب.

٨ كانت: كان تكثر، ب.

٩ الكثرة: الكثر، ب.

وأما قوله: هو مبدأ كل موجود، فيعقل من ذاته ما هو مبدأ له، فالسؤال عليه: أإنه[١] عقَل ثم أبدع، أم أبدع ثم عقل، أم عقل[٢] وأبدع معاً[٣]، أم كان عقله إبداعاً وإبداعه عقلاً؟ فإن قال: عقل ثم أبدع، لزم أن يكون المبدَع شيئاً أو تقدير شيء حتى يبدعه، ويتعالى أن يكون معه شيء أو تقدير شيء. وإن قال: أبدع ثم عقل، لزم أن يكون عقله انفعالياً لا فعلياً. وإن قال[٤]: عقل وأبدع معاً، فلم يبدع ما عقل ولم يعقل ما أبدع، وبطل[٥] قوله: فيعقل من ذاته ما هو مبدأ له. وإن قال: عقله إبداعه[٦] وإبداعه عقله، وهذا مذهب الرجل، فيلزم عليه[٧] أشياء، منها أن العقل والإبداع إن كانا مترادفين[٨] فليقل: أبدع[٩] ذاته، بمعنى أنه عقل ذاته، ومنها أن العقل قد يكون كلياً وقد يكون جزئياً، فليقل: إن الإبداع قد يكون كلياً وقد يكون جزئياً، ومنها أنه[١٠] يبطل قوله: إنه مبدأ كل وجود، فيعقل من ذاته ما هو مبدأ له، فإن تقديره يكون: يعقل كل

١ أإنه: إنه، ا ب.

٢ أم عقل: -، ب.

٣ معاً: -، ا ب.

٤ قال: -، ا.

٥ وبطل: فبطل، ب.

٦ إبداعه: إبداعاً، ا.

٧ عليه: عليها، ا.

٨ مترادفين: مترافين، ب.

٩ أبدع: ابداع، ا.

١٠ أنه: -، ب.

موجود، فيعقل ما هو عاقل له، وهذا تهافت، ومنها أنه يبطل قوله: إنه يعقل الموجودات التامة[١] بأعيانها، والكائنة الفاسدة بأنواعها، وبتوسط ذلك أشخاصها، فإن الأعيان والأشخاص تبدع، وأما الأنواع فتعقل ولا تبدع. فلو كان العقل والإبداع مترادفين بحيث يقوم أحدهما مقام الآخر لأبدعت الأنواع من حيث هي أنواع على وجه كلي بما عقلت على وجه كلي، وليس ذلك مذهب الرجل.

ثم قال: ولا يجوز أن يكون عاقلاً لهذه المتغيرات مع تغيرها.

قيل: إذا جاز أن يكون مبدأ للموجودات التامة بأعيانها ولم يتكثر بتكثرها، جاز أن يكون عاقلاً للمتغيرات ولا يتغير بتغيرها. على أن مذهب الرجل يخالف ما ذكره[٢]، فإنه ليس مبدأ للموجودات التامة بأعيانها معاً إلا بتوسط العقل الأول، فهو مبدأ لشيء[٣] واحد وعاقل لشيء واحد، وبتوسطه[٤] مبدع وعاقل للموجودات التامة بأعيانها. والأنواع والأشخاص كذلك، فإنه يعقل الأنواع[٥] وبتوسط[٦] يعقل الأشخاص. فنسبة الموجودات التامة التي هي المفارقات إلى العقل الأول[٧]

١ التامة: الثابتة، ب.

٢ ذكره: ذكرنا: ا؛ ذكرناه، ب.

٣ لشيء: الشيء، ا ب.

٤ وبتوسطه: وبتوسط، ا.

٥ فإنه يعقل الأنواع: -، ب.

٦ وبتوسط: وبتوسيط، ب.

٧ الأول: -، ا.

كنسبة الأشخاص إلى النوع، إلا أن[١] النوع لا يمكن أن يوجَد بنوعيته، ثم[٢] توجد الأشخاص، ويمكن أن يُعقل بنوعيته، ثم تعقل الأشخاص، وهذا فرق ظاهر[٣] بين الإبداع والتعقل.

وأما قوله: بل يَعقل كل شيء على وجه[٤] كلي، ولا يعزب[٥] عنه شيء جزئي، أقول[٦]: لما علم أن العلم بالجزئيات يتغير بتغير الجزئيات، والعلم بالكائنات الفاسدات كذلك، تخلص من ذلك[٧] بالفرار إلى إثبات العلم بالكليات، ثم الجزئياتُ تندرج[٨] تحت الكليات ضرورة وتبعاً[٩]. ومثال ذلك العلمُ بأن سيكون[١٠] كسوف معيّن في وقت مخصوص لا يكون علماً بالكائن وقت[١١] الكسوف، ولا بالذي[١٢] مضى من الكسوف، فلا بُدّ وأن

١ إلا أن: لأن، ا.

٢ ثم: -، ب.

٣ ظاهر: -، ا.

٤ وجه: واجه، ب.

٥ يعزب: يغرب، ب.

٦ أقول: مكرر في ب.

٧ من ذلك: -، ا.

٨ تندرج: تدرج، ا.

٩ تبعاً: ابتغا، ا.

١٠ سيكون: يكون، ا؛ سكون، ب.

١١ وقت: في وقت، ا.

١٢ ولا بالذي: وبالذي، ب.

يتغير العلم بتغير المعلوم أو يكون علم آخر[1] غير العلم الأول. لكنّ العلم بأن القمر إذا كان في برج كذا والشمس في مقابلتـه في برج كذا[2]، مع سائر الأسباب التي توجب الكسوف، فلا بد وأن يكون كسوف، فهذا علم كلي[3] لا يتغير، وهو قبل الكسوف وحالة الكسوف وبعده على وتيرة واحدة. فظن ابن سينا أنه بمثل[4] هذا المثال[5] يتخلص عن إلزام[6] التغير[7]، ولا خلاص {وَلَاتَ حِينَ مَنَاصٍ}.

فلينعم[8] المجلس العالي النظر[9] في الإلزامات التي أوردها[10] عليه والمطالبات التي أخنقه[11] بها[12]، فيعلم أن جميع ما عوّل عليه مسلمات[13]

١ علم آخر: العلم الآخر، ب.

٢ كذا: -، ا.

٣ كلي: كل، ا.

٤ بمثل: يتمثل، ب.

٥ المثال: المقال، ب.

٦ إلزام: الإلزام، ب.

٧ التغير: التعين، ب.

٨ فلينعم: فليعم، ب.

٩ النظر: -، ا؛ بإمعان نظره، ب.

١٠ أوردها: أوردتها، ا ب.

١١ أخنقه: اخنقته، ا.

١٢ بها: + ووجهتها، ب.

١٣ مسلمات: مسلمان، ب.

مشهورات[١] لا يقينيات[٢]، والقضايا المشهورة[٣] لا تنتج اليقين. فأقول[٤]: توجهت عليك[٥] المطالبة بإثبات كونه تعالى عالماً لا[٦] من طريق المتكلم، فإنه يستدل بالإحكام والإتقان في الجزئيات، وأنت لا[٧] تقول: إنه يعلم الجزئيات، إلا تبعاً وضرورة، وهو لا يصلح[٨] للاستدلال به. فإن مَن طبع خاتماً منقوشاً على شمعة فظهر فيها[٩] النقش لم يُستدل بحسن النقش على علم الطابع، ولربما لا يكون عالماً بالنقش[١٠]، بل النقش قد حصل[١١] منه[١٢] ضرورة وتبعاً للطبع، والناقش غير الطابع، فأنت بعدُ في مقام المطالبة من طريقتك.

١ مشهورات: مشهورة، ا ب.

٢ يقينيات: + مشهورة، ب.

٣ المشهورة: المشهور، ب.

٤ فأقول: وأقول، ب.

٥ عليك: عليه، ا ب.

٦ لا: -، ا.

٧ لا: -، ب.

٨ يصلح: يصح، ا.

٩ فيها: منها، ب.

١٠ على علم ... بالنقش: -، ب.

١١ حصل: جعل، ا.

١٢ منه: فيه، ب.

ونتخطى عنه في البيان قليلاً، ونقول[١]: سلمتَ[٢] كونه عالماً، أي عقلاً وعاقلاً، وقلتَ: صدقت، فقلنا[٣]: نعم[٤]، فلم قلت: إن العلم على وجهين، كلي وجزئي، وإذا لم يجز أن يكون جزئياً يجب أن يكون كلياً؟ وما[٥] أنكرت على من يثبت علماً وراء القسمين؟ وهذا كمن يقول: العلم إما تصور وإما[٦] تصديق، فيقال: إن علم واجب الوجود ليس بتصور ولا تصديق، أو يقال: العلم أوّلي ومكتسب، فيقال: بمَ[٧] تنكر على من يثبت علماً غير أولي ولا مكتسب؟ ويكفيني من حُكم النظر تحقيقُ المطالبة الحاقّة دون المثال، لكني أوردت المثال احترازاً عن وصمة المراء والجدال.

على أني أتخطى عنه قليلاً، فأقول: إن كان تغيُّر المعلوم أوجب تغير العلم فتكثّر المعلوم يوجب تكثر العلم، حتى يلزم أن تتكثر الذات بتكثر المعلومات، أو يتحد معلومه حتى لا يعلم إلا معلوماً واحداً، كما لم يُبدع إلا عقلاً واحداً، وبتوسطه[٨] يعلم سائر المعلومات على اللزوم والاستتباع، كما بتوسطه[٩] يُبدع سائر الموجودات على اللزوم والاستتباع[١٠].

١ ونقول: ويقول، ب.

٢ سلمت: تسلمت، ا ب.

٣ فقلنا: قلنا، ب.

٤ نعم: -، ا.

٥ وما: ولم، ب.

٦ وإما: أو، ب.

٧ بم: وبم، ب.

٨ وبتوسطه: وبتوسط، ا.

٩ بتوسطه: بتوسط، ا.

وعلى هذا الاعتبار سقط الحكم بأنه يعلم الكليات، بل ليس يعلم بالذات إلا معلوماً واحداً.

وإذا كان وجود العقل الأول من لوازم وجوده بذاته وتعقّله ذاتَه كان عاقلاً[1] بذاته لذاته فقط، وصار المعلول الأول من اللوازم في العلم كما هو من اللوازم في الوجود، فلا يعلم إذاً إلا[2] ذاته فقط. ابصر[3] كيف ارتقى درجة العلم عن الجزئي إلى الكلي، ثم إلى العقل الأول، ثم إلى ذات واجب الوجود، وهذا بعينه[4] مذهب قدماء الفلاسفة: أن الأول[5] يعقل ذاته بذاته فقط، وإنما يعقل العقلَ الأول وما بعده من الموجودات[6] على اللزوم، فلا يعقل الكليات من حيث أنها كليات[7] لأنه يتكثر بتكثرها، ولا الجزئيات من حيث أنها جزئيات لأنه يتغير[8] بتغيرها، وعلمه أعلى من أن يكون كلياً أو جزئياً أو يعلم به غير[9] ذاته الأعلى.

١٠ كما بتوسطه ... والاستتباع: -، ب.

١ عاقلاً: عقلاً عاقلاً، ب.

٢ إذاً إلا: إلا، ا؛ إذا لا، ب.

٣ ابصر: انظر، ب.

٤ بعينه: يعينه، ب.

٥ الأول: العقل الأول، ا.

٦ الموجودات: الوجودات، ب.

٧ كليات: كليا، ب.

٨ لأنه يتغير: لا، ب.

٩ غير: عن، ا.

وأما قول ابن سينا: لا يجوز أن يعلم الأشياء من الأشياء وإلا كان علمه انفعالياً، أقول[١]: فهذه[٢] مسألة بينهم وبين المتكلمين[٣]، أنه يعلم الأشياء قبل كونها أو مع كونها أو بعده، وأن العلم يتبع[٤] المعلوم فيتبين المعلوم على ما هو به، أم المعلوم يتبع العلم، وأن المعدوم[٥] هل يجب أن يكون شيئاً حتى يُعلم ويخبر[٦] عنه أم لا يجوز[٧] أن يكون شيئاً؟ فعلى مذهب الرجل علمُ واجب الوجود علم فعلي[٨]، أعني به أنه سبب وجود المعلوم، ويلزم أنه لا يعلم المعلوم قبل كونه ولا بعد كونه[٩]، بل علمه به تكوينه له. وعلى هذا يلزم[١٠] أن[١١] لا يعلم ذاته إذ لا[١٢] يكوّن ذاته[١٣]،

١ أقول: فأقول، ب.

٢ فهذه: وهذه، ا ب.

٣ المتكلمين: + مشكلة، ب.

٤ يتبع: يتتبع، ا.

٥ المعدوم: المعلوم، ا ب.

٦ ويخبر: ونجر، ا.

٧ يجوز: يجب، ب.

٨ فعلي: + لا انفعالي، ب.

٩ ولا بعد كونه: -، ب.

١٠ أنه لا يعلم ... يلزم: -، ا.

١١ أن: أنه، ا.

١٢ إذ لا: ولا، ب.

١٣ ذاته: معلوماً له، ب.

أو يلزم أن يكون علمه بالنسبة إلى الأشياء علماً[١] فعلياً، وعلمه بذاته علماً انفعالياً. وحينئذٍ لا يكون علمه بذاته ذاته[٢] ولا يكون علمه بذاته علماً[٣] بالأشياء. فيا لَلّه من حيرة علي حيرة[٤]، {وَمَنْ لَمْ يَجْعَلِ اللّهُ لَهُ نُوراً[٥] فَمَا لَهُ مِنْ نُورٍ} (٢٤ النور ٤٠).

المعتقد الحق[٦]

إن الأنبياء عليهم السلام تنكبوا هذه المسالك في مناهجهم ومنعوا الناس من الخوض في جلال الله عزّ وجلّ والجدال عليه والتكلم في صفاته، وامتلأت[٧] كتبهم، واشتهر قولهم بأنه[٨] {لاَ يَعْزُبُ[٩] عَنْهُ مِثْقَالُ ذَرَّةٍ فِي الأَرْضِ وَلاَ فِي السَّمَاءِ[١٠]} (١٠ يونس ٦١)، وأنه[١١] {يَعْلَمُ السِّرَّ وَأَخْفَى}

١ علماً: علم، ا.

٢ بذاته ذاته: بالأشياء علمه بذاته، ب.

٣ علماً: علم، ا.

٤ حيرة على حيرة: خيره على خيره، ب.

٥ نوراً: نور، ا.

٦ الحق: مطموس في ا.

٧ وامتلأت: مطموس في ا؛ وامتدا، ب.

٨ بأنه: انه، ا ب.

٩ يعزب: يعذب، ب.

١٠ السماء: السماوات، ب.

١١ وأنه: فإنه، ا.

(٢٠ طه ٧)، وأنه {يَعْلَمُ[١] مَا بَيْنَ أَيْدِيهِمْ وَمَا خَلْفَهُمْ} (٢ البقرة ٢٥٥ وغيرها) وأنه {عَالِمُ الغَيْبِ وَالشَّهَادَةِ} (٦ الأنعام ٧٣ وغيرها) وأنه {يَعْلَمُ خَائِنَةَ الأَعْيُنِ وَمَا تُخْفِي الصُّدُورُ} (٤٠ غافر ١٩)، من غير فرق بين الكلي والجزئي، ولا تمييز بين الثابت الدائم وبين الكائن الفاسد. وعلى هذا شرعوا العبادات المشتملة على الدعوات والمناجات التي تدل على أنه يسمع ويرى ويجيب، وهو بالمنظر[٢] الأعلى، فالقلوب تقصد نحوه، والأيدي تُرفع إليه، والأبصار تخشع له، والرقاب تخضع لقدرته وعزته، والألسن[٣] تضرع[٤] إلى عفوه[٥] ورحمته، فُيستغنى به ولا يُستغنى عنه[٦]، ويُرغب إليه ولا يرغب عنه، ولا تُفني خزائنَه المسائل، ولا تبدل حُكمه الوسائل، ولا تنقطع عنه[٧] حوائج المحتاجين، ولا يغنيه[٨] دعاء الداعين.

فهذا وأمثاله لعلمه بالجزئيات والكليات، بل علمُه فوق القسمين، وإحاطته أعلى من[٩] الطريقين، بل من مخلوقاته من هو بهذه[١٠] الصفة،

١ يعلم: اعلم، ا.

٢ بالمنظر: بالنظر، ب.

٣ والألسن: والا السن، ب.

٤ تضرع: يتضرع، ب.

٥ عفوه: العفو، ب.

٦ عنه: -، ا.

٧ عنه: -، ب.

٨ يغنيه: يعينه، ب.

٩ من: -، ا.

١٠ بهذه: بهذا، ب.

أعني العقل يدرك الكلي، والحس يدرك الجزئي، وعلمه تعالى وراء العقل والحس جميعاً {لاَ تُدْرِكُهُ[١] الأَبْصَارُ وَهُوَ يُدْرِكُ الأَبْصَارَ وَهُوَ اللَّطِيفُ الخَبِيرُ} (٦ الأنعام ١٠٣).

وقد قالت الحكماء الذين هم أساطين الحكمة: إن الأول لا يدرَك من نحو ذاته، وإنما يدرك من نحو آثاره. وإنما يدركه[٢] كل مدرك بقدر الأثر الذي أُودع فيه وفُطر عليه، فكل[٣] حيوان يسبّحه بقدر ما احتمله من صنعه[٤] ووجد أثره في طبعه. ولما كان حظ الإنسان من صنائعه أوفر[٥]، ونصيبه من ألطافه[٦] أكثر، كانت معرفته أقوى وتسبيحه[٧] أوفى. وإذا كانت رتبة الملائكة المقرّبين[٨] الذين هم في أعلى علّيين أرفع وأعلى، ولطائف الصنع في جواهرهم[٩] أسنى وأبهى، كانت معارفهم أصفى. وكما لا يمكن أن يقف الحيوان على وجوه معارف الإنسان، كذلك لا يمكن أن يقف الإنسان على وجوه معارف[١٠] المقربين من الملائكة[١١]. ولا يقف الكل على

١ تدركه: يدرك، ب.

٢ يدركه: يدرك، ا.

٣ فكل: بكل، ب.

٤ صنعه: ضعه، ب.

٥ أوفر: وافر، ا.

٦ ألطافه: الطاقة، ا.

٧ وتسبيحه: ونتيجته، ا.

٨ المقربين: المقربون، ب.

٩ جواهرهم: جوهرهم، ب.

١٠ الإنسان كذلك ... معارف: -، ا.

وجه إحاطة الباريء تعالى[١] بجميع الموجودات، جُمَلها وتفاصيلها، وكلياتها وجزئياتها، ولا يشغله كلي عن كلي[٢] ولا جزئي[٣] عن جزئي، وكلاهما بالنسبة إليه[٤] سواء. وليس لزم[٥] أن يقال: إنه علم الأشياء قبل كونها أو بعد كونها، فإن[٦] قبل وبعد ومع أحكام زمانية، وعلمه تعالى ليس بزماني، بل الأزمنة بالنسبة إليه على السواء. وليس إذا جعله كلياً[٧] خرج عن أن يكون زمانياً، كما ظنّه في الكسوف، بل العلم الزماني يتغير بتغير الزمان، والغير الزماني لا يتغير بتغير الزمان البتة[٨]. وقد يجوز أن يكون كلياً وهو في زمان[٩]، بل الكلي لا يتصور في حقه

١١ من الملائكة: والملائكة، ا.

١ تعالى: -، ب.

٢ عن كلي: -، ب.

٣ ولا جزئي: وجزئي، ا.

٤ إليه: -، ب.

٥ لزم: يلزم، ا ب.

٦ فإن: كان، ا.

٧ وعلمه تعالى ... كلياً: -، ا ب.

٨ الزماني يتغير ... البتة: وعلمه تعالى ليس بزماني، بل الأزمنة بالنسبة إليه على السواء وليس إذا جعله (+ زمانياً، ب) كلياً (+ خرج عن أن يكون كما ظنه في الكسوف، بل العلم، ب) الزماني يتغير بتغير (بتغيره، ب) الزمان (الزمان، ا) البتة، ا ب.

٩ زمان: الزمان، ب.

تعالى، كالقضايا الحملية[1] والشرطية التي استعملها في الكسوف، أعني إن كان كذا فيكون كذا، وعلم البارئ تعالى[2] أعلى من ذلك، فلا يكون مشروطاً بإن كان كذا كان كذا.

ومن العجب أنه فسّر التعقل والعلم بالتجريد عن المادّة تارة، وبالإبداع تارة، وما هو مجرد عن المادة كيف يُتصور أن يكون فعلياً؟ لأن التجريد نفي في المعنى، أي[3] ليس هو في مادة. وإذا كان فعلياً، أي موجباً للفعل والموجود، كيف يكون كلياً؟ إذ الكلي[4] ليس يوجد بالفعل في الأعيان.

فعُلم من ذلك كله أن علمه تعالى فوق القسمين، وأعلى من الوجهين، ونسبته[5] إلى الكليات والجزئيات والأزمنة المتغيرات، والأمكنة المختلفات، نسبة واحدة {أَلاَ يَعْلَمُ مَنْ خَلَقَ وَهُوَ اللَّطِيفُ الْخَبِيرُ} (٦٧ الملك ١٤).

ألسنا نختار أن حمل النطق على الإنسان وعلى المَلَك حمل[6] باشتراك[7] الاسم؟ فكذلك[8] العقل الذي هو للإنسان[9] والملك يكون باشتراك

١ الحملية: الحلية، ب.

٢ تعالى: سبحانه وتعالى، ا.

٣ أي: إذ، ا.

٤ الكلي: الكل، ب.

٥ ونسبته: ونسبة، ا.

٦ حمل: -، ا.

٧ باشتراك: اشتراك، ب.

٨ فكذلك: قولك، ا.

الاسم. فالملائكة لا يعقلون الأشياء تصوراً وتصديقاً بواسطة الحد والقياس، بل تعقلاتهم خارجة عن القسمين، فما ظنك بعلم أعلى من الأقسام كلها؟ أفيقال[1]: إنه كلي أو جزئي؟ ومن دعاء الصالحين عليهم السلام[2]: يا من لا تراه العيون، يا من لا تخاله[3] الظنون، يا من لا يصفه الواصفون[4]، أي هو أعلى من الحس والخيال والعقل. ثم يقولون: يا مَن حين[5] أبتغيه[6] أجده، يا من حين[7] أعبده أسكن إليه، يا من إذا علم بوحدتي آنسني[8] بحفظه، يا من إذا حيل بيني وبين الاستجارة أجارني[9].

٩ للإنسان: الإنسان، ا ب.

١ أفيقال: أيقال، ا.

٢ عليهم السلام: رضي الله عنهم، ب.

٣ تخاله: تخالطه، اب.

٤ الواصفون: الوصفون، ب.

٥ حين: حيث، ب.

٦ أبتغيه: ابغيه، ب.

٧ حين: حيث، ب.

٨ آنسني: أنسي، ب.

٩ أجارني: + سبحانه سبحانه سبحانه، ب.

المسألة الخامسة
في حدث العالم

إن[١] الفلاسفة[٢] على ثلاثة آراء في هذه المسألة، فجماعة من الأوائل الذين هم أساطين الحكمة من الملطية وساميا صاروا إلى القول بحدوث موجودات العالم بمبادئها وبسائطها ومركباتها، كما صار إليه جماعة من المسلمين. وطائفة من أثينية وأصحاب الرواق صاروا إلى قدم مبادئها من العقل والنفس والمفارقات والبسائط دون المبسوطات[٣] والمركبات. فإن المبادئ فوق الدهر والزمان، فلا يتحقق فيها حدوث زماني بخلاف المركبات التي هي تحت الدهر والزمان، ومنعوا كون الحركات سرمدية، ويقرب من مذهبهم مذهب جماعة من المسلمين من القول بقدم الكلمات والحروف. ومذهب[٤] أرسطو ومن تابعه من تلامذته ووافقه من فلاسفة الإسلام أن العالم قديم والحركات[٥] الدورية سرمدية.

١ إن: اعلم أن، ب.

٢ الفلاسفة: + والحكماء، ب.

٣ المبسوطات: المتوسطات، ب.

٤ مذهب: مذهبه، ا.

٥ والحركات: الحركات، ا.

ونحن نقدّم على الخوض فيما ذكره ابن سينا مقدمتين، إحداهما في بيان معنى التناهي واللاتناهي[١]، وفي أي قسم من الأقسام يجب التناهي وفي أي قسم لا يجب، والثانية في بيان معنى التقدم والتأخر والمعية وأنها على كم وجه تكون.

المقدمة الأولى

قالوا: التناهي قد يكون حسّياً، وقد يكون عقلياً. فالتناهي الحسي إنما يكون بحد حسي[٢]، وذلك على قسمين، مكاني وزماني. فالمكاني كما[٣] ينتهي[٤] حد جسم بحد جسم، واتفقوا على أن جسماً[٥] لا يتناهى[٦] بُعداً في[٧] جميع الجهات أو في جهة واحدة مستحيل. والزماني كما ينتهي[٨] حد وقت بجسم بوقت. وقد قال المتأخرون: إن أوقاتاً لا تتناهى متعاقبة في الوجود، وكذلك حركات ومتحركات لا تتناهى متعاقبة في الوجود، غير مستحيل.

١ واللاتناهي: وأن لا تناهي، ا.

٢ إنما يكون بحد حسي: -، ب.

٣ كما: ما، ب.

٤ ينتهي: + إليه، ب.

٥ أن جسماً: الجسم، ا.

٦ يتناهى: يناهي، ا.

٧ في: إلى، ب.

٨ ينتهي: + إليه، ب.

وأما التناهي العقلي[١] فإنما يكون بحد عقلي، وذلك على قسمين: حد مركب من مقومات الشيء، أو رسم مركب من لوازم[٢] الشيء، به يمنع ويجمع[٣]، وحقائق تتميز[٤] الموجودات العقلية بها من غير أن تكون مركبة[٥] من مقومات ماهيتها كالمفارقات. وقد أجمعوا[٦] على أن عللاً[٧] ومعلولات لا تتناهى هي[٨] مستحيل الوجود.

وقال المتأخرون منهم: إن نفوساً وعقولاً معاً في الوجود أو متعاقبة لا تتناهى[٩] غير مستحيل. والضابط لذلك أن كل ما له وضع حسي كالجسم، أو وضع عقلي مثل العلة والمعلول، فإن ما لا يتناهى فيه مستحيل، وما ليس[١٠] له وضع حسي كالحركات الدورية، أو عقلي كالنفوس الإنسانية، فإن ما لا يتناهى فيه غير مستحيل.

١ العقلي: العقل، ب.

٢ لوازم: اللوازم، ب.

٣ يمنع ويجمع: يجمع ويمنع، ا.

٤ تتميز: تميز، ب.

٥ مركبة: مركب، ب.

٦ أجمعوا: جمعوا، ب.

٧ عللاً: علل، ب.

٨ هي: -، ب.

٩ لا تتناهى: -، ا.

١٠ وما ليس: وليس، ب.

والمقدمة الثانية في التقدم والتأخر والمعية

التقدم قد يكون زمانياً كتقدم الوالد على الولد، وقد يكون مكانياً كتقدم الإمام على المأموم[١]، وقد يكون شرفياً[٢] كتقدم العالِم على الجاهل، وقد يكون ذاتياً[٣] كتقدم العلة على المعلول. وزادوا[٤] فيه معنى[٥] خامساً، وهو التقدم بالطبع كتقدم الواحد على الاثنين. ويمكن أن يزاد فيه معنى سادس[٦]، وهو التقدم بالوجود فقط، كتقدم الموجِد على الموجَد.

وحصر الأقسام فيما ذكرناه ليس أمراً مبرهناً[٧] عليه، فمن زاد أو نقص إذا أظهر المعنى[٨] كان مصيباً، وكما أن التقدم والتأخر يرجعان إلى هذه الأقسام المحصورة، كذلك المعية ترجع إليها بحسبها. فقد يكون الشيء مع الشيء زماناً ومكاناً وشرفاً وذاتاً وطبعاً ووجوداً، وقد يكون مع ما أنه معه زماناً متقدماً عليه ذاتاً وبالعكس، وكذلك[٩] في كل قسمين.

١ المأموم: المأم، ب.

٢ شرفياً، مطموس في ا.

٣ ذاتياً: زاتياً، ب.

٤ وزادوا: وزاد، ب.

٥ معنى: قسماً، ب.

٦ سادس: سادساً، ا.

٧ مبرهناً: مرهنا، ا.

٨ المعنى: -، ا.

٩ وكذلك: كذلك، ب.

فقال ابن سينا: العالم موجود بوجود[١] البارئ تعالى دائم[٢] الوجود بدوامه، فالبارئ تعالى متقدم على العالم بالذات تقدُّم العلة على المعلول، لكن العالم دائم[٣] الوجود بدوامه، وشرع في الاستدلال على ما قال[٤]. قال: العقل الصريح الذي لم يكذب يشهد أن[٥] الذات الواحدة إذا كانت من جميع جهاتها كما كانت، وكان لا يوجد عنها فيما قبل شيء وهي الآن كذلك، فالآن أيضاً[٦] لا يوجد عنها شيء، فإذا صار الآن يوجد[٧] منها شيء، فقد حدث في الذات قصد، أو إرادة[٨]، أو طبع[٩]، أو قدرة وتمكّن، أو شيء مما يشبه هذا لم يكن، وأن[١٠] الممكن أن يوجد وأن لا يوجد لا يخرج إلى الفعل، ولا يترجح له أن يوجد، إلا بسبب. وإذا كانت هذه الذات التي[١١] هي العلة ولا[١٢] ترجح[١٣]، فإذا ترجح[١٤] فلا بد من سبب

١ بوجود: مكرر في ب.

٢ دائم: ديم، ب.

٣ دائم: ديم، ب.

٤ قال: -، ب.

٥ أن: بأن، ب.

٦ فالآن أيضاً: مطموس في ا.

٧ يوجد: لا يوجد، ب.

٨ قصد أو إرادة: قصداً وإرادة، ا؛ قصد وأو إرادة، ب.

٩ أو طبع: اطبع، ب.

١٠ وأن: فإن، ب.

١١ التي: -، ا.

١٢ ولا: لا، ب.

مرجح، وإلا كان[1] نسبتها إلى ذلك الممكن على ما كان قبل[2]، ولم يحدث لها نسبة أخرى، فيكون الأمر بحاله وكان الإمكان إمكاناً صرفاً، وإذا حدث[3] لها نسبة[4] فقد حدث أمر، ولا بد أن يحدث في ذاته أو خارجاً عن ذاته، وكلاهما محال.

وقال أيضاً: كيف يتميز في العدم وقتُ تركٍ ووقت شروع؟ وبماذا يخالف الوقت الوقت[5]؟ وأيضاً، فإن الحادث لا يحدث إلا بحدوث حال في المبدأ، فلا يخلو إما أن يكون ذلك إرادة أو عرضاً[6]، وإلا فالطبع لا يُحدث، والقسر[7] والاتفاق باطل. وعلى كل حال فلا بد من حدوث صفة أو حال، فإن حدث في[8] ذاته صار محلاً للحوادث، وإن حدث في محل فلا محل قبل المحل، وإن حدث لا في محل فالكلام في ذلك الحادث كالكلام[9] في العالم.

١٣ ترجح: ترجيح، ب.

١٤ ترجح: رجحت، ا.

١ كان: -، ا.

٢ قبل: قبله، ا.

٣ حدث: احدث، ب.

٤ نسبة: + أخرى، ب.

٥ الوقت: -، ا.

٦ عرضاً: غرضاً، ب.

٧ والقسر: في القسر، ب.

٨ في: -، ب.

٩ كالكلام: من هنا فقد النص في نسخة ا لسقط ورقات منها.

وقال أيضاً: الحق الأول مبدأ لأفعاله، والمبدأ سابق على الفعل، فبماذا سبق، أبذاته أم بزمان؟ فإن سبق بذاته فقط فذلك حق ونحن نعترف به، وإن سبق بزمان فكلامنا في ذلك الزمان بعينه عائد، ووجوده تعالى لم يزل، فالأزمنة أيضاً لم تزل، فنقدّر في تلك الأزمنة الغير المتناهية موجودات غير متناهية[١]. وكل ما ألزمتمونا في الحوادث التى لا تتناهى نلزمكم في الأزمنة التي لا تتناهى[٢].

وكذلك كلامنا في الحركات، إذ كل متحرك[٣] يستدعي محركاً[٤]، والمحرك[٥] إن كان متحركاً لزم التسلسل، فلا بد من محرك ليس متحركاً، وهو إما جسم أو نفس أو عقل. وبالجملة يجب أن يسبق المحرِّك[٦] بذاته ويقارنه في زمانه، وهو كالضوء من السراج والشعاع[٧] من الشمس، فإنهما يتقارنان[٧] زماناً، والسراج متقدم على الضوء. ولذلك تقول: وُجد السراج فوجد الضوء، ولا يمكنك أن تقول: وجد الضوء فوجد السراج. وكذلك تقول: تحركت يدي فتحرك المفتاح في كمي، ولا يمكنك أن تعكس ذلك.

١ موجودات غير متناهية: -، ب.

٢ تتناهى ... تتناهى: يتناهى ... يتناهى، ب.

٣ متحرك: متحركه، ب.

٤ محركاً: متحركاً، ب.

٥ والمحرك: والمتحرك، ب.

٦ المحرك: المتحرك، ب.

٧ يتقارنان: متقاربان، ب.

الاعتراض عليه

نتكلم أولاً في الدعوى والفتوى ونبين فيها اشتراكاً في لفظ الدوام والوجود ، وما لم يتخلص محل النزاع عن وجوه الاشتراك لم يتبين وجه الاحتجاج. فقوله أولاً: العالم موجود بوجوده، يشتمل على قليل اشتباه، وكان[١] من حقه أن يقول: العالم موجود بإيجاده، حتى يُشعر ذلك بالتقدم الوجودي الذاتي. وقوله: دائم[٢] الوجود بدوامه، فلفظ الدوام مشترك، فإن دوام الوجود للبارئ[٣] تعالى ليس بمعنى دوام الوجود للعالم، بل دوام الوجود له تعالى بمعنى أنه واجب الوجود بذاته، والواجب ما إذا فُرض عدمه لزم منه محال، ودوام الوجود للعالم بمعنى استمرار الزمان عليه أو بمعنى[٤] أنه واجب بغيره، ولو فرض عدمه لم يلزم منه محال، فلم يتلازما في الوجود ابتداءً ودواماً. فلم يكن الدوام في الوجودين بمعنى واحد، بل بمعنيين مختلفين في الحقيقة، ولم يكن الوجود في الدوامين بمعنى واحد، بل بمعنيين مختلفين في الحقيقة. فالفتوى عنه[٥] ملخَّصة، وأكثر الاختلافات بين العلماء[٦] من اشتراك الألفاظ.

١ وكان: فكان، ب.

٢ دائم: ديم، ب.

٣ للبارئ: البارئ، ب.

٤ أو بمعنى: وبمعنى، ب.

٥ عنه: غير، ب.

٦ العلماء: العقلاء، ب.

ثم البائقة[١] الكبرى التي استعظموها من ابن سينا فهي قضايا وهمية ومقدمات خيالية، خُيل من سحره إليهم {أَنَّهاَ تَسْعَى، فَأَوْجَسَ فِي نَفْسِهِ خِيفَةَ مُوسَى، قُلْنَا لاَ تَخَفْ إِنَّكَ[٢] أَنْتَ الأَعْلَى} (٢٠ طه ٦٦-٦٨) وهي بعينها شبهة الكرامية في المكان، نقلها إلى الزمان[٣]. ولسنا[٤] ممن يُقعقَع له[٥] بالشِّنان. وقوله: إن الذات الواحدة إذا كانت من جميع جهاتها كما كانت، وكان لا يوجد عنها فيما قبلُ شيء، وهي الآن كذلك، فالآن أيضاً لا يوجد عنها شيء، قلنا: أثبتّ قبلاً وآناً وراء العالم، أو قدّرت زماناً أو زمانين، أحدهما متقدم والآخر مقارن، فإن قدّرته على مذهب الخصم، فالخصم ليس يثبت وراء العالم زماناً البتة، لا متقدماً فيسمى[٦] قبلاً ولا مقارناً فيسمى الآن، كما لم[٧] يثبت وراء العالم مكاناً البتة، لا خلاء ولا ملاء. وهذا كما يقول الكرامي: إن الذات الواحدة إذا كانت من جميع جهاتها كما كانت، وكان لا يوجد معها شيء، ثم وجد معها شيء[٨]، فلا بد وأن يكون بجهة منها مبايناً عنها بينونةً متناهية أو غير

١ البائقة: النابغة، ب.

٢ فأوجس ... إنك: -، ب.

٣ الزمان: الزيان، ب.

٤ ولسنا: وليسنا، ب.

٥ له: عليه، ب.

٦ فيسمى: فليسمى، ب.

٧ لم: -، ب.

٨ ثم وجد معها شيء: -، ب.

متناهية. وتقدير وقت للترك[١] ووقت للفعل[٢] كتقدير مكان فارغ ومكان مشغول، وأنت تعرف أنه لما لم يكن وجود البارئ تعالى مكانياً لم ينسب إليه مكان فارغ ولا مكان مشغول، كذلك لما لم يكن وجوده جلت عظمته زمانياً لم يجز أن ينسب إليه وقت فارغ ووقت مشغول حتى يسمى أحدهما تركاً للفعل والثاني فعلاً.

فإن[٣] قال: إنك إن لم تثبت قبلاً على العالم ولا زماناً متناهياً أو غير متناه، فقد قضيت بتلازم الوجودين، وجود الصانع ووجود[٤] المصنوع، وكذلك إذا لم تثبت وقتاً لترك الفعل ووقتاً للفعل فقد صرحت بالتلازم، قلت: أساء سمعاً فأساء جابة، إنما يلزم التلازم في الوجود والزمان إذا كان الموجود قابلاً للزمان، وقد بينا أن العالم لا يجوز أن يكون معه تعالى زماناً، لأنه يوجب أن يكون وجوده زمانياً، فالتلازم والاقتران الزماني مستحيل، والسبق والتقدم الزماني أيضاً[٥] مستحيل. وهذا كسؤال الكرامي: إنك إن لم تثبت بينونة وراء العالم متناهية أو غير متناهية، فقد قضيت بتلازم وجودَي[٦] الصانع والمصنوع، لكنه لا يلزم، إذ ليس وجوده تعالى مكانياً.

١ للترك: الترك، ب.

٢ للفعل: الفعل، ب.

٣ فإن: زمانا، ب.

٤ ووجود: ووجو، ب.

٥ أيضاً: -، ب.

٦ وجودي: وجود، ب.

قال: إنك إذا قلت: لم يفعل ثم فعل، فقد أثبتّ وقتاً ما عطّلته عن الفعل حتى تميز[١] فيه وقت ترك ووقت شروع، وإن لم تثبت وقت التعطل والترك فقد وافقتني[٢] في الإيجاب[٣] واللزوم، وإني أقول: لا يجوز أن يتعطل الجواد عن الجود فيتلازمان، قلت: ولا يلزم على قولنا: لم يفعل ثم فعل، وقت تعطل ووقت شروع، فإن في العبارة تجوزاً وتوسعاً. فإن في «لم يفعل» إشعاراً[٤] بالماضي، وفي «ثم فعل» دلالة على المستقبل، وليس في العدم ماض ومستقبل. وهو كما يقول الخصم[٥]: أبدع العقل، ثم أبدع النفس، ثم الهيولى، ثم الجسم، ولم يُشعر ذلك بالماضى وتعاقب الزمان بعده.

وليس في العقل وقت قبل الوقت، ولا[٦] وقت مع الوقت[٧]، كما ليس في العقل عالم آخر وراء العالم فوقاً ولا مع العالم متيامناً ولا متياسراً، ولا دون العالم تحتاً. وإني لا أثبت التعطيل عن الفعل إلا حيث يتصور وجود الفعل، اذ الفعل ما له أول، والأزل ما ليس له أول،

١ تميز: يميذ، ب.

٢ وافقتني: وافقني، ب.

٣ الإيجاب: الإيجا، ب.

٤ إشعاراً: إشعار، ب.

٥ الخصم: إنهم: ب.

٦ ولا: فلا، ب.

٧ الوقت: الفعل، ب. من البين أن السياق بالمقارنة بما يتلو من عدم وجود عالم مع العالم يقتضي قراءة «الوقت» هاهنا وإن كان نص الكلمة في نُسخ مصارع المصارع أيضاً «الفعل» أو «العقل»، فالظاهر أن التصحيف قد وقع قبل زمان الطوسي.

والجمع[١] بين ما له أول وما لا أول له[٢] محال. وأنت إذا قلت: إنه صانع في الأزل، فقد جمعت بين طرفي النقيض، أعني إثبات الأولية ونفي الأولية. فهلا قلت: لا يجوز أن يتعطل الجواد عن إفاضة الجود حيث يتصور الوجود، وإذا لم يكن الجود[٣] متصور الوجود فلا يسمى ذلك تعطيلاً. أليس لو قال قائل: إذا لم يوجِد الصانع جسماً ذاهباً في الجهات غير متناهٍ فقد تعطل عن[٤] إفاضة الجود[٥]، أو انتقص جوده عن كماله، قيل: إذا لم يمكن[٦] وجود جسم غير متناه رجع النقص إلى قابل الجود[٧] لا إلى جود المفيض.

قال: فقد تُصُور عندك[٨] في قضية العقل جوازُ أن يخلق العالم قبل وقته بزمان، وإذا كان ذلك متصوراً ولم يخلق فقد تعطل عن الجود. قلت: التصوير العقلي في الزمان كالتقدير العقلي في المكان حذوَ القذة بالقذة[٩] والنعل بالنعل، فالوهم يصوّر والعقل يقدّر وراء العالم عالماً آخر فوقاً أوتحتاً، ويقدر جرم الكل أكبر مما هو عليه وأصغر، لكن بشرط أن

١ والجمع: والجميع، ب.

٢ له: -، ب.

٣ الجود: الجواد، ب.

٤ عن: -، ب.

٥ الجود: الجواد، ب.

٦ يمكن: يكن، ب.

٧ الجود: الجواد، ب.

٨ عندك: عندكم، ب.

٩ بالقذة: -، ب.

يكون متناهي الذات، إذ قام الدليل على أن جسماً لا يتناهى غير ممكن، كذلك يقدر[١] العقل قبل العالم وقتاً أو موجوداً بزمان ولكن بشرط أن يكون متناهياً، فإن زماناً لا يتناهى غير ممكن كما سنبين[٢].

قال[٣]: للجسم وضع طبيعي، فلا يمكن فرض اللانهاية[٤] فيه، وليس للزمان[٥] وضع طبيعي، ولا ترتيب عقلي، فيتصور فرض اللانهاية فيه.

قلت: وهذا الفرق بين الصورتين ليس بمؤثّر، لأن البرهان الذي دل على استحالة وجود جسم لا يتناهى بعداً هو بعينه[٦] يدل على استحالة وجود مدة لا تتناهى زماناً ووجودِ نفوس إنسانية لا تتناهى عدداً، إذ الأوسط فيه أمور أولية، منها أنَ الأقلّ من الأعداد الموجودة لا يكون مثل الأكثر، ومنها أن الأقل والأكثر إنما يكونان في العدد المتناهي، وما لا يتناهى لا يتصور فيه الأقل والأكثر، ومنها أنه لا يتحقق في غير المتناهي جزء معلوم مثل النصف والثلث والربع.

ونحن نركب من هذه المقدمات برهاناً في كل صورة. ولنفرض الكلام أولاً في النفوس الإنسانية، فنقول: لو دخل في الوجود ما لا يتناهى من النفوس الإنسانية في يوم الأحد لما أمكن أن يزداد بأعداد من

١ يقدر: تقدير، ب.

٢ سنبين: سبق، ب.

٣ قال: + الخصم، ب.

٤ اللانهاية: الا نهاية، ب.

٥ للزمان: للبرهان، ب.

٦ بعينه: تعينه، ب.

النفوس في يوم الاثنين، فإن ما لا يتناهى عدداً لا يزداد بعدد[١]، ولكن قد ازداد، فاستثناء نقيض التالي أنتج نقيض المقدم.

وتركيب آخر أن النفوس لو كانت غير متناهية في يوم الأحد، وهي أيضاً غير متناهية في يوم الاثنين، كان الأقل مثل الأكثر. وإذا تباينت[٢] النفوس عدداً فلا بد أن تبتدئ من نفس ليس قبلها نفس فتتناهى[٣] الأشخاص، ولا بد من أن تبتدئ من شخص ليس قبله شخص فتتناهى[٤] الحركات والمتحركات، ولا بد أن تبتدئ[٥] من حركة ليس قبلها حركة فيتناهى الزمان العادّ للحركات، ولا بد أن يبتدئ من زمان ليس قبله زمان، وذلك ما أردنا أن نبين.

وتركيب آخر أن كل حادث بسببٍ فقد يتوقف وجوده على وجود سببه، ولو توقف وجود ذلك[٦] السبب على وجود سبب آخر أدى ذلك إلى التسلسل، وهو باطل لعلة التوقف، فإن ما يتوقف وجوده على وجود شيء لم يكن ليحصل[٧] وجوده إلا وذلك الشيء وجد قبله. فلو توقف كل سبب على سبب إلى ما لا يتناهى، لم يكن ليحصل هذا السبب الذي وقع

١ بعدد: بعد ذلك، ب.

٢ تباينت: تناهت، ب.

٣ فتتناهى: فتناهي، ب.

٤ فتتناهى: فيتناهى، ب.

٥ تبتدئ: يبتدئ، ب.

٦ ذلك: لك، ب.

٧ ليحصل: يحصل، ب.

الفرض فيه لتوقف[١] وجوده على وجود ما لا يتناهى متعاقبة أو محصورة في الوجود، وذلك غير ممكن.

فننقل هذا البرهان بعينه إلى الأشخاص الإنسانية، فنقول: هذا الإنسان، ونشير به إلى زيد، قد توقف وجوده على وجود النطفة التي خلق منها، ووجود[٢] تلك النطفة قد توقف على وجود إنسان آخر حصل منه النطفة، فكذلك[٣] يتسلسل إلى ما لا نهاية له، وذلك باطل. وقد توافقنا[٤] على استحالة وجود علل ومعلولات بلا نهاية[٥]، إلا أنهم أجروا هذا الحكم في العلل الفاعلية، ونحن ألزمناهم عين ذلك في العلل المادّية[٦]، والعلل في توقف المعلولات عليها متساوية. فإذا ثبت أن النفوس والأشخاص متناهية، وإنما تبتدئ من مبدأ لها[٧]، سواء كانت متعاقبة في الوجود أو كانت[٨] معاً في الوجود غير متعاقبة، ثبت بعد ذلك أن الحركات الدورية والمتحركات متناهية، لأنها لو كانت دائمة الحركة لكانت المواليد من تلك

١ لتوقف: ولتوقف، ب.

٢ ووجود: وجود، ب.

٣ فكذلك: ولذلك، ب.

٤ توافقنا: توقفنا، ب.

٥ بلا نهاية: لا يتناهى، ب.

٦ المادية: الغائية، ب.

٧ مبدأ لها: مبداها، ب.

٨ كانت: كان، ب.

الحركات دائمة الوجود غير متناهية[١] ، وقد ثبت أنها متناهية. فالزمان الذي هو عادّ للحركات[٢] يجب أن يكون متناهياً، وهذا[٣] غاية ما أردناه[٤].

ونقول أيضاً: البرهان الذي أوردتموه على استحالة بُعد لا يتناهى أو جسمٍ لا يتناهى هو أنك تفرض على سطح الجسم الغير المتناهي نقطة، وتقدّر في وهمك بُعداً لا يتناهى مبدؤه تلك النقطة، وتفرض خطّاً آخر على موازاة ذلك أقصر منها بذارع، ثم تطبّق النقطة على النقطة، والخط على الخط، فلا يخلو[٥] إما أن يبقى الخطان غير متناهيين أو ينتقص الأصغر، فلو بقي الخطان غير متناهيين كان الأصغر مثل الأكبر، وإن انتقص من الطرف الغير المتناهي بمقدار الذراع القاصر صار الغير[٦] المتناهي منقطعاً متناهياً، فما يوازيه صار[٧] متناهياً، فبان أنه لا يُتصور جسم وبعد في جسم غير متناه.

فننقل[٨] هذا البرهان بعينه إلى أعداد النفوس الإنسانية وأعداد الحركات الدورية، وهم لا يفرقون بين الصورتين إلا بأن[٩] الجسم له وضع

١ لأنها لو كانت ... متناهية، -، ب.

٢ للحركات: الحركات، ب.

٣ وهذا: هذا، ب.

٤ أردناه: أوردناه، ب.

٥ يخلو: يخلوا، ب.

٦ الغير: غير، ب.

٧ صار: صا، ب.

٨ فننقل: فينقل، ب.

٩ بأن: أن، ب.

فيمكن أن يُفرض فيه خطان[١] يبتدئان من نقطة إلى ما لا نهاية له، والنفوس والحركات لا وضع لها. قيل[٢]: مجرد الوضع وغير الوضع لا تأثير له في الفرق، فإن الخط المفروض في الجسم موهوم، وكل ما تقدره[٣] في الخط الموهوم أمكن تقديره في العدد الموهوم. فافرض زيداً واجعله نقطة وافرض آباءه[٤] إلى ما لا يتناهى خطاً مستقيماً، وافرض عمراً[٥] واجعله نقطة أنقص من زيد بأب أو بأبوين أو ثلاثة واجعل آباءه[٦] إلى ما لا يتناهى خطاً، ثم قدّر أن زيداً وعمراً توأمان في الوجود، وسُق[٧] البرهان ألى نهايته. ونحن بيّنا[٨] قبلُ نوعَ ترتيب في الأشخاص كما كان في العلل والمعلولات[٩]، والترتيب في العلل والنفوس والأشخاص كالوضع في الأجسام والأبعاد، والبرهانُ كالبرهان كفرسي رهان.

١ فيه خطان: –، ب.

٢ قيل: قبل، ب.

٣ تقدره: أمكن تقديره، ب.

٤ آباءه: اياه، ب.

٥ عمراً: عمروا، ب.

٦ آباءه: اباه، ب.

٧ وسق: وسبق، ب.

٨ ونحن بينا: وقد بيناه، ب.

٩ والمعلولات: + والترتيب في العلل والمعلولات، ب.

ثم اعلم أن الدور في النطفة[١] والإنسان والبيض والدجاج، والحَبّ والشجر، إنما ينقطع إذا عيّنتَ الابتداء من أحد طرفي الدور، وإلا لتوقّف[٢] وجود أحدهما على وجود الآخر، ولم[٣] يكن ليحصل[٤] أحدهما دون الآخر، وذلك يؤدي إلى أن لا يحصلا أصلاً، وقد حصلا، فلا بد من قطع الدور بأحدهما، والمبدأ في الأشخاص الإنسانية بالأكمل أولى.

ومما يُستدل به على ابن سينا أنه ذكر في الشفاء أن الاستدلال بالوجود[٥] على إثبات واجب الوجود، وبواجب الوجود[٦] على الأشياء، أولى وأشرف مما يستدل بغيره عليه، فعن هذا قال: لا نشُك[٧] أن وجوداً، وإنه ينقسم إلى واجب لذاته وإلى ممكن بذاته[٨]، وتكلم على القسمين. فأقول: إذا كان أحد القسمين ممكناً باعتبار ذاته، والممكن ما ليس بضروري الوجود ولا بضروري العدم، بل يستوي عند العقل طرفاه وجوداً وعدماً، فإذا[٩] ترجح جانب الوجود على جانب العدم احتاج إلى مرجح. وإلى ههنا محل الاتفاق مع وضوح البرهان. فأقول: المرجح لا يخلو إما أن

١ النطفة: النقطة، ب.

٢ لتوقف: لوقف، ب.

٣ ولم: لم، ب.

٤ ليحصل: يحصل، ب.

٥ بالوجود: بالموجود، ب.

٦ وبواجب الوجود: -، ب.

٧ نشك: أشك، ب.

٨ بذاته: لذاته، ب.

٩ فإذا: فإذ، ب.

يكون موجِداً[١] وإما أن[٢] يكون موجِباً[٣]. وبطل أن يكون موجباً لأن الممكن ما تردّد بين الوجود والعدم، لا ما تردد بين الوجوب والإمكان، فالمرجح إذاً مرجح الوجود على العدم، لا مرجح الوجوب على الإمكان، فهو مفيد الوجود لا مفيد الوجوب، بل الوجوب يلزمه بعد وجوده[٤] نظراً إلى سببه، والوجود مستفاد له من الموجد نظراً إلى ذاته، إذ الممكن غير ضروري الوجود والعدم. ولا يقال: الممكن غير ضروري الوجوب[٥] والإمكان لأن ذلك متناقض[٦] في نفسه لفظاً ومعنى، ويرجع حاصل القول إلى أن يقال الممكن غير ضروري الإمكان. وكيف يكون ذلك، والإمكان[٧] ماهيته[٨]؟ وماهيةُ الشيء ضرورية[٩] له ولا تفارق الذات ذاته، فتعين أن المرجح موجد[١٠] لا موجب[١١]، وسقط التلازم الموهوم[١٢] أصلاً.

١ موجداً: موجباً، ب.

٢ وإما أن: وأن لا، ب.

٣ موجباً: موجوداً، ب

٤ وجوده: الوجوب، ب.

٥ الوجوب: الوجود، ب.

٦ متناقض: يتناقض، ب.

٧ والإمكان: الإمكان، ب.

٨ ماهيته: ماهية، ب.

٩ ضرورية: ضروري، ب.

١٠ موجد: موجود، ب.

١١ موجب: يوجب، ب.

١٢ الموهوم: الموهم، ب.

بقي موضع بحث، أنه متى يضاف الممكن إلى الواجب، وعلى كم وجه يضاف الفعل إلى الفاعل والمقدور إلى القادر؟ فأما متى فلا[١] متى، فلا يقدّر فراغ وشغل ووقت فعل ووقت ترك[٢] إذ الأوقات[٣] متشابهة، فلا يؤثر وقت على وقت إلا بسببٍ[٤] مخصّصٍ. وإذا كان الفاعل كما كان ولم يحدث أمر فلم يحدث مخصص ومرجح سواءً لازمه وجوداً أو سبقه[٥].

وعند القوم إنما ترجح الوجود على العدم في الممكن لذاته بإفاضة ذاته تعالى، فيطالَبون بنفس الإفاضة والإيجاب[٦]، ويقال: ما الذي اقتضى كونه مفيضاً موجباً؟ كما طالبونا بوقت الإفاضة والإيجاب. وكان[٧] جوابهم أن ذاتاً يَفيض[٨] منها شيء أشرف من ذات لا يفيض[٩] منها شيء. وقيل لهم: هذا يشعر[١٠] بأنه استفاد الكمال من الإفاضة، وكامل[١١]

١ فلا: ولا، ب.

٢ ووقت فعل ووقت ترك: ووقت ترك ووقت فعل، ب.

٣ الأوقات: + متساوية، ب.

٤ بسبب: سبب، ب.

٥ أو سبقه: وسبقه، ب.

٦ والإيجاب: والإيجاد، ب.

٧ وكان: فكان، ب.

٨ يفيض: يقبض، ب.

٩ يفيض: يقبض، ب.

١٠ يشعر: مشعر، ب.

١١ وكامل: وكمال، ب.

الذات لا يستفيد الكمال من غيره. قالوا: إن الفيض منه تبع لكماله، لا أن[١] كماله تبع لفيضه. قيل: فلم يكن إذاً مفيضاً موجباً بالذات، بل فاضت منه الموجودات ووجبت من غير إفاضته[٢] وإيجابه. وهذا حكم التبع، والتابع أبداً[٣] بعد المتبوع في الوجود، ولكن لا يضاف إلى المتبوع مقصوداً وبالذات[٤]، بل تبعاً وبالعرض.

فأنتم طالبتمونا بوقت الإبداع وسببه، ونحن طالبناكم بأصل الإبداع وسببه، وألزمتونا حدوث حادث ما لأمر حادث، وألزمناكم وجود الموجودات تبعاً وبالعرض، لا بالاختيار والقصد الأول، والطبع والاتفاق باطلان لا مدخل لهما[٥] في كماله تعالى[٦].

بل نحن وجدنا الممكنات بالذات قد دخلت في الوجود، أعني ترجح جانب منها على جانب، وقلنا: لا بدّ من مرجح لا إمكان[٧] له بوجه من الوجوه، ويجب إضافة الممكنات إليه تعالى. ووجوه[٨] الإضافات مختلفة، فمنها الإفاضة والإيجاب، ومنها الطبع والميل، ومنها الغرض والحكمة، ومنها الإرادة والاختيار، والقصد والإيثار، ولك أن تؤثر

١ لا أن: لأن، ب.

٢ إفاضته: إفاضة، ب.

٣ أبداً: أبد، ب.

٤ وبالذات: بالذات، ب.

٥ لهما: لها، ب.

٦ تعالى: + وتقدس، ب.

٧ لا إمكان: لإمكان، ب.

٨ ووجوه: ووجود، ب.

الأشرف فالأشرف منها. والشرائع قد وردت بتخصيص شرف الإضافة بالاختيار والإرادة[١] والخلق[٢] والأمر والملك لما في هذه الإضافة من كمال الجلال والإكرام، ولما في سائر الوجوه من النقص[٣] والانثلام، ففي الإيجاب والإفاضة شبه[٤] التوالد والتناسل، وفي الطبع والميل شبه القسر والحاجة، وفي الغرض وطلب العلة حقيقة الحاجة، والله تعالى منزّه عنها {تَبَارَكَ اسْمُ رَبِّكَ ذِي الجَلاَلِ وَالإِكْرَامِ} (٥٥ الرحمن ٧٨).

المختار[٥] الحق

قد بينا أن التقدم والتأخر والمعية[٦] على أنحاء أربعة: تقدم بالزمان، وتقدم بالمكان، وتقدم بالشرف وتقدم بالذات[٧]، وقد زيد فيه التقدم بالطبع والتقدم بالوجود فقط. ومُيّز بينهما وبين التقدم بالذات بأن[٨] تقدم الواحد على الاثنين معلوم، والواحد لا يوجب[٩] الاثنين بالذات،

١ بالاختيار والإرادة: بالإرادة والاختيار، ب.

٢ والخلق: والحق، ب.

٣ والنقص: + والخلل، ب.

٤ شبه: شبهة، ب.

٥ المختار: والمختار، ب.

٦ والمعية: والهيئة، ب.

٧ بالشرف وتقدم بالذات: بالذات وتقدم بالشرف، ب.

٨ بأن: فإن، ب.

٩ يوجب: يوجد، ب.

ففيه[١] معنى آخر وهو التقدم بالطبع. وتقدم الموجد على الموجَد[٢] وراء العلية بالذات. وقد بينا[٣] أن مفيد الوجود غير ومفيد الوجوب غير، يقال[٤]: وُجد به فوجب، ولا يقال: وجب به فوُجد[٥].

وإذا تقررت[٦] هذه القاعدة في التقدم والتأخر تبين أن الوجوه المذكورة جارية كلها[٧] في المعية، فنعود ونقول: ليس العالم مع الله[٨] تعالى بالزمان، فإن وجود البارئ[٩] تعالى ليس زمانياً، فكما لا يسبق وجوده تعالى وجود العالم زماناً كذلك لا يكون معه زماناً[١٠]. وليس العالم معه تعالى بالمكان، فإن وجوده ليس بمكاني، فكما لا يكون فوقه مكاناً لا يكون معه متيامناً أو متياسراً مكاناً. وليس العالم مع الله تعالى بالشرف، فإن واجب الوجود لا يساوى بجائز[١١] الوجود بالشرف. وليس

١ ففيه: فنقرر، ب.

٢ الموجد: -، ب.

٣ وقد بينا: وبينا، ب.

٤ يقال: ويقال، ب.

٥ فوجد: -، ب.

٦ تقررت: ثبت، ب.

٧ جارية كلها: كلها جارية، ب.

٨ الله: البارئ، ب.

٩ وجود البارئ: وجوده، ب.

١٠ زماناً: زمان، ب.

١١ بجائز: الجائز، ب.

العالم مع الله تعالى[١] بالذات، أما عندهم فلأن الموجَب لا يكون مع الموجِب بالذات، وأما عندنا فلأن الموجَد لا يكون مع الموجِد بالذات. وليس العالم مع الله تعالى بالطبع، فإن وجوده[٢] لا من طريق العدد، وكان الله ولم يكن معه شيء. وقد سئل النبي[٣] عليه السلام عن بدء[٤] هذا الأمر، فقال: كان الله ولم يكن معه شيء[٥]، فأخبر عن سر المسألة، ونص على متن الحكمة وقطع الأمر بما يفلّ الحد[٦] ويصيب[٧] المفصل[٨].

فإذا لم يكن معه شيء بوجه من وجوه المعية كان[٩] تعالى متقدماً على كل شيء بكل[١٠] وجه من وجوه التقدم، ولا يجوز أن يقال: واجب الوجود يتقدم على ممكن الوجود بالذات ويكون معه بوجه آخر كتقدم السراج على الضوء وتحرك اليد على تحرك الخاتم. فإن الشيء قد يتقدم على الشيء بالذات ويكون معه بالزمان كالمثالين المذكورين، فإن

١ تعالى: -، ب.

٢ وجوده: وجود، ب.

٣ النبي: عنه، ب.

٤ بدء: بدو، ب.

٥ شيء: + قط، ب.

٦ الحد: الحر، ب.

٧ ويصيب: ونصيب، ب.

٨ المفصل: من هنا يستأنف نص نسخة ا.

٩ كان: + الله، ب.

١٠ بكل: -، ب.

وجودهما زماني. ولا يجري هذا الحكم[١] في حق الباريء تعالى، فإنه يتقدس عن الزمان، فلا[٢] يجوز أن يتقدم بالذات ويقارن بالزمان، ولا أن يقارَن بالوجود، فإنا قد بينا أن الموجِد يتقدم على الموجَد في الوجود، ولهذا قالوا: الوجود به[٣] تعالى أولى وأول. فأسفر وجه المسألة كفلق الصبح، وتبين مثار[٤] الشبهة، وعاد الخلاف إلى أن حوادث لا أول لها[٥] محصورة بالوجود معاً أو متعاقبةً متتالية مستحيل الوجود، وقد بينا ذلك بما فيه مقنع.

ومن الموجودات العلوية مفارقات للمادة، مجرّدات عن الهيول قدّيسات[٦] عن الأحياز المكانية والأحوال الزمانية والأعراض الجسمانية، لها مبدأ ذاتي وأول وجودي، ابتدعها الباريء تعالى بقدرته ابتداعاً، واخترعها[٧] على[٨] مشيئته اختراعاً، وهي مظاهر[٩] الكلمات التامات، الطاهرات[١٠] الزاكيات، والكلمات مصادرها، وما دونها الكواكب

١ هذا الحكم: -، ا.

٢ فلا: ولا، ا.

٣ به: لله، ا؛ الله، ب.

٤ مثار: مشار، ب.

٥ لها: -، ا.

٦ قديسات: قد نشأت، ا ب.

٧ واخترعها: واخترعهم، ا.

٨ على: في، ا.

٩ مظاهر: من مظاهر، ب.

١٠ الطاهرات: الطاهرة، ا ب.

والأفلاك المتحركات، التي هي هياكل تلك الروحانيات. فإنما يبتدئ الدهر والزمان حيث حدوث الحركة، وإنما تبتدئ الحركة منها[١] حيث الشوق الطبيعي، والنزاع الطلبي إلى كمالاتها، فالأولية الزمانية لن تكون إلا[٢] للمتحركات، والأولية الذاتية[٣] لن تكون إلا[٤] للمفارقات. والربّ تعالى هو الأول بلا أول كان قبله، الآخر بلا آخر يكون بعده. فهو {الأَوَّلُ وَالآخِرُ} (٥٧ الحديد ٣) أي ليس وجوده زمانياً، {وَالظَّاهِرُ وَالبَاطِنُ} (٥٧ الحديد ٣) أي ليس وجوده مكانياً.

وأمثال هذه المتناقضات لفظاً متفقات[٥] في حقه تعالى معنىً، والزمان والمكان توأمان تراكضا في رحم واحد، وارتضعا من ثدي واحد، ونوغي[٦] عليهما في مهد واحد، فاضرب الدهري بالجسمي والجسمي بالدهري[٧]، واطلب دين الله تعالى بين[٨] الغالي والمقصّر، وجلال الله تعالى فوق الأوهام والعقول، فضلاً عن المكان والزمان.

١ وإنما تبتدئ الحركة منها: -، ب.

٢ لن تكون إلا: لمن يكون أولاً، ب.

٣ الذاتية: -، ا.

٤ لن تكون إلا: لمن تكون أولاً، ب.

٥ متفقات: متفقة، ا.

٦ ونوغي: ولوعي، ا.

٧ بالدهري: -، ب.

٨ بين: من، ا.

وحيثما اتسعت[١] العبارة باستعارتها في آفاق الفكر الجائل في عرصات[٢] المطلوب صار ما يُرام وضوحه[٣] غامضاً[٤]، وما يُتمنى فيضه غائضاً، وكلّت الآلة، وضلت الحالة، وعاد العقل الإنساني عنده هباء، والحيلة استحالت عَياء[٥]، فلا وجه بعد هذه المعاني التي طلعت عليها شمس العظمة، فطبختها[٦] في أمواج البحار، ونسحتها[٧] في أدراج الرياح، إلا الركون إلى الشرع الظاهر، والحنيفي الطاهر[٨]، فإنه يؤنس كل الأنس وليس يوحش[٩] كل الإيحاش، ولو أنه لم يُرو كل الإرواء لم[١٠] يُعطش كل الإعطاش.

١ اتسعت: اشتقت، ا.

٢ عرصات: غرضات، ا.

٣ وضوحه: -، ب.

٤ غامضاً: ايضاً، ب.

٥ عياء: عفاء، ا ب.

٦ فطبختها: فطيحتها، ب.

٧ ونسحتها: وسيحتها، ا؛ وسبختها، ب.

٨ الطاهر: -، ب.

٩ يوحش: يتوحش، ا.

١٠ لم: ولم، ا.

ولما أنهيت الكلام في هذه المسألة[١] إلى هذه الغاية، وأردت الشروع[٢] في المسألة السادسة والسابعة، شغلني عن بيانهما[٣] ما قد تكاءدني ثقله، وبهظني[٤] حمله، من فتن الزمان، وطوارق الحدثان، فإلى الله المشتكى، وعليه المعوّل في الشدة والرخاء، فاقتصرت على إيراد رؤوس المسائل من أسئلة وشكوك وإشكالات ومَحارات[٥] عقول[٦]، فمَن حلّها فهو أولى بها، إن شاء الله تعالى.

١ في هذه المسألة: -، ا.

٢ الشروع: السير، ب.

٣ عن بيانها: عنها، ا.

٤ وبهظني: وبهضني، ا.

٥ محارات: مجازات، ب.

٦ عقول: -، ا.

محارات[١] العقول

إن الحكيم يطلب العلة في كل شيء والسبب لكل حادث، إما علة فاعلية، أو علة مادية، أو علة تمامية[٢]، وقلّ ما يطلب العلة[٣] الصورية[٤]. فأول ما يسأل عن حصر المبادئ، أهي محصورة[٥] في عدد[٦] معلوم أم[٧] غير محصورة ولا متناهية؟ فإن كانت محصورة بعدد فلا عدد أولى من عدد[٨]. وإن من الأوائل من قال: المبادئ أربعة، الأول والعقل[٩] والنفس والهيولى[١٠]، ومنهم من قال: خمسة، وزاد الطبيعة، ومنهم من قال: ستة، وزاد الخلاء[١١]، ومنهم من قال: سبعة، وزاد الدهر والزمان.

١ محارات: محادات، ا؛ مجات، ب.

٢ تمامية: غائية، ب.

٣ العلة: علته، ا.

٤ الصورية: التصورية، ب.

٥ أهي محصورة: وهي محصورة، ا.

٦ عدد: عدم، ا.

٧ أم: -، ا.

٨ أولى من عدد: -، ب.

٩ والعقل: العقل، ب.

١٠ والهيولى: -، ا.

١١ الخلاء: اخلا، ب.

وابن سينا يميل إلى أنها تسعة، هي العقول المفارقات[١]، وربما يزيد على ذلك حتى يبلغ بها[٢] نيفاً وأربعين عقلاً، وربما يقول: تعددت المفارقات بعدد النفوس المدبرات، وتعددت النفوس بعدد الأفلاك، ولربما دل الرصد على أنها تسعة. فما الذي ينجينا من[٣] هذه الحيرة، ومن الذي يخلصنا من[٤] هذه الورطة؟

إشكال[٥]

المفارقات تتمايز[٦] بالفصول النوعية كالنطق للإنسان، أو بعوارض شخصية كالشكل والصورة للإنسان، أم بوجه آخر كما نص عليه أنها تتمايز بالحقائق الذاتية. وهذا القسم[٧] ليس معلوماً، فإن اسم الجوهرية قد شملها شمولاً ذاتياً كالجنس، فلا بد من تمييز بفصل ذاتي نوعي، ولا بد من عوارض شخصية عينية حتى يمكن أن يشار إلى كل واحد إشارة[٨] عقلية بهذا أو ذاك[٩]. ولا يكون ذلك إلا بأبدان لها

١ المفارقات: والمفارقات، ب.

٢ بها: -، ا ب.

٣ من: عن، ب.

٤ الذي يخلصنا من: الذين يخلصان من، ب.

٥ إشكال: -، ا ب.

٦ تتمايز: يتميز، ا.

٧ القسم: التقسيم، ا ب.

٨ إشارة: اشار اليه، ب.

٩ أو ذاك: وذاك، ا ب.

كالأفلاك، فلا تكون إذاً مفارقة مجردة عن المادة من كل وجه، ولا يحصل فرق بينها[١] وبين النفوس الإنسانية، وحينئذ تتمكن فيها هيآت من أحوال حركات الأفلاك كما تمكنت في النفوس الإنسانية[٢] من حركات الأبدان. وبالجملة، فتخرج عن أن تكون مفارقات من كل وجه.

إشكالات

الجسم مركب من مادّة وصورة ويستدعي علة فاعلية، فما العلة لوجود المادة، وما العلة في وجود الصورة، وما العلة لتركبهما[٣] معاً؟ فإن كان الإمكان في ذات العقل الأول هو العلة لوجود المادة فالإمكان في كل موجود غير واجب الوجود كذلك، فليناسب وجودَ المادة. بل الإمكان طبيعة عدمية، فلا يناسب وجود شيء ما، والعلة في وجود الصورة لا يجوز أن تكون إمكان وجوده، بل وجوب وجوده بالغير، ووجوب الوجود بالغير في كل موجود عن[٤] العقل الأول على وتيرة واحدة، فليناسب كل صورة. وبالجملة كلُّ ما يذكرونه[٥] من وجوه[٦] المناسبات في العلل فهو موجود في المعلولات، فليست العلة أولى[٧] بعليتها من المعلول.

١ بينها: بينهما، ا.

٢ وحينئذ ... الإنسانية: -، ب.

٣ لتركبهما: لتركبها، ا؛ في تركبهما، ب.

٤ عن: غير، ب.

٥ يذكرونه: تذكرونه، ا.

٦ وجوه: وجود، ا.

٧ أولى: بأولى، ب.

ثم الاستعداد في المادة ليس متشابهاً[١] في جميع المواد، بل مختلف[٢]، فما سبب الاختلاف فيها؟ فإنما[٣] تختلف الصور فيها لاختلاف استعدادات المواد[٤]. والهيولى الأولى لا تختلف[٥] استعداداً، بل هي مستعدة[٦] لقبول صورة[٧] الجسمية فقط. فأما مقادير الصور والأشكال في الصغر والكبر، والأقلّ والأكثر، والخاصية[٨] والأثر، فتستدعي[٩] عللاً تناسبها. فما تلك العلل، وما الذي أوجب اختصاص الهيولى بقبول[١٠] صورة الجسم الكل[١١] على المقدار الذي هو عليه، ليس يزيده ولا ينقص؟

وإنكم طلبتم العلة لكُريته[١٢]، فقلتم: إن العلة إذا كانت واحدة، والمادة واحدة، وجب أن يكون الجسم متشابه الأجزاء، وهو شكل الكرة،

١ متشابهاً: متناهياً، ا.

٢ مختلف: يختلف، ب.

٣ فإنما: وإنما، ا.

٤ المواد: المراد، ب.

٥ الصور ... تختلف: -، ا؛ فما سبب الاختلاف ... تختلف: الجملة مكررة في ب.

٦ مستعدة: مستعد، ب.

٧ صورة: صور، ب.

٨ والخاصية: والخاصة، ا.

٩ فتستدعي: ويستدعي، ا ب.

١٠ بقبول: لقبول، ب.

١١ الكل: الشكل، ا؛ المشكل، ب.

١٢ لكريته: لكريتها، ا ب.

إذ لا زاوية فيها تتخصص[١] بها شكلاً[٢] مربعاً أو مثلثاً أو غير ذلك، فهلا طلبتم لمقدار الكرة علة أخرى؟ وهلا طلبتم لكل كرة سماوية، نجماً أو فلكاً، علة، فيعرف بها مقادير الأعظام والأجسام؟ وكذلك[٣] القول في أبعادها وأماكنها[٤] وحركاتها وأزمانها، فإن المجسطي ليس يقرر[٥] إلا ما عليه وجودها، وليس يطلب علة[٦] وجودها، والإلاهيات تشتمل على بعض عللها الغائية لا الفاعلية والمادية. والمطالبة توجهت عليهم في هذه المسائل[٧] توجّه مطالبة الغريم[٨] علي الغريم المماطل، وإذا أعيتكِ جاراتك فعوّلي على ذي بيتك {مَا أَشْهَدْتُهُمْ خَلْقَ السَّمَوَاتِ وَالأَرْضِ} (١٨ الكهف ٥١) الآية[٩].

١ تتخصص: بتحصص، ا؛ تخصيص، ب.

٢ شكلاً: شكل، ب.

٣ وكذلك: كذلك، ب.

٤ وأماكنها: وأمكنها، ب.

٥ يقرر: يقدر، ب.

٦ علة: علل، ب.

٧ المسائل: المشاكل، ا.

٨ الغريم: الغرم، ب.

٩ ما أشهدتهم ... الآية: -، ا.

سؤال وإشكال

إن كان كل متحرك يستدعي[١] محركاً، فإن كان[٢] المحرك متحركاً، استدعى أيضاً[٣] محركاً، وتسلسل[٤] القول فيه إلى أن يستند إلى محرك غير متحرك، فلا يخلو بعد ذلك إما أن يكون ذلك المحرك[٥] الأول ساكناً أو غير ساكن ولا متحرك. فإن كان[٦] ساكناً فالسكون لا يوجب الحركة التي هي ضده[٧]، وإن كان غير ساكن ولا متحرك فيجب أن يكون جوهراً عقلياً، فما الذي أوجب فيه أن يكون محركاً لغيره، أشوق يحمله، أم كمال يطلبه؟

ثم لا يخلو بعد ذلك، أيمكن الوصول إلى كماله أم[٨] لا يمكن؟ فإن أمكن ووصل فيجب أن يقف عن التحريك فتسكن[٩] المتحركات كلها، وإن[١٠] لم يمكن ولا يصل إلى كماله البتة فهو[١١] إذاً[١٢] متعب دائم العذاب،

١ يستدعي: فيستدعي، ا.

٢ كان: -، ا.

٣ أيضاً: -، ب.

٤ وتسلسل: فيتسلسل، ب.

٥ المحرك: المتحرك، ا.

٦ كان: -، ب.

٧ ضده: ضدها، ا.

٨ أم: لم، ب.

٩ فتسكن: فيسكن، ا.

١٠ وإن: فإن، ا ب.

متواصل[١] الأحزان، متزايد[٢] النقصان، لا يزداد بحركته[٣] إلا شوقاً إلى كماله، ولا بشوقه[٤] إلا بُعداً عن كماله. وإن قيل: إنه ينال في كل حركة كمالاً جزئياً، فالتذاذه بكماله الجزئي يلهيه[٥] عن أذى الشوق إلى كماله الكلي، قيل[٦]: وقصوره عن نيل كماله الكلي يلهيه[٧] عن الالتذاذ بكماله[٨] الجزئي.

١١ فهو: فهذا، ا.

١٢ إذاً: + أيضاً، ب.

١ متواصل: متواصد، ب.

٢ متزايد: متزيد، ب.

٣ بحركته: بحركة، ا.

٤ بشوقه: شوقه، ا؛ بشوقها، ب.

٥ يلهيه: تلهية، ا.

٦ قيل: + من مواقف العقل، ا.

٧ يلهيه: ملهية، ا.

٨ بكماله: بكمال، ب.

من مواقف العقل[١]

إن كان الجسم الكل[٢] كرة متناهية فليس لها[٣] سطح أعلى، إذ ليس وراءها خلاء ولا ملاء فيظهر عليه سطح هو[٤] أعلى، فإذا توهمت شيئاً ما إما خلاء أو ملاء[٥] فحينئذ يتصور لك سطح أعلى. ثم إذا تحركت الكرة ظهر القطبان متوازيين، فما الذي أوجب تعيّن القطبين بالمكان الذي هما فيه[٦] الآن[٧]، وأجزاء الكرة متشابهة متساوية، وليس جزء[٨] أولى من جزء[٩]؟ و إنما أطلب بهذه المطالبة العلة الفاعلية لا الغائية[١٠]. ثم إن كانت حركات الأجرام مكانية أوجبت خرق تلك الأجرام، وهي لا تقبل الخرق. وإن كانت وضعية فالحركات الوضعية إنما تحدث إذا سبقتها حركة المكان، والأينُ كالمربع ذو وضع، فإذا تحركت رجله إلى شكل آخر غير التربيع حدثت[١١] له حركة[١٢] هي في نسبة الأجزاء بعضها إلى بعض، فلا بد من

١ من مواقف العقل: -، ا ب.

٢ الكل: للكل، ا؛ الكلي، ب.

٣ لها: -، ب.

٤ هو: وهو، ب.

٥ فيظهر ... أو ملاء: -، ا.

٦ هما فيه: هو فيهما، ا.

٧ الآن: -، ب.

٨ جزء: جزبه، ب.

٩ جزء: جزيه، ب.

١٠ الغائية: الغايبة، ب.

١١ حدثت: حديث، ب.

حركة النقلة لبعض الأجزاء حتى تتبدل نسبة[١] سائر الأجزاء بعضها إلى بعض، وإلا فالحركة في الوضع لا يُتصور[٢] وجودها.

شك

العلة والمبدأ يقال على كل ما استتم له[٣] وجوده ووجد[٤] منه شيء آخر، ثم قد تكون تمامية[٥] وجوده من ذاته وقد تكون من غيره، وما يكون من غيره فقد يكون كالجزء لما هو معلول[٦] له، كالصورة والمادة للجسم، أو لا يكون، كالفاعل والغاية، على التقسيم الذي ذكره ابن سينا في كتبه، وغرضه حصر العلل في أربعة، المادة والصورة والفاعل والغاية. فالشك عليه أن المادة لم يتم لها وجود ووجد منها شيء آخر، بل إنما يتم وجودها بالصورة حتى يوجد منهما[٧] جسم، وما لم يتم وجوده في نفسه كيف[٨] يوجد منه شيء آخر؟

١٢ حركة: جزكت، ب.

١ نسبة: بسببه، ا.

٢ يتصور: يتور، ب.

٣ له: -، ب.

٤ ووجد: ووجود، ب.

٥ تمامية: بماهية، ا؛ وماهية، ب.

٦ معلول: معلوم، ب.

٧ شيء آخر ... منهما: -، ا.

٨ كيف: فكيف، ا.

ثم التقسيم الذي أورده ليس بحاصرٍ لجميع[١] أقسام العلل[٢]، ويمكن أن يوجد شيء آخر سوى الأقسام التي أوردها، كما عدّوه من الآلة. وما ذكره من التقوم به احتراز لفظي ليس يمنع معنى العلّية والسببية[٣]. ولو قيل: الفاعل والغاية كافيان في العلية، والمادة كالآلة، والصورة كالصورة[٤] في نفس الفاعل، فمن زاد أو نقص من التقسيم كان له مجال[٥]، ولم يلزم منه مُحال.

إثبات النبوة من مدارك العقل ومناهجه

مُخرِج العقول[٦] الهيولانية الإنسانية من القوة إلى الفعل يجب أن يكون عقلاً بالفعل، فإنها لا تَخرج بذواتها إلى الفعل، ولا يُخرجها ما هو مثلها في القوة، مبرهن[٧] مسلم. فلِمَ ينبغي أن يكون ذلك المخرج الذي هو عقل بالفعل واحداً بعينه هو العقل الفعال المدبر لفلك القمر، فيسمّى[٨]

١ بحاصر لجميع: مطموس في ا.

٢ العلل: المعلل، ب.

٣ العلية والسببية: الغلبة والنسبية، ب.

٤ كالصورة: -، ب.

٥ مجال: محال، ا ب.

٦ مخرج العقول: ويخرج للعقول، ب.

٧ مبرهن: مبرمين، ب.

٨ فيسمى: فسمى، ا.

واهب الصور دون العقول التي هي مدبرات لسائر[١] الأفلاك، أو معها بالشركة؟ ولِمَ لا[٢] تضاف الصور كلها إلى العقل الأول الذي هو واسطة الكل، فيكون هو الواهب الفعّال، ولا تتكثر ذاته بتكثر الصور، كما لا تتكثر ذات العقل الأخير؟ بل ولِمَ لا[٣] تضاف الصور كلها إلى واجب الوجود الأول تعالى وتقدس، فلا تتكثر ذاته بتكثر الصور؟ تبارك الله الواحد القهار، العزيز الجبار، الكريم الوهاب.

وإن طلبتم شيئاً قريباً من السماويات وجعلتم الفلك الأخير ومدبره[٤] هو الأقرب، فيكون هو المفيض على المواد[٥] الصور التي استُعدّت لها، فلم اعتبرتم القرب[٦] المكاني في الجواهر العقلية؟ وهلا قضيتم بأن الجواهر العقلية في البعد والقرب[٧] على السواء؟ وهلا اعتقدتم أن واجب الوجود أقرب من كل قريب، فهو المخرج لما بالقوة إلى الفعل من العقول؟ {اللَّهُ وَلِيُّ الَّذِينَ آمَنُوا يُخْرِجُهُمْ مِنَ الظُّلُمَاتِ إِلَى النُّورِ}. أو هلا[٨] جوزتم أن يكون من العقول الإنسانية ما هو عقل بالفعل، فيكون هو السبب

١ لسائر: كسائر، ا.

٢ لا: -، ب.

٣ لا: -، ب.

٤ ومدبره: مدبره، ا.

٥ المواد: المراد، ب.

٦ القرب: القريب، ب.

٧ البعد والقرب: القرب والبعد، ب.

٨ أو هلا: وهلا، ا ب.

القريب المؤيَّد بالقوة القدسية، كما جوزتم[1] امتياز بعض العقول بالقوة الحدسية[2]؟ وأوجبتم في النفوس تفاضلاً وفي العقول ترتباً، والمتفاضلات[3] المترتبات تنتهي إلى واحد هو الأفضل فلا[4] تتسلسل. {يَا أَيُّهَا النَّبِيُّ إِنَّا أَرْسَلْنَاكَ شَاهِداً وَمُبَشِّراً وَنَذِيراً وَدَاعِياً إِلَى اللَّهِ بِإِذْنِهِ وَسِرَاجاً مُنِيراً} (٣٣ الأحزاب ٤٥-٤٦). اللّهم انفعنا بما علمتنا وعلّمنا ما تنفعنا به، بحق المصطفين من عبادك[5] عليهم السلام[6].

١ جوزتم: جودتم، ا.

٢ الحدسية: الجذبة، ا؛ الجدسية، ب.

٣ والمتفاضلات: والمتفاصلات، ب.

٤ فلا: ولا، ا.

٥ عبادك: + الصالحين، ب.

٦ السلام: + وصلواته على سيدنا محمد وآله [و]صحبه أجمعين، كتبه الفقير إلى رحمة الله تعالى فضائل بن أبي الحسن الناسخ الشافعي، رحم الله قارئه وكاتبه، آمين، وكان الفراغ من نسخه في العشر الأخير من صفر سنة تسعين وخمسمائة، وحسبنا ونعم الوكيل، ومن يتوكل على الله فهو حسبه، ا؛ برحمتك يا أرحم الراحمين، هذا آخر المصارعة، تم، ب.

الفهارس

١ - الأعلام

٢ - الجمعات والفرق

٣ - الأماكن

٤ - الكتب

١ - الأعلام

ابن سينا، أبو علي الحسين بن عبد الله، ٣، ٨، ١٦، ٢٤، ٢٩، ٣١، ٤٠، ٤١، ٤٣، ٥٣، ٥٥، ٥٦، ٦٠، ٦٨، ٧٣، ٨٢، ٨٦، ٩٤، ٩٧، ١٠١، ١١٠، ١٢٢، ١٢٩.
أرسطو ٩٣.
زيد ٤٧، ١٠٩.
علي بن جعفر الموسوي، المجلس العالي مجد الدين ١، ٤، ٨٢.
عمرو ١٠٩.
محمد ،النبي ١، ١١٦.

٢ - الجمعات والفرق

آل محمد ١.
أصحاب الرواق ٩٣.
الأنبياد ٦٠، ٦١، ٨٧.
الأوائل ١٢١.
الجسمية ١١٨.
الحاكة ٢٨.
الحشوية ٢٨.
الحكماء ٣٣، ٥٠، ٥٥، ٨٩، ١٢١.
الدهرية ١١٨.
الغالية ١١٨.
الفقهاء ٥٥.
الفلاسفة ٧، ٨، ٦٤، ٦٧، ٨٥، ٩٣.
القاصة ٢٨.
الكرامية ١٠١، ١٠٢.
المتكلمون ٧، ٦٧، ٨٦.
المسلمون ٩٣.
المقصرة ١١٨.
الملائكة ٦٣، ٨٩، ٩١، ٩٢.
النصارى ٧٣.

٣ - الأماكن

أثينية ٩٣
ساميا ٩٣.
الملطية ٩٣.

٤ - الكتب

الإشارات ٣.

إلاهيات الشفاء ٣، ١٢٥.

التعليقات ٣، ٥٦.

الشفاء ٣، ٢٧، ٧٠، ١١٠.

المجسطي ١٢٥.

النجاة ٣، ٨، ٥٣.

Muḥammad b. ʿAbd al-Karīm b. Aḥmad
al-Shahrastānī

Kitāb al-Muṣāraʿa